AUTOPSY OF AN UNWINNABLE WAR: VIETNAM

COLONEL (RET) WILLIAM C. HAPONSKI WITH
COLONEL (RET) JERRY J. BURCHAM

CASEMATE
Philadelphia & Oxford

AN AUSA BOOK
Association of the United States Army
2425 Wilson Boulevard, Arlington, Virginia, 22201, USA

Published in the United States of America and Great Britain in 2019 by
CASEMATE PUBLISHERS
1950 Lawrence Road, Havertown, PA 19083, USA
and
The Old Music Hall, 106–108 Cowley Road, Oxford OX4 1JE, UK

Hardback Edition: ISBN 978-1-61200-719-9
Digital Edition: ISBN 978-1-61200-720-5 (ePub)

A CIP record for this book is available from the British Library

Printed and bound in the United States of America

Typeset in India by Versatile PreMedia Services. www.versatilepremedia.com

For a complete list of Casemate titles, please contact:

CASEMATE PUBLISHERS (US)
Telephone (610) 853-9131
Fax (610) 853-9146
Email: casemate@casematepublishers.com
www.casematepublishers.com

CASEMATE PUBLISHERS (UK)
Telephone (01865) 241249
Email: casemate-uk@casematepublishers.co.uk
www.casematepublishers.co.uk

Front cover: A North Vietnamese tank entering the smashed-down gate of Independence Palace,
April 30, 1975. (Roger-Viollet/TopFoto)

DEDICATED TO

General of the Army (Ret, French) Jean Delaunay
Geneviève (de Galard) de Heaulme, "The Angel of Dien Bien Phu"
Colonel (Ret, French) Jean de Heaulme
Lieutenant Colonel Nguyen Minh Chau (Former Marine Corps,
Republic of Vietnam)
Dr. Charles Lamb
Sandra Haponski
Maura and Stephen Cornell
Troopers of 11th Armored Cavalry Regiment, Vietnam and Cambodia
Troopers and Soldiers of Task Force 1/4 Cavalry,
1st Infantry Division, Vietnam
Troopers of 2/5 Cavalry (Airmobile), 1st Air Cavalry Division, Vietnam

"You cannot kill an idea with bullets"

General Jacques Philippe Leclerc
Commander, French Expeditionary Corps entering Vietnam 1945

Contents

Foreword

In the eight years from 1775 to 1783, American revolutionaries astounded observers in capitals all across Europe by defeating—against all odds—mighty Great Britain. They did so on the wings of a supremely motivating dream: to gain independence and to create a single nation united.

Nearly two centuries later, in the 30 years from 1945 to 1975, Vietnamese revolutionaries, driven by that very same dream, shocked the world by defeating, one after the other, three powerful foes: France, the United States, and their fellow countrymen in the southern half of Vietnam.

That is more than a coincidental similarity of aspirational ideas and surprising outcomes. Ho Chi Minh, the revered Communist and Nationalist leader of Vietnam's revolutionaries from well before World War II, dramatically proclaimed his movement's basis to a huge cheering throng in Hanoi in 1945. "All men are created equal," he said. "The Creator has given us certain inviolable Rights; the right to Life, the right to be Free, and the right to achieve Happiness." After pausing for effect, he continued, "These immortal words are taken from the Declaration of Independence of the United States of America in 1776. In a larger sense, this means that: All the people on earth are born equal; All the people have the right to live, to be happy, to be free." He then invoked a second declaration, one guiding the later French Revolution, saying, "Men are born and must remain free and have equal rights. Those are undeniable truths."

In the light of that animating vision—the unwavering idea of a united Vietnam free of foreign influence—William Haponski holds that no French or American or South Vietnamese general could have gained a victory in Vietnam. That is his central theme as he tells the story of those three decades of war.

His telling is as unique as his thesis. Although the book itself is solid history, Haponski's style is far from that of the traditional historian. While he writes often in the first person and does not shy away from placing himself in the story where appropriate, the tone is not that of a memoir. That out-of-the-ordinary approach reflects the author himself. Haponski has examined the war exhaustively for half a century, at every level from reflections on his first-hand experiences to post-doctoral research. The result is an absorbing blend ranging from the deeply personal to the academically professional. He has created a multi-dimensional narrative, at once alive and lucid.

A most valuable facet of the book is its focus on events *inside* Vietnam, placed in the clarifying framework of the four distinct phases of the long war. First, from 1945 to 1954, was the fight against the French. Next came a decade of transition, 1954 to 1964, as American military elements gradually took the place of French forces. Then, from 1965 to 1972, was the ill-fated American effort to defend South Vietnam. And finally, 1973 to 1975, the conquest of South Vietnam. To understand the Vietnam War, to really understand it, one must know the essence of all four phases.

Ever since North Vietnamese tanks rolled into Saigon in April 1975, journalists and generals and politicians and historians have debated heatedly over why America lost. Conclusions abound…. It was a default, not a defeat. It was lost in Washington, not in Vietnam. Poor generalship is to blame. And on and on.

This book might not stop the debate, but it deftly rearranges the arguments. Haponski contends no general—no general—could have mustered military forces to defeat the enduring idea of a free and unified Vietnam. That idea, so fervently held, provided the Vietnamese the will to persevere unto victory no matter how long it took or how painful the cost.

He asserts that in the end, willpower trumped firepower.

Lieutenant General (Ret) Dave R. Palmer

Preface

"The politicians, media, and hippies lost that war for us!" Since the April 30, 1975 fall of Saigon how many times have we heard it, or something like it? Especially from veterans who sacrificed so much, having buddies killed, getting wounded themselves, getting Dear John letters, acquiring cancers from toxins, trying to deal with their physical wounds and PTSD?

Many vets have expressed their feelings more colorfully: "The ******* *politicians*, ******* *media*, and ******* *hippies* lost that ******* war for us!"

Can the vets who fought close in—down in the jungles and rice paddies, on the inland waterways, or overhead engaging the enemy—be faulted for such a view when it also came as a post-war assessment from the very top? The senior American commander in charge of prosecuting the war during its buildup and peak of fighting was Admiral U.S.G. Sharp, Commander in Chief Pacific. As such, he was in overall charge of U.S. operations in the war—on land, on water, and in the air. He concluded his memoir, saying: "The real tragedy of Vietnam is that this war was not won by the other side, by Hanoi or Moscow or Peiping. It was lost in Washington, D. C."[1]

This remains an all too common belief. The stark facts, though, are that the Vietnam War was lost before our first American shot was fired. In fact, it was lost before the first French Expeditionary Corps shot, almost two decades before us, and was finally lost when the South Vietnamese after us fought partly, then entirely, on their own. It was not a war in which the generals of France, America, or South Vietnam could have led to victory.

It is important to understand why.

America's inability to win in Vietnam cannot be just dumped conveniently onto the laps of the Washington politicians who established the rules of engagement within which the war could be fought. In essence those parameters were restrictions on crossing borders during the ground war in South Vietnam, blockading North Vietnamese ports, and conducting the air war over North Vietnam. Washington rejected the "kick ass and take names" approach of tough-talking men such as General Curtis LeMay and presidential candidate Senator Barry Goldwater. Their utterances on how to win the Vietnam War—bomb them back to the Stone Age; make that place a mud puddle—were roundly rejected by the American people and decision makers in Washington, and rightly so.

The ultimate American intention after the 1954 Geneva Accords was to enable the Republic of Vietnam (South Vietnam) to remain a sovereign nation. After commitment of ground combat units in 1965, the commander of Military Assistance Command Vietnam (MACV), General William C. Westmoreland, was given authority to fight the ground war within South Vietnam as he saw fit and was afforded enormous resources to do so. This same authority was passed on to his successor, General Creighton W. Abrams, who had still substantial but steadily diminishing resources. History shows that despite great odds and burdensome limitations, victory had sometimes been snatched from the jaws of defeat. Why that was not to be the case in Vietnam needs exploration.

Shortly after World War II ended, a hero of that war, General Jacques Philippe Leclerc, commanded the French Expeditionary Corps entering Vietnam. President De Gaulle gave him the mission of restoring the status quo, that is, returning Indochina to its prewar colonial condition. Quickly Leclerc committed French Union troops to action in this hostile environment and soon began to discover what an enormous task it would be. He concluded, "You cannot kill an idea with bullets."[2]

He urged his government to negotiate.

France chose bullets.

The rest is tragic history.

Causes of American failure stemming from high-level politics and policies have been profusely dissected, analyzed, and argued, and there is little need to go there again except to provide background. This book, rather, is the story of the roots, and then the 30-year war *within Vietnam*, 1945–75. It is by a combatant not only in six violent, large battles and many smaller firefights, but a leader with a full range of pacification duties, a commander who lost 43 wonderful young men killed and many more wounded, men who were doing what their country asked of them. This story is the result of a quest for answers by one who, after decades of wondering what it was about—*what was it all about?*—turned to a years-long search of French, American, and Vietnamese sources and conducted a multitude of queries of participants.

It is a story of success on the one hand, defeat on the other, and the ingredients of both, inspirational or sordid as they may be.

It is a story mostly lived and revealed by the people *inside Vietnam* who were directly involved in the war: from French, American, and Vietnamese leaders in high positions, down to the jungle boots and sandals level of the fighters, and among the Vietnamese people who were living the war. Because of what was happening *inside Vietnam itself*, no matter what policies and directives came out of Paris or Washington, or the influences in Moscow or Beijing, it is about a *Vietnamese idea* which would eventually triumph over bullets.

Lieutenant General Harold G. "Hal" Moore, 1975. (NARA)

Hal Moore, Twelve Inches, and Another Couple Inches

Our story of an idea is perhaps best opened by Hal Moore. As a lieutenant colonel, Harold G. (Hal) Moore commanded his battalion of 1st Air Cavalry Division in what many recognize as the first major battle of the American war, fought at LZ X-Ray in the Ia Drang Valley, November 14–16, 1965. His book, written with reporter Joe Galloway, *We Were Soldiers Once … and Young*, and the resulting movie, *We Were Soldiers*, powerfully depict the very best that America had to offer: its soldiers locked in mortal combat with highly capable, determined soldiers of North Vietnam.

Hal Moore is one of the greatest American soldiers to come out of Vietnam alive. Certainly, he is one of the most highly respected—even loved—by not just his veterans of that battle, but by many other soldiers who in one way or another have known him, either personally, through his writing, or through his continuing efforts to help all veterans and their families. Retired Lieutenant General Moore and Joe Galloway, the courageous journalist who was at Hal's side during the fierce fighting, made trips back to Vietnam beginning in 1990 and ending in 1999. Their first trip was to meet commanders who had fought against them in those hellish days in the Ia Drang Valley. They were unsuccessful in their attempts to meet Hal's counterpart or other commanders. On a following trip, though, because of his book in which he fully accorded the North Vietnamese the respect they deserved as formidable opponents, he and his party were granted permission to tour the battlefield itself, accompanied by the lieutenant general who as a lieutenant colonel had commanded the forces Hal had fought.

In a book which resulted from those return trips, again with Galloway as coauthor, *We Are Soldiers Still*, Hal said, "When my soldiers spoke harshly, with anger, of our enemies, I told them to remember that these men had mothers who would be shattered by the news of their deaths; that they, like us, had been caught up in great power politics and were doing their duty as we were."[3]

Across the years I have tried to tell my veterans much the same thing. Like Moore's veterans, some of my men understand and accept this and feel compassion for our former enemies and their families, and some don't.

On his 1990 trip to Hanoi, Moore met an official in the Ministry of Foreign Affairs, a tough old soldier who had fought the French. Moore said,

> He seemed bemused by our total focus on our war in Vietnam and suggested that we might profit from a visit to the Vietnam Historical Museum nearby…. The high point for us was not the exhibits but finding a huge mural that stretched across one long wall that was both a timeline and a map of Vietnam's unhappy history dating back well over a thousand years. There on the wall we saw thick red arrows dropping down into Vietnam from the north, depicting half a dozen invasions and occupations of Vietnam by neighboring China, and some of those occupations lasted hundreds of years before Vietnamese patriots and rebels drove them out, again and again and again. The Chinese section of the timeline stretched out for fifty feet or so. The section devoted to the French and their 150 years of colonial occupation was depicted in about twelve inches. The miniscule part that marked the U.S. war was only a couple inches.

A couple inches!
Moore continued,

> It put everything into a perspective few Westerners seemingly had ever considered before marching their soldiers off into the jungles of a nation full of ardent nationalists who had demonstrated that they were fully prepared to fight for generations until the foreign occupier got tired of war, or choked on his own blood.[4]

I have never seen the map, confining my 2005 and 2010 visits back to Vietnam to the boondocks north of Saigon where in 1969 as a lieutenant colonel I commanded the armored cavalry task force of 1st Infantry Division. But anyone who can envision the mural that Moore described has gone a long way toward understanding why no French or American general could ever have "won" the wars France and the U.S. fought in Vietnam.

Neither could any South Vietnamese general have defeated his opponents. Not necessarily because he was a bad general—there were some good South Vietnamese generals, and many heroic and dedicated South Vietnamese soldiers and civilians—but because of what so many North Vietnamese and Viet Cong had and too many South Vietnamese lacked—*fire in the belly!*

That fire started way back on the left edge of the mural. It blazed at times, fell back into glowing embers, then grew bright again, fell back and blazed again, and again. Without forgetting the huge portion of early invasions and domination that forged Vietnamese spirit, we can focus on the "twelve inches" that was the French portion and the "couple inches" of American. Such small segments. Such huge tragedies.

The French failed. Subsequently no American general, regardless of how skilled or how good his strategy and tactics, could have led to victory in that war. Not General Westmoreland. Not General Abrams. Not General Weyand who followed Abrams. And not any American generals who might otherwise have been selected to command the effort instead of them. And most definitely not any of the South Vietnamese generals who carried on the war to its conclusion in 1975.

Why?

The essence of the answer lies in an idea expressed by these closely related words: *Independence* and *union*, or *unification* as it came to be called. The idea was a *Vietnamese* idea that was virtually the lifeblood of the Vietnamese people.

Acknowledgments

Immense thanks to Colonel (Ret) Jerry J. Burcham, my dear friend, who is profoundly important in the final shaping of this book through years of discussion of experiences and ideas and who at places within the book contributed anecdotes of his similar combat experiences and conclusions about the war, and who in the final stages of publication edited the proofs during an extended period in which I was unable to do so.

Lieutenant General (Ret) Dave R. Palmer for his contribution of the Foreword.

Merle L. Pribbenow, Jr., retired CIA officer with vast experience in Indochina matters, for translations from Vietnamese histories and documents, and for sharing his insights to the nature of South and North Vietnamese and their conduct of the war.

General of the Army Jean Delaunay, former French Army Chief of Staff who as a lieutenant fought the Viet Minh, who put me in contact with other French generals and Vietnam combatants, and who for decades has sent me material and provided invaluable insights to the French conduct of the war.

Lieutenant Colonel (Marine Corps, RVN) Nguyen Minh Chau. If all district chiefs had been as capable, honest, and dedicated to the people as my deceased friend Chau, America might never have fought a Vietnam War.

Anne Le Dimna Marsilio, formerly of the French Air Force, who ensured the accuracy of my translations from the French.

Research team of 1–4 Cavalry, especially Ronald M. Halicki for getting research started, Colonel (Ret) Carl H. "Skip" Bell III, for heading the team; archivists (former) Sergeant Michael T. O'Connor, and Sergeant First Class (Ret) Terry L. Valentine, for their years of efforts and insights; Major (Ret) James C. Pitts, for his significant input; Lieutenant Colonel (Ret) James A. "Jay" Ward, for map research and production; Major (Ret) Thomas C. Witter, for insights to the nature of civil affairs and pacification efforts.

Maps

Indochina. (David Rennie, from original sketches by Colonel (Ret) William C. Haponski)

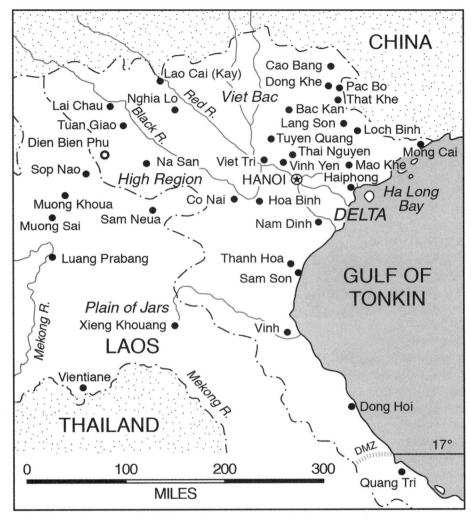

North Vietnam. (David Rennie, from original sketches by Colonel (Ret) William C. Haponski)

South Vietnam. (David Rennie, from original sketches by Colonel (Ret) William C. Haponski)

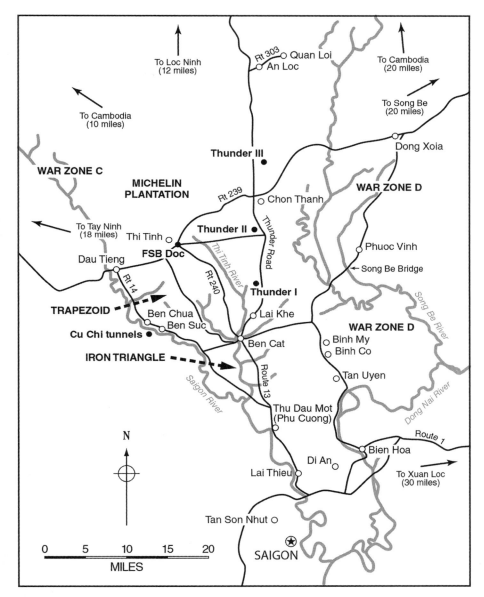

Area of Operations 1st Infantry Division. (David Rennie, from original sketches by Colonel (Ret) William C. Haponski)

PART ONE

THE FRENCH WAR—THE IDEA, AND BULLETS

***

General Vo Nguyen Giap:

"C'est fini. It's over. We will yield no longer."

Hanoi, December 18, 1946

***

CHAPTER I

Independence, Union

Those words—*independence, union*—came to illuminate the aspirations of millions of Vietnamese, North and, yes, South.

The consuming desire for independence had been imbedded in the Vietnamese for two thousand years. They hated foreign domination, whether Chinese, Mongol, Champa, French, Japanese, French again, or American. Independence and union of their country became a passionate credo of not just the 20th-century Vietnamese Communists, but of other independence-minded Vietnamese nationalists as well. It was the Communists, however, who organized early and well, and from a slow beginning spread this desire to a sufficiently large core of adherents that ultimately it became the driving force of the North as well as many in the South throughout thirty years of Indochina wars. In Saigon on April 30, 1975, after decades of enormous sacrifices and losses on both sides, the gates of the Diem-named Independence Palace were smashed down, and a new government took charge. From all the tragic waste emerged a new Vietnam. That it was deeply flawed then, and to a large degree still is, does not seem as important to most Vietnamese as the fact that after desperate struggle, Vietnam since 1975 has been one nation, independent, unified.

***

I served as a lieutenant colonel in two combat units in Vietnam—11th Armored Cavalry Regiment, and 1st Squadron, 4th Cavalry, 1st Infantry Division. In 11th Cav in 1968 I was first the plans and operations officer, then executive officer, the two top staff roles. In 1/4 Cav (QuarterCav) in 1969 I was the commander. In these assignments I was deeply into pacification and violent combat against our enemy's guerrilla, local and regional, and main forces. I reacted to their attacks and planned and directed a variety of actions against them. I was with my men, many times shot at on the ground and in the air, mortared and rocketed. I narrowly missed mines and being hit, and like them I unknowingly sucked in the defoliant toxins that have killed, or is killing, many of us. In the gory business of war, I had direct or indirect responsibility in the killing of many enemy. And at very close range I killed one man, perhaps three men, who came near to killing me. I knew from fighting the enemy and interrogating prisoners that, like my soldiers, most of my enemy were incredibly dedicated, courageous young men.

In 11th Cav we lost 64 troopers KIA while I was with the regiment, not counting the soldiers from our Vietnamese Ranger battalions or U.S. battalions under our operational control. In Task Force 1/4 Cav I lost 36 task force soldiers killed and seven others I had responsibility for protecting. Around 100 of my soldiers were evacuated from the battlefield with serious wounds, and many others were patched up and returned to duty. These soldiers were wonderful young men, called to perform tasks well beyond their 18, 19, 20 or so years, day after day, night after endless terrible night, to the end of their tours, medical evacuations, or deaths. I have experienced agonizing sorrow for those men killed and dreadfully wounded, and for their families and loved ones. Those great guys served their country magnificently. They were the best.

For years afterward I found myself pondering the enormous tragedy, wondering what it was about. *What in hell was it all about?*

In 1998, 29 years after I had come home, I was cleaning my storage shed and found myself looking at my old GI footlocker. I do not know why, but I opened it. The footlocker still smelled of Vietnam, an unmistakable musty smell of jungle. I pulled out my journals, maps, letters, audiotapes, and other memorabilia, then put everything back except the journals: three large notebooks full of entries. I placed the journals on a shelf in my bedroom. On the Internet I came across a reference to my old unit. That led to contact with Mike O'Connor, who, I discovered, as a young sergeant had commanded a tank in my B Troop during our fierce QuarterCav battle in the Michelin Plantation, and we began corresponding. But for another year I could not bring myself to read my journals. When I finally looked into the first of them I knew I had to revisit that fantastically agonizing—and compelling—experience.

Mike had developed a unit website, and with his help I began contacting former troopers (cavalry soldiers) and soldiers of my task force and, my curiosity piqued by what they told me, I began researching in earnest. Having committed so much of myself to this war, I had arrived at the point of wanting to know what it was about—not for our president and national leaders who committed us to a war to contain Communism, citing the domino theory—not even so much for our nation which had seemed to come apart as a result of that war. I wanted to know what it was about for *me*, for *my men*.

Soon I established a research team of over a dozen of my veterans, and we met and recovered thousands of pages of original documents from National Archives. A few were in my handwriting; some others were typed operation orders bearing my signature. I began studying the war in earnest, doing Internet research, buying books, making several more trips to National Archives, corresponding with Frenchmen who had fought in the Indochina War, querying my troopers and other veterans. Within a year I had collected copies of all unit records from squadron and battalion and higher units up to MACV which related to our 1968–69 11th Cav and 1/4 Cav experiences, and I added to this collection in the next several months and years.

During the war in Vietnam I had been profoundly curious about our enemy. I took every opportunity to root out and absorb information. Through my interpreters I extensively interviewed many prisoners. I probed intelligence personnel in my headquarters, adjacent and higher headquarters and in district and province advisory staffs. I had many conversations with a Vietnamese district chief and his village chiefs, all with long experience in fighting our common enemy. I talked with residents of hamlets about the Viet Cong and NVA. At scenes of our small contacts and large battles I tried to discover how our enemy lived and fought. What did they believe? Why did they do the things they did? I tried also to learn as much as possible about the South Vietnamese with whom I came into contact, soldiers and civilians.

From my decades-later research, I learned much more than I knew when I served in Vietnam, particularly about the enemy—the fighters themselves, their units, their terrain, and especially their motivations. Much of the enemy story was contained in our records, in particular, interrogation of prisoner-of-war reports and other intelligence reports. I collected hundreds of books and articles, and thousands of original documents in French and English. Also of great interest were translations of books and other material that had been written by our former enemy. One such book was the official, comprehensive history of the People's Army of Vietnam, *Victory in Vietnam*, translated by Merle Pribbenow. I contacted him and learned that he was an Indochina expert, retired from the CIA. After countless exchanges of information by mail and email, I found that Merle had given me a unique opportunity to discover much more about the actual enemy who had faced my units. His keen insights into our former enemy's order of battle, personnel, combat practices, mannerisms, and motivations have been invaluable.

My sources are:

1) My Vietnam journals. 2) Letters and audio tapes to and from my wife, daughter, friends and family, and many photos and films I took in Vietnam. 3) A multitude of interviews, letters, e-mails, personal conversations, recorded and unrecorded phone calls with former members of my task force. 4) Original records of participating U.S. and South Vietnamese units from squadron/battalion through Army levels (over 15,000 pages of documents, most from National Archives, some from other repositories). 5) Original North Vietnamese unit histories and articles, some translated specifically for me by Merle Pribbenow. 6) Endless queries of an important South Vietnamese official, Lieutenant Colonel Nguyen Minh Chau. 7) Original materials from French colonial times, supplemented by personal accounts

sent to me by French combatants in the Indochina War. 8) All the books, articles and other secondary sources I could find on American, South Vietnamese, North Vietnamese, French, and British units in our area of operations, their commanders and methods, especially those written by combatants. 9) A trip to Vietnam in 2005 to study the scenes of our actions, talk with Vietnamese participants on both sides in the war, and meet one of my "adopted daughters" from the hamlet that was the center of our 11th Cav pacification operations. 10) Additionally, for this current book I made another trip to Vietnam in 2010 to get more information and meet the remainder of my "adopted" Vietnamese family. Also, I added substantially to my secondary sources of books and articles.

***

My experiences in Vietnam combat and my subsequent research led me to conclude that:

1. The Vietnam War was lost before French expeditionary corps or American combat units came ashore. Said another way, there was never a war there which could be won. The reasons lie in the history of Vietnam and the character of its people going back more than 2,000 years.

2. From about 1930 forward, the desire for independence from foreign domination was so strong among the Vietnamese that it would sustain its growing number of adherents no matter how long the effort, no matter what the sacrifice. From about 1944, the desire for unification of their nation began to coalesce with the desire for independence. From 1945 to 1954 the Viet Minh fought and ultimately defeated the French Expeditionary Corps. The bulk of the Vietnamese people, North and South, so much resented French domination that no French high commissioner(s) or general(s) could have brought victory in Vietnam.

3. Following the 1954 Geneva Accords, the Communist leaders were able to reenergize the North and many Vietnamese in the South to fight the Southern government and military. They would outlast any other power which threatened their view of independence and unification.

4. By mid-1964 the intensive U.S. military and economic aid program in South Vietnam had failed. It would have failed under any MAAG/MACV commanding general or American ambassador because so many South Vietnamese people would not support their government. The North could govern and harness the will of the people; the South could not.

5. After the March 1965 insertion of U.S. ground combat forces, the People's War strategy of Ho Chi Minh and Vo Nguyen Giap proved flexible in adapting to changed circumstances, just as it had during the French war. They were able to fight using guerrillas, local and regional forces, and main forces simultaneously, with some pauses in intensity which enabled them to regroup and go at it again.

They were aided by an extensive intelligence and espionage network which persisted despite vigorous attempts to counter it. No American generals, followed after 1971 by South Vietnamese generals, could permanently diminish the recuperative powers of their enemy.

6. The one chance for success—pacification—could never succeed in the South, no matter how promising, for two basic reasons. First, the South Vietnamese government could not gain the loyalty of a sufficient number of its people. Second, virtually every pacification effort was planned and supported by Americans instead of South Vietnamese. Even had the South Vietnamese planned and conducted the operations, they could not have succeeded because the efforts, almost always corrupted by an inbred manner of doing business, came from the top down and not the village up. Importantly, South Vietnam's regular army, ARVN (Army, Republic of Vietnam), was widely despised by the people. While I was with my "adopted" Vietnamese family in 2010 I asked them many questions about their experiences as children and young adults during the war. They had lived in a tiny agricultural hamlet up against the jungle of War Zone D northeast of Saigon. Among my questions, I asked if they were afraid of the VC (Viet Cong)? Of the Americans? No, they were not afraid of either. But they didn't like and were afraid of the ARVN.

***

One commentator said, "To begin the story of America's 'longest war' in the Johnson years—or even in the Kennedy Thousand Days—is like coming into a darkened theater in the middle of the picture. You can gather what has happened after a while, but the relationship between what you are seeing happen on the screen and what had gone before remains fuzzy."[1] Yet that is what not just many historians but also key players in the war itself have done. William Colby, one of the most important among them in his role as America's Vietnam pacification manager, entitled his book, *Lost Victory: A Firsthand Account of America's Sixteen-Year Involvement in Vietnam.* He said we must investigate "the 'dilemma of defeat' …. from the perspective of the War on the ground and in the villages, jungles, mountains, and rice paddies of South Vietnam. We must review the long span of the years from 1959, when the Vietnamese Communists decided to open the 'Second Indochinese War' against the 'American-Diem' Government of South Vietnam, to their final victory in 1975."[2]

Colby's book, based on his experiences from then forward, provides much-needed insights into the later stages of pacification as he built toward his conclusion that we lost a war which should have been a victory. This dedicated American who sacrificed much to serve our country went on to become the director of the CIA. He investigated well, and he pulled together many useful pieces from his research, contacts, and own experiences. But by starting in 1959 "in the middle of the picture" without considering the long Vietnamese history of struggle against foreigners, without understanding the Confucian nature of Vietnamese character, without considering the French war, compounded by gravely misunderstanding the American war despite his close involvement in it, he came to the wrong conclusion. There was no Lost Victory. There was never a victory to be won.

***

During the dark days of 1963, Under Secretary of State George W. Ball told President Kennedy,

> To commit American [ground combat] forces to South Vietnam would, in my view, be a tragic error. Once that process started, I said, there would be no end to it. "Within five years we'll have three hundred thousand men in the paddies and jungles and never find them again." ... To my surprise, the President seemed quite unwilling to discuss the matter, responding with an overtone of asperity: "George, you're just crazier than hell. That just isn't going to happen."[3]

Reflecting on Kennedy's assassination, General Bruce Palmer who had two command assignments as a lieutenant general in Vietnam wrote, "Since that day I have often asked myself what would have happened with respect to South Vietnam if President Kennedy had lived."[4]

It is tempting but ultimately fruitless to indulge in what might-have-been, could-have-been, shoulda-coulda. "History" has a multitude of definitions, depending on the source. Common to most of them, however, is the word *events*. In this book I attempt to present *events* as they *were*. These events show that neither the French nor the American nor the South Vietnamese governments and militaries could ever have won a war in Vietnam regardless of who led the efforts.

The thinking, planning, and efforts in Paris, Washington, Beijing, and Moscow of course were important to the conduct and outcome of the war—important in just that order, with Paris leading (for without the tragic mistakes in Paris, the Vietnamese struggles for independence and unity would inevitably have had a profoundly different character, though most likely the same outcome—an independent, unified, Communist Vietnam). But that is matter for speculation. This book deals with what actually happened.

In *Autopsy* I try to present as succinctly as possible the essence of the contest itself inside the political and social framework that constrained and guided it on both sides—that is, within Vietnam—and leave it to the reader to discern what lessons could have been learned. There are several, crucial to America's approach to current and future wars.

I have long been deeply interested in what Vietnam combatants revealed about their experiences. I consider the term "combatants" to include all those who planned and/or fought within Vietnam—from Ho Chi Minh and Le Duan down to the Viet

Minh and Viet Cong guerrilla; from the French high commissioner of Indochina down to the *soldat* sloshing in the rice paddy, from Ngo Dinh Diem and Nguyen Van Thieu down to the ARVN sergeant who was my interpreter; from General Westmoreland and General Abrams down to the American sergeant who was my radioman. Writings of the highest-level combatants and information about them of course are crucial to an understanding of the war. But interesting, and in many respects, the most revealing, stories were written by combatants who at the time thought and fought at the mid- and lower levels. Their stories are usually unburdened by high-level politics. Crucial matters were being debated and decided in Paris and Washington. But it was the matters in Hanoi and Saigon and throughout Vietnam, *among the combatants themselves which ultimately decided the war*. It is what the combatants believed, what they felt, what they *did*, that made all the difference.

CHAPTER 2

Indochina to September 1945

The recorded history of Vietnam is nearly 3,000 years old. From 207 BC for about 1,100 of those years, Chinese dynasties either ruled directly or dominated the Vietnamese. A revolt in AD 40 led by two Vietnamese sisters named Trung succeeded in recapturing a significant portion of Vietnam from the hated Chinese, but it was crushed within two years. Another woman, Ba Trieu, in AD 225 led a revolt that was longer lasting, almost a quarter century. The hate for foreign rule resulted in inherent resentment of the Chinese specifically, and any type of foreign domination generally. Vietnamese children were inspired by stories of heroes who fought against domination. The fact that for some periods the Vietnamese were able to gain independence gave much later Vietnamese hope they could do it again.

French Colonialism

The arrival of Roman merchants in 166 BC seems to have been the earliest contact with Westerners. Many centuries were then to pass before Marco Polo came to trade in 1292. The first modern Europeans appeared in the early 16th century. French colonialism in Indochina then arose from the compulsion to spread Catholicism and the perceived need to keep up with the British and Dutch in economically exploiting Southeast Asia. In 1847 the emperor Tu Duc "ordered execution of all foreign missionaries, the exiling of Vietnamese Catholic leaders, and prohibition of trade with Westerners. Tu Duc's harsh policy toward his approximately 400,000 Christian subjects was the single most important factor in Vietnam's coming loss of independence. To pro-colonial Frenchmen, it provided moral justification for their encroachments."[1]

The depredations of Vietnamese rulers against French Catholic missionaries and their Vietnamese converts gave France excuse for outright conquest. In 1858 gunships bombarded the port of Tourane (Da Nang) and then moved south to enable capture of what became Saigon. The French annexed three provinces around Saigon and in 1867 three more in an effort to quell the bands of armed guerrillas who were making life intolerable for the resident French *colons*—French colonial residents.

The earliest French military forces were naval with their usual component of marine infantry on board for shore action. Supplementing the white French forces since 1859 were the *Jaunes*—Yellows—Indochinese troops in French service. Troops employed in Indochina were of four types: Regular French Forces (all white); Coloniale (most from North Africa, dark-skinned with mostly white officers); Nationale (Vietnamese and some Cambodian and Lao—again with a predominance of white officers); and French Foreign Legion (of many nationalities with French and German constituting the majority, and mostly French leaders).

By 1893 five regions of Indochina emerged, each with somewhat different means of French governance. Cambodia and Laos lay to the west of Vietnam, which consisted of Tonkin in the north, Annam in the center, and Cochinchina in the south. Cochinchina was linked closest of all to Paris, having been designated a colony and sending a delegate (French of course) to the French National Assembly in Paris. A French governor general (sometimes called high commissioner) of all five parts of Indochina established himself at Hanoi in Tonkin, and for decades thereafter the capital effectively migrated semiannually between Hanoi (in the summer) and Saigon (winter) to take advantage of differing seasonal weather. Many Vietnamese resented not just their loss of independence but, with the codified division of Vietnam into three regions, their unity.

A prime minister of France in the period 1880–85, expressed the views of the fervent pro-colonialists in a speech to the Chamber of Deputies in Paris, telling them that the higher races have a duty to civilize the lower races. On the positive side, the *mission civilisatrice* (civilizing mission) of the French showed itself in many improvements: suppression of malaria, building of roads, railroads, docks, canals, hospitals, schools, construction projects of all kinds. Many, perhaps most, Vietnamese were caught in a love-hate relationship with the French, admiring and emulating their Western culture and the improvements, but hating them for their domination. From the beginning of French colonization, the stage was set for a Vietnamese struggle once again to throw off the foreign yoke and gain independence.

Ho Chi Minh and Early Indochinese Communism

The Russo-Japanese War of 1904–05 had profound consequences for Vietnam. The war ended in a surprising, humiliating defeat for the Russians. The fact that an Oriental power was able to defeat a European nation was not lost on Vietnamese groups gearing up to move for independence from the French, least of all on Nguyen Sinh Cung, if in fact that was his name. The details of his early life are sketchy, with conflicting accounts. Later, among other aliases, he was known as Ho Chi Minh (The Enlightened One).

Ho was born in Nghe An Province of Annam on May 19, 1890. His father, Nguyen Sinh Sac, was a minor mandarin-style official and teacher, educated but impoverished. Ho's father disdained both the French and the imperial court of Annam at Hue and imbued his son with patriotic deeds of heroes who struggled against oppression. Sac guided him too in studying the "inner ethical content of Confucian philosophy."[2] The Confucian values of patience, perseverance, and patriotism were ingrained in Vietnamese culture, and young Cung would make them tenets of his life. Ho and his adherents "combined the traditional value system inculcated by Confucianism—loyalty and service to the national community based on moral and ethical values—with the new revolutionary and scientific values of Marxism-Leninism."[3]

A South Vietnamese lieutenant general, Dong Van Khuyen, highlighted the Confucian ethic which historically so shaped Vietnamese culture:

> Almost all leaders of Vietnamese history upheld the Confucian principle of "People First, Government Second." The people were a major force that enabled Vietnam to survive as a nation despite foreign invasions and domination. It was the Vietnamese people who helped the Viet Minh win the War of Resistance against the French. For the South Vietnamese government soldiers, [however,] winning popular sympathy was an uphill task because, in the people's eyes, they were the successors of the French Union forces.[4]

Ho understood the people, and he never stopped telling his followers that in the revolution, the people had to come first—and he meant it. The people responded in massive numbers not just by following and admiring him, but with many loving him. To them he was "Uncle," a most affectionate term in Vietnamese culture.

Ho advocated independence and had to move quickly at times to keep out of the reach of French authorities. From 1911, he spent some time at sea as a kitchen helper, then in New York and Boston restaurants as a helper and pastry chef.

After the outbreak of World War I in 1914 "some 50,000 Vietnamese troops and 50,000 Vietnamese workers were sent to Europe … 80,000 Vietnamese were either fighting for the French Army or working in French factories side by side with French women."[5] The Vietnamese also had to pay taxes to help support France's war efforts. What, Ho certainly wondered, would the Vietnamese receive in return?

The 1917 Russian Revolution provided impetus to social movements worldwide, especially in underdeveloped countries. After some time in London, Ho had gone to France and become a spirited speaker among French socialists and labor groups. He was particularly enamored of Lenin who knew that revolution would take organization, hard work, and force—revolutionary violence. By the time of the Versailles Peace Conference of 1919 Ho was trying to see the leaders of France, Great Britain, and the United States to get their support, but failed. He seems to have had to settle for passing out his flyer, a petition demanding political autonomy and traditional freedoms of a democratic society—freedom of religion, assembly, press, and equality with the French in Vietnam. Up to this time he was much more a nationalist proselytizing for independence than a Communist, but it was the Communists who were disrupting the comfortable world order of nations, and Ho joined others as a founding member of the French Communist Party.

> Ho … traveled extensively throughout France in 1919–21, addressing large crowds of Vietnamese war workers and soldiers awaiting repatriation to the Far East. Thus, tens of thousands of Vietnamese who had come into contact with the white man's world and seen its failings from close up, were for the first time given an interpretation of what they were seeing and how it could affect their future. That interpretation was both nationalist and Communist, and its seeds matured slowly over the next two decades.[6]

In 1924 Ho was invited to Moscow. Surreptitiously he left France, successfully evading the Sûreté (Security and Intelligence Service). In Russia Ho studied Marxist and Leninist thought, and participated in and addressed an early Comintern Congress. He had passed from relatively unknown revolutionary into one who was acquiring international recognition.

Later in 1924 Ho went on to China and organized revolutionary gatherings while beginning to be recognized as an important figure in the worldwide Communist movement. "Vietnamese Communism was born, if so amorphous a development as a modern mass movement has a fixed time and place of birth, in Canton in 1925."[7]

At first Ho got support from Sun Yat-sen's nationalist Kuomintang Party (KMT), presumably because he and those around him were fiercely nationalist. Some of Ho's adherents were trained in China until the KMT realized that Ho and those around him were not only nationalists who would fight for Indochinese independence, but also Communists, the enemies of KMT.

It was in Canton that the person who eventually was to become known as a nation's kindly uncle first revealed the cruel lengths he would go to in order to ensure the success of the revolution he envisioned. Ho had sent cadre back into Indochina to conduct subversive works. Some among them had proven unreliable or refused to follow Communist orders, so "Their names were leaked by the Communists to French Intelligence, and the Sûreté in Vietnam was only too glad to pick them up on arrival."[8]

By 1927, with the KMT against him, Ho left quickly for Moscow.

Rubber Plantations, Hotbeds of Communist Recruitment

In Vietnam the terrible conditions for workers in the mines of the North and rubber plantations of the South provided hotbeds for early Communist recruitment. The French had trouble attracting Vietnamese laborers in the areas around the plantations in the South, largely because these people knew what life on the plantations was all about. In Tonkin, though, there was starvation and incredible hardship which killed hundreds of thousands. Unscrupulous French and Vietnamese recruiters exploited the situation, signing up hordes of desperate people and transporting them in slave-like conditions for labor in the southern plantations. Many of them would die there of disease brought on by overwork, mistreatment, and unhealthy conditions that were part and parcel of jungle life as they cleared the primeval forest, planted rubber trees, maintained the plantations, and harvested the latex.

The Michelin Company's huge plantation 40 miles northwest of Saigon would seem to have been hospitable, flat as it was, with more than one road running through it, and on the bank of the Saigon River. But the work conditions were terrible. In clearing the jungle and planting the rubber trees, workers weakened by malnutrition contracted malaria and died by the dozens from lack of medicine and proper health care.

"The workday was long, from ten to twelve hours [six days a week].... On Sunday [the coolies] had to work half a day.... Every village had its own counting field—the place where the workers gathered for a head count by their assigned contract numbers (workers were assigned numbers—names were not used).... At the counting field they beat people very brutally."[9]

In 1927, soon after the Companie Michelin began developing its second plantation at Thuan Loi near Phu Rieng to the northeast, a worker there killed a French foreman, the first instance of serious revolt by the workers. Growing unrest was followed by the worldwide Great Depression, which had a devastating effect on workers everywhere. Thuan Loi was hit by a general uprising on February 3, 1930, suppressed by the French military, gendarmes (national military police), and provincial Vietnamese security units. This event naturally affected the workers at the primary Michelin plantation in Dau Tieng, and they too rose in protest, calling out to the plantation manager just transferred down from Thuan Loi, "Soumagnac, get out. You will not be allowed to make the workers eat spoiled rice and rotten fish, you will not be allowed to beat the workers."[10] Security troops at Dau Tieng fired on and killed two of the demonstrators, ending the open protest.

Ho as Communist Party Organizer

In 1930, now in Hong Kong, Ho was instrumental in drawing together bitterly divided Communist organizations. He addressed them and all countrymen:

> Workers, peasants, soldiers, youth, and pupils!
> Oppressed and exploited compatriots!
> Sisters and brothers! Comrades! ....
>
> The Vietnamese Communists, formerly working separately, have now united into a single party, the Communist Party of Indochina [ICP] to lead our entire people in their revolution....
> From now on we must join the Party, help it and follow it in order to implement the following slogans:

1. To overthrow French imperialism, feudalism, and the reactionary Vietnamese capitalist class.
2. To make Indochina completely independent....[11]

Here at age 40 was Ho, the leader of a movement in a small area of the world largely dismissed by the West, the Soviet Union, and China alike as inconsequential. From this unlikely beginning, Vietnamese Communism would grow to have enormous global consequences.

Communists and Nationalists

Plantation violence plus unrest and disobedience among mineworkers were only part of the problems for French colonial authorities. Nationalist, non-Communist independence groups had been developing since the last half of the 19th century. In fact, by the 1920s and 1930s they were stronger than the Communists. One of these independence groups, the Viet Nam Quoc Dan Dang (VNQDD—Vietnamese Nationalist Party) had directed its recruiting efforts toward not just civilians but also Vietnamese members of the French colonial forces. Shortly after the February 1930 uprising at the Michelin's Thuan Loi plantation, the VNQDD incited a mutiny of over 50 soldiers at Yen Bai garrison northwest of Hanoi, supported by a large number of civilians who had forced their way inside the compound. The mutiny failed when other Vietnamese soldiers in Yen Bai units refused to follow the mutineers. Shortly afterward the guillotine was busy dealing with soldier and civilian nationalists.

All the while, the Communists grew in number, starting with not many, and spreading through the plantations. The Dau Tieng Communist Party Chapter was formed in late 1936. In 1937 there was another large worker strike in Dau Tieng in which four workers were killed and 41 arrested. And so it went on. The French struck back hard, and "as 1939 began, because of the savage suppressions by the enemy, the Dau Tieng Party Chapter was shattered."[12]

Both the so-called "nationalist" parties and the "Communists" were nationalists—that is, patriotic independence organizations. In terms of parties, however, the various groups were properly termed Nationalist or Communist. They were locked in mortal combat, out of which one would emerge as the much more powerful party—the Communist. The Nationalist VNQDD was modeled after the Chinese KMT from whom they got support. Their organization was loose, often fractured, inefficient, in comparison to the more tightly knit, efficient and disciplined Communist organization. The Nationalists were impetuous and wanted independence *now*. The Communists planned for the long haul and chose their targets and methods far more carefully.

In 1939 the French had outlawed the ICP, and its leaders fled to China or went underground, mostly in the Viet Bac, the mountainous region north of Hanoi where Communist recruiting had been quite successful. Many unlucky leaders were caught and sent to the notorious prison, Poulo Condor, on an island in the South China Sea. Later, Vietnamese who survived the horrible prison experience, there and in other prisons, took it as a badge of honor in their fight against the French.

Indochina in World War II

World War II broke out on September 1, 1939 with the German invasion of Poland. Then in 1940 the Germans invaded France. Colonel Charles de Gaulle had commanded his armored regiment well, was promoted to brigadier general and given command of the 4th Armored Division. De Gaulle wanted to set up a resistance government in North Africa, the complications of which led to the rise of Marshal Philippe Pétain to head a collaborationist government (the Vichy regime), and the flight on June 17 of de Gaulle to England where he later in absentia was condemned to death for treason by the Pétain government. De Gaulle made the famous June 18, 1940 radio call on BBC to all Frenchmen to resist and fight the enemy until once again France was free. "France is not alone! She is not alone! She is not alone! She has a vast Empire behind her. She can align with the British Empire that holds the sea and continues the fight. She can, like England, use without limit the immense industry of the United States." The French Resistance was created, and by September 1941 de Gaulle had established the Free French government-in-exile.

At the time of the German invasion of France, French Indochina was in a pitifully weak condition. There were fewer than 40,000 French people in the five parts of Indochina with only about 30,000 troops of all kinds in the ground forces.[13] De Gaulle was in no position to provide support, Britain was fighting for its very survival, and America was trying to stay out of the fighting while it supplied arms and other support to Allied forces.

The mighty Japanese military had invaded China, were set on conquering all of Asia, and now were at the northern border of Vietnam. The French in Indochina, ill-equipped and cut off from their support base half a world away, were faced with the prospect of defending Vietnam against Japan. Sailing out of Vietnamese ports, the French navy had only one cruiser and four cutters to defend a 1,500-mile coastline against the powerful Japanese Navy. The French air force had about 100 outdated planes, mostly observation and utility or transport, whereas "sleek Japanese bombers and fighter aircraft made prewar French biplanes and Potez transports look quaint indeed."[14]

General Georges Catroux, Governor General of Indochina, was in a tough spot. He had no respect for a Vichy regime but felt it was his duty to keep Indochina French so long as possible. The Japanese began pressuring him for concessions to make Indochina an asset in their plan for domination of East and Southeast Asia. The immediate problem for the Japanese was the rail line and the roads from northern Vietnam running across the border with China. American weapons and other military equipment and supplies were making their way from the harbor at Haiphong in Vietnam to Chiang Kai-shek's KMT forces in southern China. The Japanese demanded that Catroux cut off this supply line. Washington said it could give no support to Catroux who then was forced to acquiesce. Back in France, the Vichy government thought Catroux had given in too easily and sent Admiral Jean Decoux to replace him. This well suited Catroux who flew to join the Free French and eventually became commander of French forces in the mid-East.

In September of 1940 the Japanese were coercing the Vichy French administration of Indochina, now under Decoux, into transit agreements, and when negotiations seemed to be too slow, Japanese troops came across the Chinese border and overran border posts, fiercely resisted by the French defenders who took heavy casualties. The Japanese then pressured Decoux into turning over three airfields in Tonkin, followed in July 1941 by eight more in southern Indochina, accompanied by withdrawal of the French garrisons from those places. On July 28, 1941, four months before Pearl Harbor, the Japanese marched into Saigon and established their complete supremacy by occupying key positions throughout Vietnam. The Japanese saw it to their advantage to leave the Vichy French administrators and plantation managers largely in place. For the next nearly four years Admiral Decoux tried to preserve as much as he could of Indochina from Japanese encroachment but was forced by circumstances largely to cooperate with them. The dreaded Japanese Kempeitai kept the French Sûreté and the rest of Decoux's government under close surveillance.

Ho Chi Minh saw the war as a marvelous opportunity. In his 1941 "Letter from Abroad," he wrote:

> Elder citizens!
>> Sages and heroes!
>> Scholars, farmers, workers, merchants, and soldiers!
>> France has been lost to the Germans, French strength here is dissipated, yet still they [the Vichy government] raise our taxes to loot us, still they mount white terror against the people. In foreign dealings they hold their breath fearfully, giving some land to Siam [later named Thailand], kneeling down in surrender to Japan. Meanwhile our people have to wear two yokes, continuing to serve as buffaloes and horses for the French, but now also being slaves of the Japanese. In such painful, tormenting conditions shall we simply fold our arms and wait to die? No, absolutely not! More than twenty million descendants of Lac and Hung [ancient heroes] are determined not to be perpetual slaves without a country![15]

Despite Ho's optimism, the combination of the Japanese and the French Vichy government caused the Communists serious problems. The workers' *History* said, "These two fascist, colonialist powers worked together to oppress and exploit our people."[16] The Michelin plantation at Dau Tieng became a refuge for Party members and sympathizers in surrounding provinces.

Fearful though the times were, and wary of the Japanese, independence-minded Vietnamese were nevertheless heartened by recognition that once again Oriental troops had vanquished Westerners, this time the French in Indochina. Although Vietnamese loyal to Communists were hunted and persecuted by Decoux, the Communists had no love for the Japanese either, and in time would come to resist them. Despite the unfavorable odds, Ho was determined that the Indochinese Communist Party would take advantage of the times to strengthen themselves, enlarge their ranks, and when circumstances were right, defeat both the Japanese and the French.

Ho's Early Work in Tonkin

Ho had not set foot in his homeland since 1912. Twenty-nine years later, in February 1941, he crossed the border from China into northern Tonkin and set up his headquarters in a cave at Pac Bo, a small hamlet near the border in the Viet Bac. From the 1930s a small number of Vietnamese Communists had done well in this region in propagandizing their *doc lap*—independence—theme, and as the years passed, more of the locals became not just willing listeners and sympathizers, but proponents of the cause. In 1940 and 1941, Ho's close follower and later general, Vo Nguyen Giap, made trips to the Viet Bac to contact committed and potential recruits. Many of these were from various Montagnard (hill-dwelling) tribes. A local Nung tribesman, Chu Van Tan, became a close friend of Giap, and he later became a general and the first Viet Minh defense minister.

At Pac Bo, Ho conferred with Giap, Truong Chinh, Pham Van Dong, and other early leaders on the course to take. A young revolutionary asked,

> "How can we have a revolution without arms and where are we going to find guns?" … Ho replied, "We must rely on our own force with some outside help. When the people absorb this beautiful idea of revolution, they will create the strongest of forces. Everything because of the people; everything for the people. People first, guns last. If we have the people on our side, then we will have guns. If we have the people, we will have everything."[17]

This belief became the heart and soul of the long Communist-led wars against the French and Americans: politics aimed at gaining popular support were much more important than military force.

In May, in a hut near the cave while sitting on a block of wood at a wooden table, Ho convened the Eighth Plenum of the Indochinese Communist Party. It established the League for the Independence of Vietnam: *Việt Nam Độc Lập Đồng Minh Hội*, or Viet Minh, that provided the armed element of the Party. A decision which was to guide their war policy from then until the end in 1975 was "that the demands of ideology and class war must be subordinated to those of the anti-imperialistic struggle for national independence."[18] This was a crucial concept. Ho would strongly express Communist views, only later to amend them, abandon them temporarily, deny them, adapt to any change in circumstances so long as by doing so the struggle could continue and eventually succeed. At one point he would even disband the Indochinese Communist Party in order to give the impression that the independence movement was not controlled by Communists, but by revolutionaries, all of whom were nationalists.

Ho's Privations

In August 1942 Ho set out once more for China, headed for Chungking, the provisional capital of the Chinese Nationalist government. Located there were the headquarters of a sizable Soviet delegation, the command post of U.S. operations in the China-Burma-India theater, and a detachment of the OSS (Office of Strategic Services), forerunner of the CIA. The Chinese Nationalists and Communists were bound by a temporary, uneasy cooperative arrangement with the common purpose of driving the Japanese out of China. Thus, if Ho was lucky, he could contact high-level people in the Chinese, Soviet, and U.S. governments, seeking information on operations that would affect Indochina, and hoping for support of his cause.

Ho and his Vietnamese companion walked through dangerous country of southern China until they were stopped by police. Suspected of being a spy, Ho was arrested. This began a period of severe hardship during which he somehow managed to get some writing materials and compose poems, recording his experiences and thoughts. He estimated he had passed through 18 prisons. The final prison was a den of thieves, cutthroats, and miscellaneous unfortunates, and the only place he could find to rest was next to the filthy latrines. "Ho spent time with men who had fallen into ruin and suffered both social and moral ostracism, which taught him more about mankind than he could have learned from a course in psychology."[19] A biographer described his condition: "By now his body was emaciated and covered with sores, his hair had begun to turn gray, and his teeth were falling out."[20]

After months of such inhumane conditions, while the Chinese authorities were assessing his potential usefulness, Ho was treated better. No longer shackled at night, fed better, he was even allowed to read books and write to comrades in China and Vietnam. In September 1943 he was released from jail and when the Chinese had decided Ho was the best person to lead a Vietnamese resistance movement against the Japanese, restrictions were further eased, and he traveled, lectured, and continued political work in southern China.

***

Ho Chi Minh, 1944. (NARA)

In November 1942 the Allies landed in North Africa and caused the collapse of Vichy there, resulting in large numbers of Vichy units going over to the Allies. The Germans quickly took over Vichy southern France, and the Vichy government became a shadow of its former self. The question now as to Indochina was whether Decoux could continue to maintain administrative control. The Kempeitai began keeping an even closer eye on his government.

Events in Pac Bo

In September 1944 Ho was granted freedom by the Chinese, and after arduous travel he arrived back in Pac Bo. While he had been gone, his Communist colleagues had done a considerable amount of proselytizing throughout Vietnam and had gained significant support among the people. Especially in the Viet Bac stronghold, called the "Liberated Zone," the Party leadership had notably improved in recruiting and organizing civilians for resistance, and in training men and women for military service.

For two years the war had been going badly for the Axis Powers both in the Pacific and North Africa and was getting progressively worse. In June 1944 the Allies had landed in Normandy. In the Pacific, the Japanese were being relentlessly pushed back. Relative to colonialism, in July 1944, de Gaulle said, "The aim of French policy is and will remain to raise all these territories to as high a level as possible, so that every one is able to look out for its own interests and to be represented within a federal system. This is the policy France will pursue, in particular for Indochina."[21] De Gaulle's words rang hollow. In Vietnam the Communists believed in independence, not continued subjugation within a French system. The time for decisive action was drawing near.

In Pac Bo, Ho held a meeting of comrades, of which Giap said,

> Uncle put forth the question of organizing the National Liberation Army. Turning to me, he said in conclusion, "This you should carry out. Can you do that? We are still weak, the enemy is strong. But we must not let them annihilate us, must we?"
> I answered, "Yes, I'll do it."
> Ho insisted, "The first battle must be successful."[22]

Later, Ho had a stroke of good luck. On November 11, 1944, a U.S. reconnaissance plane over mountainous terrain along the Chinese-Vietnamese border had an engine failure and the pilot, Lieutenant Rudolph Shaw, bailed out. Viet Minh got to him just ahead of both a Japanese and a French patrol. Ho soon heard of this and directed that the pilot be delivered to him at Pac Bo. After nearly a month of negotiating virtually impassable terrain with guides whose only English was "America! Roosevelt!," the weak, despairing Shaw was greeted in English by Ho, who also spoke fluent French and Chinese: "'How do you do, pilot! Where are you from?' Shaw was reportedly so excited that he hugged Ho and later said to him, 'When I heard your voice, I felt as if I were hearing the voice of my father in the United States.'"[23]

Ho and his small party set out walking, headed for Kunming to deliver Shaw back to the Americans. Just across the border, Chinese authorities sent Shaw on ahead by air to Kunming, leaving Ho's group to get there the best way they could. A Vietnamese comrade "recalled that Ho Chi Minh looked sickly and emaciated, and ate little. His uniform was patched and worn, and his thin canvas shoes were full of holes.... Ho had recently caught a fever ... and he seemed uncharacteristically depressed. Yet his mind was still focused on his cause."[24]

Giap's Early Leadership

During Ho's absence, at Pac Bo Giap prepared for a military strike. Finally, in early December instructions came in a letter from Ho. A unit was to be formed, the Vietnam Propaganda Unit for National Liberation. The letter said, "It shows by its name that greater importance should be attached to the political side than to the military side.... At first its size is small; however, its prospect is brilliant. It is the embryo of the Liberation Army and can move from north to south, throughout Vietnam."[25]

Giap had no formal military study or training. He had a baccalaureate degree in political science from the University of Hanoi, followed by one year of teaching history in a private school before his revolutionary activities consumed him. But from his teens, Giap had avidly studied military history, and he knew the intricacies of numerous historical battles so well that in his teaching he left students spellbound. In December 1944 at Pac Bo, instant "General" Giap gathered an "army" of 34 comrades to go forth to battle, 31 men and three women. He sent a 12- or 13-year-old boy into the nearby garrison of Phai Kat to spy. The young fellow performed useful tasks for the French in the garrison while gathering information on their layout, personnel, and daily activities. This tactic of careful acquisition of advance information before attack was to persist throughout the thirty-year war.

Giap's group was armed with "two revolvers, seventeen rifles, fourteen flintlocks, and one light machine gun [actually, probably a submachine gun]."[26] Giap three decades later wrote, "We forgot that we were only 34 human beings equipped with rudimentary weapons. We imagined ourselves to be an army of steel, not to be defeated by any force, ready to destroy the enemy. Confidence, eagerness prevailed."[27]

On Christmas Eve his small force assembled around their red flag with gold star. They took a ten-point pledge, the first of which was "To sacrifice everything for their fatherland so as to make Vietnam independent."[28] They set off, dressed as a mandarin patrol with fake authorization papers, talked their way into the Phai Khat outpost and quickly overcame the defenders. When the French commander rode up shortly after, they killed him and his horse. During that night they then marched 20 miles to the Na Ngan post, disguised by uniforms captured at Phai Khat, posing as a patrol which had captured some Communists. Again they gained entrance, and this time shooting broke out within the post, killing five occupants. The others were taken prisoner (and by some accounts were killed, as had been the Phai Khat defenders—the accounts are murky). The 9th Colonial Infantry Regiment of the Tonkin Division retaliated with a powerful sweep of the area, rounding up suspects, seizing some arms, killing 75. No one could possibly recognize the tremendous significance of this first direct combat of Giap's Viet Minh unit against French, that it would be precursor to an all-out, thirty-year war.

From Phai Khat, Giap went to other bases in the Viet Bac, significantly adding to his military strength. Caves near Cao Bang became his first headquarters, and there in addition to his main forces he created regional and district armed militias and village self-defense forces. The latter were 30-man platoons poorly armed but trained in putting out mines, booby traps and punji pits. In all types of forces more time was spent on political indoctrination than military training:

> At first, everything was lacking: food, weapons, coverlets, medicine. The troops often had nothing to eat, yet they remained in an eager and joyful mood…. Not long afterward our strength increased from a few dozen to several hundred. Young people came in great numbers to enlist into the army. The Viet Bac people extended eager assistance in all fields. Some people

even sold their buffaloes and lands to help, and people in other places also extended all-out assistance…. Not only did the liberated zone [northwest, north and northeast of Hanoi] come into existence, but base areas were built up everywhere.[29]

Nationalist or Communist?

About at the time in 1944 when Giap was forming the nucleus of his army, in a military academy just north of Hanoi two young Vietnamese cadets were preparing for regular commissions in the French Army. One of them, Tran Van Don, wrote,

> One afternoon the bugle sounded, calling us to fall in ranks for a special ceremony. The symbol of the foreign country we were serving, the French tricolor, flapped in the gentle evening breeze. The flagstaff flew no other; nothing of our own to honor as we stood at rigid attention. The ceremony came to an end and we were dismissed. Xuong and I faced each other, evidently moved by the same thoughts. There were tears in our eyes. At that moment, in the splendid effusiveness of youth, we swore that we would from now on dedicate our whole lives to serve only one country, Vietnam, and to defend only our own national colors in independence and freedom.

Xuong kept his oath. Under the red flag with gold star in the middle he went on to become a reputed guerrilla fighter and province chief in the North. Tran Van Don also kept his oath. Under the yellow flag with three horizontal red stripes, in the South he rose to become a lieutenant general and finally, Defense Minister in President Thieu's cabinet.[30] Independence and unity. Both wanted it desperately, each in his own way. Only one, Xuong, would see his aspirations realized.

Also about then, other young men and women were graduating from the high schools of Hanoi and the University of Hanoi with a burning nationalist spirit. Many of them, such as the young man Bui Diem, would oppose the Communists not as soldiers but as members of secret non-Communist nationalist parties. He was not related to the later President Ngo Dinh Diem of the Republic of Vietnam (South Vietnam). Rather, he came from a prominent mandarin family and had been one of Giap's history students at the high school Lycée Thang Long in Hanoi:

> We students felt that our country was on the verge of striking out for its freedom, and there wasn't a soul who didn't want to be part of that…. New nationalist groups were forming a number of different parties under the name Dai Viet (Great Vietnam).
>
> When Giap disappeared from the Lycée, rumor had it that he had gone to the Viet Bac to train revolutionaries. Bui Diem, a bit later a University of Hanoi student in mathematics, was intrigued by nationalistic youth groups. The students bicycled on weekends to historic sites honoring past heroes.
>
> The French authorities could hardly object to such orderly excursions. Sitting around campfires, we would discuss how the Trung sisters had overthrown the Chinese occupiers of the first century…. Afterward we would sing, so loudly the woods seemed to reverberate: "Brothers, students, stand up! Answer the call from rivers and mountains. Go forward, always forward. Have no regrets ever about sacrificing your lives."

> In public the students were united. In private it was a different story. Gradually, each of us joined one or another of the parties that promised to mold a reality from the desire for freedom. At that time, in 1943 and 1944, few had any idea of the distinctions between these parties, or even a good concept of which was which. They all said they were fighting for independence. That was enough.... It was not generally known ... that the Viet Minh was Communist controlled. Ho Chi Minh was not a name anyone had yet heard of.[31]

The Communists were much more organized than the various nationalist groups, who were plagued by infighting. The Communists had a broad-based strategy of appealing to the people on many levels—personal, societal, economic, political; the nationalists were much more single-mindedly focused on getting the French out, without a strategy as to what would then happen to the people. The Communists were much better trained, with many of their leaders having close ties to Moscow or Beijing or both, and they were more disciplined, insisting on adherence to Party guidance. And they began early to build a spirited, disciplined armed force.

The 1944–45 famine resulted in deaths estimated from the hundreds of thousands to two million Vietnamese. The Communists gained considerable support when they worked assiduously to try to get food to the masses.

The Japanese Coup

By early March 1945, the Japanese in Indochina were in an increasingly precarious position. Advancing American forces across the Pacific had placed them in a stranglehold. Burma, Iwo Jima, the Philippines—all had been lost. The possibility of the Vichy French forces within Indochina suddenly taking the side of their enemy was real and immediate.

In Saigon, in the late afternoon of March 9, 1945 the Japanese secretly gave Admiral Decoux an ultimatum: turn over administrative control of all Indochina to the Japanese and disarm and confine French troops to barracks. Decoux refused. Under arrest, the admiral could not get an order out to his forces to resist. Pre-positioned Japanese troops swept down upon startled French garrisons throughout Indochina, and in most cases the confused French, not hearing from their command in Saigon as to what they were to do, had no choice but to obey the Japanese. Some got word, though, of what had happened and managed to retain their arms and fiercely fight back. Had the coup not occurred, quite certainly Decoux would have delivered Indochina back to de Gaulle's new Provisional Government at the end of the war. Instead, he was taken up to the Loc Ninh rubber plantation north of Saigon to be confined and contemplate his fate until war's end.

Taking advantage of the confusion, Vietnamese prisoners all over the country escaped as French jail guards abandoned their posts and tried to escape from the Japanese.

The Japanese coup caused considerable consternation in U.S. intelligence circles. The Americans needed information on Indochina, and it was possible that the small bands of French Resistance there would no longer be able to communicate with Ceylon and Kunming. An OSS officer in China, Lieutenant Charles Feng, wanted to meet Ho, which would be a wonderful opportunity for Ho. OSS Major Archimedes Patti wrote of this encounter. "Feng described their first meeting [on March 17, 1945 in China]: 'I asked [Ho] what he wanted…. He said—only recognition of his group' …. They met again three days later and worked out details for Ho to return to Indochina where intelligence listening posts would be set up with OSS radios and OSS-trained Vietnamese operators."[32] Soon Ho was to meet Patti, the newly appointed head of the OSS mission to Indochina.

The OSS was aware of President Roosevelt's attitude about France and Indochina. FDR had an unfavorable impression of de Gaulle from the very beginning. Roosevelt basically did not want to do anything to assist France in regaining its colonies, but of course he also did not want to help Communists. The OSS in China, well out of earshot of the head shed in the U.S., felt that Ho could be of use in the war against Japan. Also by 1944 they were turned off by the Chinese Nationalists whom they saw as corrupt and not committed enough to fight the Japanese. Ho seemed eager to do so.

On March 24, 1945 the French government in Paris announced an Indochinese Federation of Allied States, covering the five Indochinese areas: Laos, Cambodia, and the three parts of Vietnam. While it offered much broader privileges within a French Union than had been the case with pre-war Indochina, Ho and other nationalist leaders denounced the Federation decree as falling far short of true independence.

Post-coup, in April the Japanese formally gave Indochina its independence (while they still of course pulled the strings). The Vietnamese Communists began making full use of five months of total Japanese control of the French by strengthening themselves for the struggle they felt sure was soon to come. By May, working out of the Viet Bac, they had "liberated" nine Tonkin provinces and parts of two others, and Giap proclaimed the formation of the People's Liberation Army. He also was named a member of the Central Committee of the Indochinese Communist Party, an important formal juncture of his military and political duties.

In July one of Patti's OSS teams in southern China parachuted into the Viet Bac and contacted the Viet Minh, with the eventual mission to raid a Japanese position. The OSS team leader was taken to a hut with a banner over the entrance in English: "Welcome to our American friends." The team members gave the Viet Minh some weapons, but their greatest gift was to save Ho's life. He was trembling and had a high fever, so they gave him "quinine, sulfa drugs, and vitamin capsules," and within a few days he was "well on his way back to health."[33]

The raid for which the OSS team had prepared never happened. Astonishingly, on August 6 an atom bomb was dropped on Hiroshima, and on August 9 another on Nagasaki. On August 15 Japan gave notice of unconditional surrender.

***

De Gaulle had long been planning for an expeditionary force of two divisions to fight the Japanese in the Pacific arena, which included Indochina. When in 1944 he had offered this idea to the Americans and British he was given the cold shoulder. FDR saw the plan as a way for French colonialism to regain a toehold. De Gaulle nevertheless had gone ahead with plans, and two early units, the 5th Régiment d'Infanterie Coloniale (5th RIC) and a commando naval air parachute detachment, were already in Ceylon. De Gaulle felt that Free French blood spilled on Indochinese soil could make an impressive claim for reestablishment of control in Indochina. At the Yalta Conference in February 1945, to which de Gaulle pointedly was not invited, a very ill FDR was said to have told Stalin that no U.S. ships would carry French troops to Indochina (a policy which Truman initially would continue).

Ho's Provisional Government

With Japanese announcement of intended surrender, the Viet Minh were ecstatic. At least one enemy had been taken care of, and the way now seemed clear to go after the French. On August 16, 1945 in Hanoi, having taken over the French Résident Supérieur's mansion as the seat of a new government, the Viet Minh People's Congress proclaimed a provisional government under President Ho Chi Minh. On August 19, in celebration as part of the famed "August Revolution," the Viet Minh orchestrated a huge demonstration in Hanoi.

Ever since the Japanese coup, Emperor Bao Dai at the imperial capital of Hue had been propped up on his throne by the Japanese as the nominal ruler of Vietnam. He sensed what would lie ahead for France and Vietnam if de Gaulle's France were to reassert its rule over Indochina. On that same day of August 19 the emperor sent a message to de Gaulle:

> I address myself to the people of France, to the country of my youth. I address myself as well to its chief and liberator [de Gaulle], and I wish to speak as a friend rather than as Chief of State.
>
> You have suffered too much during four deadly years [of World War II] not to understand that the Vietnamese people, who have a history of twenty centuries and an often-glorious past, no longer desire and can no longer endure any foreign domination or governments.
>
> You will understand still better if you could see what is happening here, if you could feel the will for independence which has been smoldering in the hearts of all and which no human force can hold in check any longer. Even if you were to come to re-establish French government here it would not be obeyed: each village would be a nest of resistance, each former collaborator an

enemy, and your officials and your colonists themselves would ask to leave that unbreathable atmosphere.

I beg you to understand that the only means of safeguarding French interests and the spiritual influence of France in Indochina is to recognize unreservedly the independence of Viet-Nam and to renounce any idea of reestablishing French sovereignty or French administration here in any form.

We would be able to understand each other so easily and to become friends if you would stop hoping to become our masters again.

In making this appeal to the well-known idealism of the French people and to the great wisdom of their leader, we hope that the peace and the joy which has come for all the peoples of the world will be equally ensured to all the inhabitants of Indochina, native as well as foreign.[34]

If de Gaulle had heeded this sage advice, France, America, and the people of Vietnam—North and South—might have been spared many long years of agony. But he could not. The colonial concept was imbedded in French politics and culture. It would have taken almost superhuman sensitivity and courage for de Gaulle or any other leader of the French nation to make decisions that would entirely upset that order. So de Gaulle remained determined that France should first reestablish the status quo before he took up the idea of independence for Vietnam, a form of which he preferred but, as events took their tragic turns, he was later powerless to negotiate.

On August 20, Giap attacked a French garrison in Thai Nguyen just north of Hanoi, and the French provincial governor quickly capitulated, resulting in seizure of 160 Vietnamese troops of the French forces, along with their arms and ammunition. Giap directed this battle dressed in a white suit, tie, and brimmed dress hat, the "uniform" he chose to wear for the first months of the war.

After the emperor's surrender announcement, the Japanese in Vietnam basically tried to help the Viet Minh and impede French efforts to regain control. In several places they opened their arms depots to the Viet Minh. Additionally, they continued to hold their French prisoners for another month and in some instances provided training for the Viet Minh. Many, especially Kempeitai, deserted, joined, and led Viet Minh units. A few Japanese were still fighting the French in Indochina until the French war with Ho's government ended nine years later.

The immediate problem for the French in Paris after the Japanese surrender announcement was to establish the new French Indochina administration before the Communists grew any stronger. De Gaulle's forces had long planned on first entering Saigon with military units to ensure the security of their administration rather than entering Hanoi. This was for two main reasons.

First, Cochinchina had long been an actual colony, not just a protectorate. It had representation in the National Assembly in Paris, and it had the most *colons*. It was the most modern and economically developed of the five areas of Indochina. When Frenchmen thought of Indochina, they thought first and foremost of Saigon, "Pearl of the Orient."

Second, the strongest nationalist movement was in the North. The Viet Minh and other independence groups had been developing both political and military strength there that could pose a serious problem for French troops from the exterior if they tried to land in the North. Considering the strength of Communists and non-Communists in the North, every faction being nationalists and vying for dominance, and all fiercely committed to freedom from French rule, it was better for the French to gain a solid foothold in the South before turning militarily to the North.

The "Return" of the French to Indochina

By late August 1945, in Paris the French Fourth Republic was on the way to being constituted with de Gaulle as its provisional president. Although of course "the French" had never left Indochina, several historians refer to the early post-World War II period in Indochina as the "return" of the French. The problem now was to get French troops into Indochina quickly enough to prevent a Communist takeover and to establish conditions for a federal union of Indochina states.

The OSS and the DRV

On August 22, Major Patti flew into Hanoi to establish a second OSS headquarters there and soon was visited by Giap. Patti wrote,

"In impeccable French, Giap conveyed President Ho's personal welcome.... We were to consider ourselves guests of the Vietnamese government." Giap led Patti and his staff outside where there seemed to be a ceremony of some kind awaiting them. "A fifty-piece military band had been formed directly across the street facing us. Waving in the breeze were five huge flags representing the United States, Great Britain, the Soviet Union, China, and the Democratic Republic of Vietnam [the name which Ho intended for all of Vietnam but had not yet officially announced]. To our left was a military unit of about a hundred men standing at 'present arms.' ... To our right were smaller units of unarmed youths in sparkling white uniforms.... Giap pointed with pride to 'my troops who have just arrived from the mountains.' ... Within seconds all flags were dipped except the Stars and Stripes, and the band struck up the 'Star Spangled Banner.'"

Then the units passed in review, followed by a large crowd of civilians carrying placards of welcoming and political messages, then teens and adults singing their national anthem accompanied by the band.

When all was done, Giap said, "This is the first time in the history of Vietnam that our flag has been displayed in an international ceremony and our national anthem played in honor of a foreign guest. I will long remember this occasion."

Then Giap took Patti to see Ho. Patti wrote, "A wisp of a man came forward. I was pleased to see him again but thoroughly shocked. Ho was only a shadow of the man I had met … four months earlier. Ho introduced me as 'our American friend from Washington.'"[35] The position of the OSS had been not to side openly with either the French or Viet Minh. As a professional, Patti gathered, processed, and analyzed information from all sides but tried to avoid giving the impression of supporting one or the other. Above all he was wary of any word or action which implied that the United States supported Communism. One cannot read Patti, though, without detecting his obvious admiration, even personal liking, for the little man who had persevered through such strenuous circumstances in his attempt to forge an independent nation.

The pressure of events on Bao Dai had been too great. His tenuous rule as emperor ended on August 25 when he abdicated in favor of Ho's provisional government. The former emperor soon left for France. Bao Dai was not pro-French politically, just culturally with his fondness for wine, women, and song. In Hanoi and at Hue (the emperor's palace) the matter seemed to be settled, and by August 25 in Saigon the Viet Minh more than any other liberation group was in control of what government existed, nearly completing the "August Revolution" of the Communist Party.

All the world knew that on September 2, 1945 General MacArthur would receive the formal surrender of Japan aboard the battleship *Missouri*. Ho Chi Minh chose that same day to announce the independence of Vietnam under the new government, the Democratic Republic of Vietnam (DRV). On the eve of Independence Day in Hanoi, Patti had dinner with Ho and Giap at the Bac Bo Palace, formerly the Résidence Supérieur and now the headquarters of Ho's new government. Ho invited Patti to be on the official platform the next day during the announcement.

That next day broke bright and clear. General Leclerc, the highly respected commander of the French 2nd Armored Division which had been chosen to liberate Paris, had been on his way to Indochina when he was detoured north to sign the Japanese Instrument of Surrender for the French. On the USS *Missouri*, General MacArthur, well aware of the difficulties of fighting Orientals in jungle conditions, gave Leclerc some advice: "*Amenez des troupes, des troupes, encore des troupes.*" Bring troops, troops, and more troops.[36]

And that is what the French, and then the Americans would do.

Ho's Democratic Republic of Vietnam

Meanwhile, on that same day in Hanoi, Ho Chi Minh proclaimed the founding of the Democratic Republic of Vietnam (DRV). Patti had declined Ho's invitation to be on the platform, no doubt concerned that his appearance might be taken as an official U.S. endorsement of Ho's DRV. He chose instead to stand in the crowd to observe reactions. The preparations in the days preceding the ceremony had been elaborate. Armed groups, both Communists and Nationalists, and civilians alike had thronged into the capital, carrying their flags, crying out slogans, singing patriotic songs, chanting *Doc lap–Doc lap*.

The crowd had begun arriving early in the morning, but they had a long wait. After several hours, troops were called to attention and a hush came over the crowd, by some estimates, a half million. Patti wrote,

> The suspense was broken by a voice at the microphone introducing Ho as the "liberator and savior of the nation." The crowd, led by well-placed party members, intoned the chant, *Doc-Lap* (Independence), repeated over and over for several minutes. Ho stood smiling, diminutive in size, but gigantic in the adulation of his people. Raising his hands in a paternal gesture, he called for silence and began his now-famous proclamation with the words:
>
> "All men are created equal. The Creator has given us certain inviolable Rights; the right to Life, the right to be Free, and the right to achieve Happiness."
>
> Ho stopped short and asked his listeners: "Do you hear me distinctly, fellow countrymen?" The crowd roared back: "YES!"
>
> Ho continued,
>
> "These immortal words are taken from the Declaration of Independence of the United States of America in 1776. In a larger sense, this means that: All the people on earth are born equal; All the people have the right to live, to be happy, to be free."
>
> Then turning to the Declaration of the French Revolution [in 1789] on the Rights of Man and the Citizen, Ho said "it also states: Men are born and must remain free and have equal rights. Those are undeniable truths."[37]

Chaos in Saigon, and British Intervention

World War II had dealt an all but fatal blow to colonialism. The United States led the way before the war by positioning the Philippines for independence, a move interrupted by the war, then granted after war's end. The breakup of the British Empire began with withdrawal from India in 1947, followed by widespread decolonization by European powers. France was the holdout.

Since the Japanese surrender two weeks earlier, Hanoi had been generally in a hopeful, celebratory mood, but elsewhere tensions were building. The Indochinese Communist Party (ICP) was inciting demonstrations all over the country. North of Saigon,

> Rubber plantation workers gravitated toward the Loc Ninh–Saigon railway line, then walked south to Ben Cat and the provincial seat [Thu Dau Mot village (Phu Cuong)], where they joined with Vanguard Youth groups, townspeople, farmers, and a sprinkling of Stieng minority members [Montagnards] to sing revolutionary songs, salute the Viet Minh flag, listen to speeches, yell "Long Live the ICP!" and eventually occupy government facilities.[38]

Mandarins had been killed in Hue, and murders of Frenchmen and those Vietnamese who opposed the Viet Minh had begun in earnest.

On September 2 in Saigon, simultaneously with the Hanoi celebration, a rally of a quarter million people of various independence groups paraded under banners that read: "Down with fascism and colonialism!" "Vietnam has suffered and bled under the French yoke!" "Long live the USSR and the USA!" "Long live Vietnamese independence!" Vietnamese youths taunted French soldiers still imprisoned under Japanese guard in a Saigon prison whereupon the soldiers draped the tricolor from their cell windows, sang the *Marseillaise* and traded insults with the crowd. By mid-afternoon the crowd in the center of Saigon became frenzied and shots were fired. Father Tricoire, a Catholic priest who was watching the demonstration, was dragged from the steps of the Saigon Cathedral and murdered. Other French people were killed, and many were beaten."[39]

Major General Douglas Gracey, the British commander of the excellent 20th Indian Division, had been tasked by South East Asia Command (SEAC) with getting quickly to Saigon to restore order and disarm and repatriate the Japanese troops in Indochina south of the 16th Parallel. This amounted to the southern half of Annam, some of Laos, and all of Cambodia and Cochinchina. The Nationalist Chinese were to do the same with the Japanese north of that line, which included the northern half of Annam, most of Laos, and all of Tonkin. Ho had already gotten the upper hand in the North. If the Viet Minh were not to do likewise in the South, immediate action was needed.

On September 5, 1945 a British medical team parachuted into Saigon, and the next day, the first British troops began arriving at Tan Son Nhut airfield. The first French detachment from the exterior arrived on September 12. Gracey himself landed at Tan Son Nhut on September 13. On hand was a guard of Japanese soldiers surrounding the airfield to provide security, a small group of the most senior Japanese officers to greet him, and a large crowd of French civilians. The crowd cheered as each arriving aircraft loaded with soldiers taxied to a stop on the tarmac. A roar went up for Gracey as finally he exited and was driven off toward his new headquarters. "The road to Saigon was lined with Union Jacks and a cheering throng; most of the French population were in the streets to greet the senior Allied officers."[40]

Soon the Nationalist Chinese troops of Chiang Kai-shek would plunder their way from the border, enter Hanoi, and thus begin a period of uneasy coexistence with the Vietnamese. Ho's government occupied the former Résident Supérior's mansion, but the Chinese general wielded the supreme authority by virtue of having almost 150,000 troops in Tonkin.

In Saigon, other than the detachment of Frenchmen that had been flown in on the 12th, the only other French troops were what was left of the 11th Colonial Infantry Regiment (11th RIC), the unit that for decades had been stationed in Saigon and Thu Dau Mot and since the Japanese coup had been decimated and imprisoned for six months in Saigon under severe conditions. Only perhaps 1,000 were anywhere near fit for service. Most of the survivors were still suffering from starvation, mistreatment, and disease. With what forces could be mustered, on September 17 the French took control of two munitions supply points in the Saigon area, an important development since when the 11th Colonial men were first released from confinement they had only bamboo staves and a few old firearms to protect themselves and French citizens from hostile Vietnamese. The 11th RIC men, many of them embittered by the treatment they had received from Vietnamese jailers, began taking out their resentment on any Vietnamese they encountered, beating some, and Gracey had to order them back to barracks.

The situation in Saigon had become increasingly dangerous for the Allied forces and *colons*, and many more troops were needed. Viet Minh and other revolutionaries had taken over key positions in the civil administration to include the police headquarters, Radio Saigon, and some of the most powerful financial institutions. Gracey knew that big trouble was ahead if he allowed this to continue, so he quietly retook control of a few of these critical positions and then, on the night of September 22/23 accomplished what some describe as a coup, sweeping aside weak resistance and seizing critical points to include bridges that controlled access to the city. By evening of the 23rd the Viet Minh had been largely evicted and the French government reinstalled in Saigon, but, as events were soon to show, at great cost. Some of the bitter French former prisoners treated their Vietnamese jailers and others brutally, and Vietnamese scrambled to strike back.

Street fighting erupted and many on both sides were killed and wounded. By the following night, the Saigon area had exploded in violence.

> On 24/25 September 1945, the Viet Minh began their long war. Truong Chinh [a member of the National Liberation Committee, later First Secretary of the Communist Party] wrote not long after those events: "People's power had scarcely been founded in Viet Nam when the British forces … landed in Indo-China…. On September 23, armed and protected by the British forces, the French colonialists launched their attack and occupied Saigon. Our people replied by force of arms, *and from that moment, our heroic resistance began.*"[41]

On the night of the 25th in the northern outskirts of the city, the resistance did not seem so heroic when "[Vietnamese] broke into the Cité Heraud, a residential area outside the perimeter controlled by the British forces, where mostly minor French administrators of modest income lived, as well as non-commissioned officers and mixed-breed families. The slaughter which followed was violent and the killers retreated carrying 64 hostages with them, few of which were to be recovered alive."[42] By some accounts, as many as 150 men, women, and children were horribly slaughtered. If anyone had any doubts as to what kind of war would result from the French "return" to Indochina, the question was settled in those days and nights of September 23–25, 1945. This would be *une guerre sans merci*, a war without mercy, fought by men on both sides who often resembled crazed beasts tearing at one another, exacting the maximum of pain and suffering to the last drop of blood.

The editors of *The 30-Year War, 1945–1975*, published in Hanoi in 2000, state that beginning on September 24, 1945, "weapons, money, medicines from North and Central Vietnam were urgently sent to the South. Young people volunteered to enlist in the army and various units urgently left for the South."[43] Despite denials by the North, often repeated throughout the war, this statement acknowledged what the leaders of South Vietnam, the French, and (later) the American authorities well knew: the North, under Ho and his compatriots, was in charge of the war.

The North soon designated a commander of forces in the South. In many instances, leaders of the Viet Minh, and later the Viet Cong, had some latitude in the South, but from earliest times it was the North which would direct the war, in North, Central, and South Vietnam.

CHAPTER 3

General Leclerc,
October 1945 to June 1946

The First French General

Philippe François Marie de Hauteclocque was born in 1902, descendent of a noted family which included a knight of the Crusades in the 12th century. A distinguished Saint Cyr cadet, upon commissioning he joined the cavalry. After North African assignments, as a captain in 1935 he was appointed to the coveted post of commandant of cavalry at Saint Cyr. On a maneuver, his horse suddenly bolted from an auto, fell, and crushed his rider's leg under him. In extreme pain, Philippe remounted, led his squadron back to campus and passed them in review. Thereafter, because of the seriously broken leg he used a cane. During the German occupation of World War II Hauteclocque took the nom de guerre, Philippe Leclerc, to protect his family in occupied France.

Among the French generals of World War II, Leclerc stood out, and was chosen in 1944 to liberate Paris. At war's end, he was named head of the Expeditionary Corps, the overall French military command in Indochina. Leclerc's military experience had been in North Africa, France, and Germany. He had none in Indochina.

The general landed in Saigon on October 5, 1945. Following the brief ceremony, Leclerc was driven through the streets of Saigon and welcomed by a deliriously joyful French population. "We have come," he told them, "to reclaim our inheritance." (Not good news to Vietnamese.) Two days later in a tropical downpour he spoke to a mostly French crowd of 10,000. "The Indochinese, lost momentarily in a disastrous [Communist] propaganda, are not our enemies. They will soon also play their role in the French community [of nations].... *They are not our enemies!*"[1]

Leclerc had been instructed that, before the anticipated arrival a few weeks later of Vice Admiral Georges Thierry d'Argenlieu, High Commissioner for Indochina, he was also to assume that higher role which was principally to reestablish French sovereignty in Indochina.

General Philippe Leclerc troops the line of General Douglas Gracey's 20th Indian Division honor guard which is greeting him at Tan Son Nhut airbase on October 5, 1945, with Gracey behind Leclerc. (NARA)

> Tonkin and Annam, already under the authority of the national government [of Ho Chi Minh] in Hanoi, were in open revolt [against the French]. The two realms of Cambodia and Laos expressed their friendship for France but asked that it recognize their independence in the French Union. As for Cochinchina, it seemed still little affected by the Viet Minh revolution except for Saigon... Practically speaking, the means for certain operations in the Center [Annam] and in the North [Tonkin], already solidly held by the Viet Minh, would exceed the possibilities of the French army forces—only Cochinchina might be suitable for a military pacification operation.[2]

"Pacification" to the French meant something different from what it came to mean to the Americans. Although the French attempted to provide security for villages and work with local officials to enable a better life for the people, too often "pacification" meant simply establishing fortified areas and eliminating any opposition within or just outside them.

General Leclerc, 41 years old, deeply religious, was as good as they came—in any army. General George S. Patton's diary extracts reveal the spunky Leclerc to be not unlike Patton himself. The French troops who knew him best held him in the highest professional regard and, moreover, liked him. He was at once hard taskmaster and nice man, able to smile and laugh easily among his troops.

Leclerc should have had his 9th Colonial Infantry Division (9th DIC) ashore, but they had repeatedly been held up for months due to lack of ships. Only the

Americans had them available. At first Truman seemed noncommittal, but then expressed his support for the French. Eight American ships were finally allotted, and the 9th DIC set sail. Leclerc, his commanders and their men were to learn quickly what a formidable foe they faced. Most of the basic features characterizing the entire nine-year French war were played out in these early days.

Although Leclerc was a four-star general—equivalent to three stars in the U.S. Army—he wisely chose to place himself and all arriving French forces under Gracey's (two-star) command until he could get enough troops on the ground to ensure that he himself could exercise control of the French units. Leclerc recognized that this war would be unlike anything he had encountered in North Africa and Europe. Adolphe Vézinet, Leclerc's chief of staff, reported that when Leclerc gained experience in Indochina he said there was no military solution and pronounced: "You cannot kill an idea with bullets."[3]

The "idea" that could not be killed by military force was a Vietnamese idea: the yearning of so many of them for independence and unification.

Ponchardier and Massu

Because the Free French had played a minor role in the Pacific War, at the time of the Japanese surrender there were few troops under the French tricolor in the Far East. In southern China, northern Laos, and Tonkin were scant remnants of the poorly equipped French Regular, Colonial, and Foreign Legion troops who had barely escaped the Japanese coup of March 9, 1945. The French military within Indochina who had been imprisoned by the Japanese were in no shape to receive a Japanese surrender or to combat the Viet Minh. After more than five months of brutal imprisonment or fighting a rearguard action, many of them resembled Auschwitz survivors. However, in relatively nearby Ceylon was Commando du Special Air Service Bataillon (SASB) with available ship transport. This unit was called "Commando" or "SAS Ponchardier" after its colorful leader, Lieutenant Commander Pierre Ponchardier. It was almost battalion-size, a three-company unit, one of elite naval paratroops and two of colonial infantry. Because of his exploits in the French underground, Ponchardier was already a legend, and he was soon to become even more famous.

Ponchardier's unit was destined to be fed quickly into a war unlike that which French and other Allied troops had fought in Africa, the Middle East, or Europe. Even though the Allies had gained considerable experience in jungle warfare in the Pacific and Southeast Asia, it was in locations where the indigenous populations largely were with them or neutral, and not against them—a huge difference. Even in that war the French participation had been minimal. Facing the early French fighters arriving in Indochina and all later French units was a war in which Maoist People's War principles would be used first to frustrate and ultimately to defeat them in an alien climate, terrain, culture, and language.

With gruff affection Ponchardier's men called him "le Ponch," or "Pompon"—loosely translated, "He takes the cake!" Of medium height, he was built like a blockhouse with a head that thrust up almost without a neck from his broad shoulders. Barrel-chested, strong-bodied, he was imposing, an original. His men came to love him and take courage from him. Superbly intelligent, unconventional, high-spirited, he was a quick but careful planner.

Ponchardier was first a line officer aboard ships, then a submariner, then a naval aviator. When the Germans took northern France in 1940 he and other aviators without planes to fly went to Morocco. But wanting to fight Germans, he made his way back to Paris to join his younger brother Dominique who was setting up a Resistance network, and they narrowly escaped death. With Paris back in French hands, in autumn 1944 the admiral commanding the naval air arm had asked Pierre what he wanted to do.

"I would like to form a commando of aeronaval parachutists. Along the lines of the British SAS, against the Japanese."[4]

Ponchardier's Resistance buddies scoffed at the idea—*sailor* parachutists! As it turned out, the French war in Indochina, like World War II, was a war *par excellence* for parachutists, running the gamut from a jump by a single clandestine person to several hundred dropped for specific missions that could not be accomplished otherwise. But the commando unit was destined for other, non-parachute, missions.

On August 2, 1945, only days before the first atom bomb, the sailors had disembarked at Ceylon where Ponchardier was given two additional companies, colonial infantry parachutists. This created a furor among the soldiers of those two companies who had trained with their infantry regiment comrades and now were being split off to be led by—of all things—a *sailor!* But the soldiers were soon to sing the praises of *their* sailor—when they were not cussing him.

On October 8, Ponchardier was summoned to Leclerc's headquarters in Saigon. He had now been in country six days, three more than the general, and he was in ill humor, waiting for a mission. A cease fire was in effect, but in minor ways it was being violated daily. Ponchardier's big mouth often got him into trouble with senior officers. Today this lieutenant commander bluntly asked the four-star general if *he* (Ponchardier) had been brought to Indochina to fight or be a tourist. Leclerc raised his eyebrows, took a breath, and told Ponchardier he had received three complaints from the Japanese about gangsters in commando uniforms who had hijacked their cars. Ponchardier lowered his eyes, not responding to the accusation, and in a non sequitur replied that the Viets were mocking them with their "truce." Leclerc, no doubt with a sigh, tacitly agreed and told him that the Brits could not act offensively right now due to the truce until the enemy made a big mistake.

On the 11th, the Viet Minh made the big mistake, assassinating a British officer and a Gurkha. The normally good-natured and now incensed Gracey thundered, "We'll give them hell!"[5] The next day the British and French launched a joint land and riverine operation at the eastern edge of Saigon to clear out Viet Minh.

Before long, the troops were in among a large nest of Japanese-trained snipers up in trees and taking casualties—two killed, four wounded. Aspirant (cadet) Bussières, the first to be killed, was later buried in Saigon, a reflection of what was to be the fate in nine years of war for so many other French, French Union, and Vietnamese incorporated into French units: 77,333 dead, wounded, or missing.[6]

The first major French unit from the exterior had killed enemy and had its men killed in return. On the other side, many locals were further embittered and joined the Viet Minh.

To not waste precious time, Leclerc was committing piecemeal what small forces he could get as soon as he could lay hands on them. Even the French sailors from the ships that had just debarked troops were not spared. He asked for and got several hundred volunteers from those ship crews. They formed into "battalions," some not larger than companies, and they would fill in for a while as infantry "grunts."

***

Leclerc had naturally turned to his former command, the 2nd Armored Division, to supply an advance force for Indochina. Among them was Lieutenant Colonel Jacques Massu who said, "The idea of leaving such a leader never occurred to me."[7]

Major Raymond Dronne took command of a Muslim infantry battalion from Chad, mounted on M5 half-tracks which, as with all other vehicles, were American. Massu added a reconnaissance squadron (company-size) of Spahis (Moroccans) equipped with M8 Greyhound armored cars, a tank company of M5A1 Stuart light tanks, and supporting units. Two-person teams for each ambulance were the famous Rochambelles, women who had performed heroically as part of Leclerc's division. All personnel were volunteers.

Leclerc told Massu that getting rice transported from the Mekong Delta was a problem. He needed Massu to take the villages of Go Cong, My Tho, and Can Tho south of Saigon and control them. They were key to unlocking road and rail movement to Cholon/Saigon, and water transport to Saigon and Phnom Penh, capital of Cambodia.

Opération *Moussac*, the first all-French military action, was a late October thrust, a pincer movement directed at My Tho. Commander Francois Jaubert of the French navy had begun to develop a riverine force from whatever resources were at hand: Japanese junks, barges, private boats now pressed into war service—anything that could float, had a motor that could be made operable, and carry troops. Jaubert quietly said to Leclerc, "*Mon général, Cochinchine n'etait pas le Sahara.*" Cochinchina indeed was not the Sahara where Leclerc had operated in wide-open, sweeping armored movements.

Groupement Massu with its tanks, scout cars, and infantry in half-tracks, would move south out of Saigon by a main road bordered by swampy land. Ponchardier's Commandos and a detachment of sailors-now-soldiers would move down rivers and canals on Jaubert's makeshift vessels. Massu would have under his command his own groupement, Company A/5th RIC, and Ponchardier and his commandos with a unit of sailors from the battleship *Richelieu*.

Massu put one of his officers up in a two-seater Japanese Zero to reconnoiter the route. Leclerc listened to the man's report of many impassable cuts the enemy had made in the road and told him, "You are a pessimist." If the report was correct, though, this meant big trouble for Massu.

The Mekong Delta south of Saigon is a wet lowland only a few meters above sea level, cut up by many natural rivers and streams as well as hundreds of canals, small and large. To put it mildly, it was not very inviting territory for Massu's armored force.

After the operation, Massu's headquarters began publishing periodic booklets, *Coups de Massu*—Massu's Strikes—which documented the unit's experiences. The first booklet said,

> At dawn on the 25th, Groupement Massu went to war. At 4 A.M. one felt the excitement of these days of attack... the tank engines roaring, the grating of the half-tracks, the clicks of the machine guns being armed and the bands of cartridges as they unrolled, the jeeps which passed by the column, the shouted orders, the blaring radios.... [The column proceeded] at a heady speed until the first cut in the road.[8]

They discovered the truth of the aerial reconnaissance report. Engineers passed to the head of the column with their bulldozer and trucks carrying girders and began filling in the first of 24 large cuts in the road. These zig-zag obstacles were designed so Vietnamese could use the road on their bicycles or oxcarts, and jeeps sometimes could also make the passage. However, a column of trucks or armored vehicles could not navigate it.

Massu's engineers and lead unit filled in the obstacles, one by one, enough so the column could pass, and came finally to a blown bridge. It was evident they would not be able to enter My Tho on the 25th as planned but would have to work all night on a passage and continue the advance the next day. Massu said, "Around us, indifferent to our tribulations, the peasants worked in the rice paddies."[9] (They were doing the same type of thing two decades later during the American war. When one of our armored vehicles would hit a mine, the people would go on with their field work, seeming not even to notice us, while we suspected with good cause that among them was the person who planted or detonated it.)

***

Late in the afternoon of October 24, Ponchardier's small flotilla had headed south. Aboard an American LCI (landing craft infantry) left over from World War II were about 400 men consisting of 300 of Ponchardier's SASB and a company of 100 sailors from the *Richelieu*. A gunboat and barges loaded with the other *Richelieu* men would use an alternate water route.

The men in the LCI were packed in like sardines, hunching their backs under a downpour. About two hours after sunset they came to the entrance of the canal that led directly upstream to My Tho. It was blocked across its entire width with large junks linked together with a heavy chain. Bullets from both banks of the canal began striking the metal of the LCI and ricocheting off. The captain of the boat, a young British ensign who that night performed like a seasoned veteran, called for full speed ahead, steered directly into a junk and smashed it. The chain made a sinister noise scraping the bow of the LCI and then snapped. The enemy fire redoubled, and the LCI opened up with its 40mm cannon. Gasoline-powered junks burst into flames and in a matter of minutes the LCI was upstream.

The night fell silent. Beautiful rubber plantations lay on both sides of the canal—but also a Japanese guard post. The LCI slowed so that a French captain who spoke Japanese could yell out and negotiate with the guard, telling him that aboard were British troops of General Gracey, charged to go disarm Japanese garrisons in accordance with terms of the armistice. The Japanese sentinel presented arms in salute, and the LCI proceeded upstream, slowing to repeat the procedure with other sentinels every two or three kilometers.

My Tho lay directly ahead. The LCI slowed, and in a few minutes had put out men both up and downstream from the village to lie under trees in ambush positions. Ponchardier called for Jean LeRoy, a half French, half Vietnamese intelligence officer who had lived in the area and asked him if he thought they could take My Tho without waiting for Massu's armored column to arrive by road.

"According to my information," Leroy replied, "it is only weakly defended."

At 0300 the LCI slid quietly up to the wharf of My Tho. Three Vietnamese sentinels armed with lances were on guard. One they shot dead, and the other two fled. Leroy jumped onto the wharf in chase, caught one and slapped him hard across the face, demanding to know where other defenders of the post were. His prisoner turned out to be a terrified 16- or 17-year-old kid who fell on his knees and begged for his life.

Leaving him, Leroy continued on with three men to the public works building, kicking the butts of the startled inhabitants who then, mouths open and arms raised, fearfully watched as his party quickly searched the premises. A phone rang. Leroy answered. It was the Viet Minh at the command post of My Tho wanting to know what was going on and, by the way, who was he? Leroy barked he was the chief of police of Tan An making an inspection and hung up.

***

As the men with Ponchardier were quickly getting My Tho under control, encountering only light resistance, the experience of the *Richelieu* detachment with the gunboat turned out to be not nearly so pleasant as they debarked to attack the nearby village of My Loi.

Ensign Yannick Guiberteau from the *Richelieu*'s sailor crew described how everything had gone according to plan as their barges rendezvoused with the gunboat *Gazelle* during the darkness of the 25th. But then as some of the 80 men on his barge were put ashore at My Loi they received heavy fire from the underbrush. He said, "Our inexperienced troop was incapable of surviving night combat against a large well-armed enemy force." The barges piloted by the terrified Japanese helmsmen backed off rapidly to a safe position behind the *Gazelle* which with its 90mm cannon laid down a barrage on the riverbank. The troops ashore were in a bad spot, losing men dead and wounded, but managed to position themselves for rescue.

A salient trait of the enemy which was to persist throughout thirty years of war was demonstrated in this early action. Whereas Ponchardier's enemy had largely melted from his superior force at My Tho, those facing the many fewer *Richelieu* men inflicted heavy casualties. In accordance with Ho's and Giap's plan for People's War, when their enemy was perceived to be weaker they would attack them fiercely; when stronger they would withdraw and prepare for another day.

At daybreak, still aided by fire from the gunboat and using additional troops to assault, the second attempt to land succeeded without opposition. The enemy had disappeared. On the afternoon of the next day, the landing party assembled and rendered honors to their four comrades, buried not more than 100 meters from where they had fallen. The men of the *Richelieu*, with some bitterness, talked about why the intelligence had depicted an unoccupied hamlet for them to assault, and why an inexperienced group, sailors turned instantly into infantrymen, was chosen in the first place for such a mission. The realities of the war had begun to set in.[10] Young Frenchmen, eager to perform their duties well, had many more such realities to face in the months and years to come.

***

Ponchardier had heard by radio of the slow progress of Massu and was amused. On this day, October 26, as darkness fell, the lead unit of Massu's column finally got into My Tho. Major Dronne, known for his great sense of humor, called out to one of Ponchardier's cadet-officers who was bare-chested, Japanese helmet on his head, and a red bandana around his neck: "What is it with the disguise? Couldn't you get a proper uniform?"

The cadet yelled back, "We left with what we had on our backs. We don't have trucks to transport our dining halls."

Dronne cracked up laughing and continued on his way without another word.[11]

Massu, though, was in understandably ill humor. He was welcomed to town by a grinning Ponchardier who had taken My Tho totally by surprise on the first night. The enemy, they found, had put virtually all of their resources into defending against

Massu's attack by land, a mistake the Viets would not repeat in this vast Mekong Delta where movement by water was much more certain than by land.

Meanwhile, Leroy and his men made a gruesome discovery—mutilated cadavers floating in a stream. Their bodies were recovered and buried in a mass grave. These were civil servants and leading citizens of the region that the Viet Minh had tortured, then killed. Later, along the route to nearby Go Cong, they found large puddles of blood congealed at the base of poles where the red flag with gold star still hung. Leroy said that according to the intelligence they got, "the Viets had tied men and women to these poles."[12]

In the next few days after having taken My Tho, Ponchardier and his men quickly took the important villages of Vinh Long, Can Tho, and Cai Rang in waterborne operations and, for the time being, these actions reasonably well reestablished French control over the Mekong.

Pacification, and Atrocities

Leclerc knew from the beginning that for any overall success in regaining Indochina he would have to not just take key villages but then provide security for the people in them.

Jean Leroy tells how in those first few days of November the French expanded their operations and divided the zone into subsectors for pacification. He said it was, however, by no means pacified. The French troops were far too few, and the Viets would lie low during the day, reappear at night and menace and assassinate inhabitants in the villages. Families scattered by the fighting could be returned to their homes, but they needed to be protected. How and with what? Leroy said an idea came to him in a flash of intuition. To fight effectively against the Viet Minh who were indigenous to the Delta he would have to raise a group of men from this same area to combat them—partisans. *Catholic* partisans. The first group of twenty was formed from the prisoners Leroy had rescued that first night at My Tho. Each man was outfitted with sneakers and a rifle taken from My Tho's Japanese garrison. From this nucleus Leroy was to develop a regional force that would be first a source of amazement and later consternation at the highest government levels.

Incidents happened that brought home even more forcefully that this would be a war unlike any these Frenchmen could have imagined. Ensign Guiberteau told how two soldiers from a unit that relieved them had gone out on a foraging mission to steal chickens. They were surprised by a Viet Minh patrol who captured one of them while the other managed to hide himself under a bush. As the latter watched in utter horror, frozen in place with fear, the Viet Minh cut off his friend's head with a machete.[13]

No quarter given, none expected. Viet Minh and French—men who could weep over the tragedies brought upon their own troops and innocent civilians by war—they were themselves the cause of those tragedies. Such was the nature of this *guerre sans merci*. God help any combatant captured by the other side. For the remainder of the French war, many on both sides would submerge themselves in unspeakable atrocities.

Viet Minh Weapons and Munitions

As soon as Opération *Moussac* was completed, others were launched. Beginning in early November Gracey's forces (Indian, Japanese, French) pushed outward from Saigon. Massu would command an attack on Tay Ninh to the northwest, and again he would have a waterborne force. They would proceed upriver to Tay Ninh while Massu with his groupement would advance by road.

Massu's ground contingent soon encountered a series of ambushes near Trang Bang, 25 miles northwest of Saigon. The first cost them three dead and six wounded. The enemy would fire from the brush lining the road, then disappear into the forest. A subsequent ambush succeeded in killing a truck driver, which immobilized his truck and blocked the column behind it. The medical officer was seriously wounded while aiding others, and a captain was killed. The head of the Rochambelles was in a nearby ambulance and she drove through the gunfire to rescue a man who certainly would have died. Then she climbed into the stopped truck and drove it so the column could advance. In the continuing fight, a mounted 75mm gun moved forward to engage the enemy with direct fire, and its commander was killed by a bullet to the head. Then the crew was shot at—with *arrows*. In his book, Massu exclaimed, "A '75 against arrows! But the brush gave an absolute advantage to the prehistoric weapons!"[14]

The Viet Minh would not long have to resort to such means, though, as they were increasingly successful in equipping themselves with captured weapons, most of them American of World War II, as well as arms they managed to manufacture.

In the North, Giap was quite successful in capturing weapons or getting the Japanese to turn caches over to him, but he needed more to support his army, guerrillas, and self-defense forces, which toward the end of the year perhaps totaled 5,000. One source was Chinese firearms to be bought from corrupt Chinese officers in the occupying army around Hanoi. But they were expensive. In running the government, Ho found that he needed more funds than were at hand for many purposes—to buy munitions, to purchase rice and distribute it to the tens of thousands of people who were once again on the brink of starvation due to another drought, to buy trucks, medicines, many things. He appealed to the people of the North and got a warm response. Women sold their jewelry, men sold their chickens and pigs, children sold their toys or pets in what became known as "Gold Week." So it was not just the shouts of acclaim they gave him, but the sacrifice of their hard-earned possessions that demonstrated their support for Uncle Ho.

The three men in whose hands the fate of Indochina largely rested in late 1945: left to right, British General Douglas Gracey, French Admiral Georges Thierry d'Argenlieu, French General Philippe Leclerc. (NARA)

Situation, End of 1945, Beginning of 1946

America had finally supplied sufficient ships for the Expeditionary Corps, and during the last months of 1945, French strength increased notably with the arrival of the 9th and 3rd Colonial Infantry Divisions plus Spitfires acquired from the British, flown now by French pilots. Continuing the focus on Cochinchina first, Leclerc would try to pacify it before any move on the North. The general began sending his units farther out from Saigon.

In January 1946 Leclerc's units pushed from Saigon to the southeast to Cap St. Jacques (Vung Tau) on the South China Sea and south to Ca Mau at the very southern tip of Vietnam. French garrisons now located throughout much of the land south of the 16th Parallel had to be supplied, so the necessity for convoy protection became pressing. The French did just as we did so many years later: they reconnoitered likely ambush sites, cut back the trees and brush from the road, and set up checkpoints. And the Viet Minh did just as the Viet Cong and North Vietnamese Army did those many years later: they found ways to ambush convoys and neutralize checkpoint systems.

Thanks initially to the British and somewhat to the Japanese who, depending on the time and local circumstances were both a hindrance and help to the Allied effort (in some actions, Japanese were actually fighting Japanese), the French had gained nominal control over the South.

Nominal is the keyword. Bernard Fall, a correspondent with keen insight gained from several years' experience in Vietnam, wrote, "Cochinchina was in French hands—to the extent of 100 yards on either side of all major roads."[15] Although the French Union forces usually could move freely about in the daylight with only moderate concern for security, the nights were another matter, then as in our day. The Viet Minh owned the night. In the darkness, they moved, held meetings, conducted small-scale but fierce operations to kill their enemy, capture weapons, train their cadre and build their strength. They prepared for bigger fights ahead.

Toward the end of 1945, given an improved Cochinchina situation, the French had necessarily begun turning more of their attention to the North. Jean Roger Sainteny had led the French military mission in China and was now both the commissioner for Tonkin and North Annam as well as special envoy of the French government. In Hanoi he and General Raoul Salan, military commander in the North, began talks with Ho Chi Minh about bringing French forces back into Tonkin and a Vietnamese nation into a French Union of Allied States. In early November, Ho, ever flexible to accommodate changing circumstances while moving forward his agenda, had found it politic to dissolve the Indochinese Communist Party (ICP). This step, he believed, would attract many Vietnamese to work with the DRV—those who were anti-French and wanted independence but were not Communists. "For the next five years, officially and publicly, there was no Communist party in Vietnam. In fact, however, Party recruitment continued, Party leadership activities went on as usual, and high-level ... congresses were staged."[16]

To the French, the time seemed right for a new series of moves. Although De Gaulle startled France and much of the world on January 20, 1946 by abruptly resigning as head of the Provisional Government of the Republic of France because of parliamentary discord, the direction of the war in Indochina remained basically unchanged. Through many later shifts in government heads, one thing remained more or less constant: the desire to bring all Indochina states firmly into a French Union. The question was *how*.

CHAPTER 4

Occupation of the North, 1946

The French Move on Tonkin

Ever since Admiral d'Argenlieu had arrived on October 31, 1945 and consulted with General Leclerc, the need for doing something about Tonkin had grown into an increasingly pressing problem. Ho and his government were getting stronger. And the Nationalist Chinese, 150,000 strong, showed no intention of withdrawing.

Ho handled what the Vietnamese called "the Chinese problem" in his characteristic fashion: "Our main enemy at present is French colonialism. We need time to consolidate the political power, build up forces and make preparations for a nationwide resistance in case they extend the war to the north. Therefore, we should now take a conciliatory attitude toward Chiang Kai-shek's troops, cleverly avoid a conflict, carry out the motto about 'Chinese-Vietnam friendship' and rely on the support of the entire people to foil the design of Chiang Kai-shek's troops." Ho well knew that "the Vietnamese were full of hatred for them. President Ho always advised local people and officials to avoid clashes with them."[1]

Admiral d'Argenlieu, High Commissioner, had been given the mission of "reestablishing French sovereignty in the territories of the Indochinese Union." He had no experience in administering a large civilian population or commanding ground troops. Leclerc, his subordinate as Supreme Commander, had the mission "to take, under the authority of the High Commissioner, all measures for the reestablishment of that sovereignty."[2] D'Argenlieu, an austere celibate, was a strange duck. "It was said of d'Argenlieu in France that he possessed one of the most brilliant minds of the twelfth century."[3] He expected respect from the Indochinese and ostensibly got it, as shown in a June 16, 1946 film of a parade in which a troop of elephants in a long line approaches the reviewing stand. One by one they face the High Commissioner, kneel under command of the mahout, and then move on. It is a scene one can only imagine being played out in an Eastern emperor's court. One wonders what Leclerc, seated behind d'Argenlieu, must have thought.

The admiral's driving ambition was to be the engineer of France's reclamation of its past role of dominance in Indochina, and he saw force as the way forward. Leclerc urged him to adjust to the conditions and negotiate insertion of French forces in the North. By the end of February 1946, French Union losses were about twelve hundred killed and thirty-five hundred wounded or missing. Leclerc recognized the even greater costs that would be ahead if the war were to continue mainly as a military contest. However, Leclerc and his staff necessarily began planning for a military move to the North even as they were still trying to consolidate in the South, and negotiations between General Salan, Commissioner Sainteny, and Ho were ongoing in Hanoi.

Chiang Kai Shek's Nationalist troops, which had been given the mission of disarming and repatriating the Japanese troops north of the 16th Parallel, had been in Tonkin now for five months. They had proven more adept at rape and pillage than in carrying out their assignment. Would they interfere with the French move to the North?

Vézinet said of Leclerc:

> Very soon convinced that the military action he had to take in the South without prolonged political discourse had no chance of success in the North, he envisaged that a foothold in Tonkin could come about only with political preparation and accompanying diplomacy. He thought that the sole means would be to negotiate with Ho Chi Minh, and to hasten, simultaneously, by negotiations, the departure of the Chinese.[4]

Leclerc's stance made d'Argenlieu furious. At the beginning of January, while de Gaulle was still in office, the admiral had written to the president scornfully about Leclerc and his "capitulators." He told others, "I am amazed—yes I am *amazed* that France has in Indochina such a fine Expeditionary Corps and that its leaders prefer to negotiate rather than fight!"[5]

On March 6, 1946, the British mission of repatriating Japanese troops was completed, with SEAC turning over control to the French. From that point forward, the French were entirely on their own. Sainteny had been busy shuttling between Hanoi and Chungking trying to arrange an accord that both Ho Chi Minh and Chiang Kai-shek would accept. Every time the parties seemed close to agreement, something would intervene to prevent it.

The end of March would mark the beginning of the monsoon season in Tonkin when French military operations would become extremely difficult. As days in late February proceeded without an agreement, one after another, relentlessly, Leclerc decided he had to act. He tasked the recently arrived lead elements of 3rd Colonial Division and the Brigade of the Far East with relieving units in place and continuing pacification efforts in the South, an enormous task for 20,000 men. This released

Massu's Groupement and the 9th Colonial Infantry Division to effect the previously planned embarkation for movement north. The tides at Haiphong would be the most favorable on March 6, and that was selected as the target date for debarkation in the North.

On February 26, 1946, a flotilla of some thirty ships began forming for Leclerc's move north. Two days later, the French and Chinese negotiators in Chungking arrived at an agreement that the French thought allowed a landing at Haiphong. It soon became apparent, though, that this "agreement" in fact depended upon the French coming to terms with Ho Chi Minh. The news was the same for the flotilla all the way up the coast. Close, but no actual agreement. Finally, on March 6, the day on which Leclerc said he had to land because he would lose the high tide, an agreement was announced, the so-called 6th of March Accords:

> France made three major concessions.... First, it recognized the Vietnamese Republic as a free state (*etat libre*), with its own government, parliament, army, and finances, although it would be integrated into the Indochinese Federation, which in turn would be a part of the French Union. The term "free" was a compromise between the Vietnamese demand for "independence" and the French offer of "autonomy" or "self-government," and the question of full independence was left to the future. The second concession was to promise a referendum among the "populations" to resolve the question of the unity of the three Vietnamese lands, Tonkin, Annam, and Cochinchina.... And the third was to accept ... that the French military presence north of the 16th Parallel would be limited to 15,000 troops, and to a period of five years.[6]

In his book, *Sept ans avec Leclerc* (*Seven Years with Leclerc*), Massu describes how the convoy of ships entered the estuary of the river at Haiphong, the cruiser *Triomphant* leading, followed by Massu's two LSTs (Landing Ship Tank). Massu and his men were admiring the scenes on both banks when the ships began receiving Chinese fire and taking casualties. In return, naval gunfire raked the Chinese positions, and later Massu learned they were furious. Some of their huge piles of booty waiting to be taken back to China had been set afire by the cannonade and burned up. Evidence pointed to a Chinese commander who very well knew of the Accord but wanted to give the French a different kind of welcome.On March 18, with Sainteny seated beside him, Leclerc drove his jeep into Hanoi at the head of his troops.

They made a visit to Ho, with Leclerc saying in greeting: "Well, Mr. President, here we are, now friends."

The discussion soon turned from cordial into confrontational, with Ho stating, "If faced with French unwillingness [to comply with the terms of the agreement], he would not hesitate to kill one or two million men and to practice the policy of scorched earth in order to obtain satisfaction in the matter of union of the three [parts of Vietnam]."[7]

Ho's willingness to come to some kind of agreement with the French is another instance of his flexibility in matters of highest importance—parrying, shifting position, waiting for better opportunity. Paul Mus, a French scholar and author who

Leclerc, riding in his jeep at the head of his column of French Union troops, being welcomed to Hanoi by a delighted mostly French crowd. (TopFoto)

had been brought up in Vietnam, had fought for the Free French then returned to Vietnam, said that Ho was reported to have remarked, "It is better to sniff the French dung for a while than eat China's all our lives."[8]

Continuing Discussions on the Future of Indochina

An old Indochina hand, General Salan was respectful and cordial, but he was not deceived by the friendly manners of his hosts. Salan said he knew Giap's history, "that he didn't pardon us for the death of his wife in our prison. He is a dangerous debater, very bright, who never remains in one place and attacks without ceasing. He spoke an impeccable French and often reflected on the [French] island prison of Poulo Condore where he had spent numerous years."

Salan was mistaken about Poulo Condore, the most infamous of the French prisons. Giap actually was imprisoned at Lao Bao near the Laotian border. Giap's brother and a 15-year-old fervent revolutionary girl, Nguyen Thi Quang Thai, were also held there. Giap fell in love with the girl, later married her, and they had a baby girl. Thai, like so many other famous revolutionary women, left her child in the care of her husband's mother and carried on clandestine activities until she was again imprisoned. Both she and her older sister were to die in 1941, some accounts saying the French tortured her to death. Giap's bitterness over the death of his wife and sister-in-law, and later his father, at the hands of the French was never to leave him.[9]

During these days of negotiations, High Commissioner d'Argenlieu wrote a letter to the French government saying that Leclerc and Salan were insubordinate, and he requested their relief from Indochina duties and assignment elsewhere. Leclerc told the Army's chief of staff that because his mission was completed, he could return to France. But Leclerc was incensed. As for d'Argenlieu's allegations against Salan, Leclerc heatedly stated that Salan had done excellent work and was beyond reproach. Salan's opinion of d'Argenlieu was that he lacked integrity and was a coward, not daring to tell his subordinates this news face to face.[10]

One day Ho sent Giap to Salan with an invitation to join him as he visited a garrison of French troops, and Salan accepted. Ho took the platform in a gymnasium where Massu and some of his troops were in formation,

> "I have been in France,'" Ho said, "in that beautiful country that is yours, and I say to your mothers, your sisters, your fiancées, that all of you have comported yourselves well and that you do honor to your country."
>
> At these words, Colonel Massu faced his troops and cried out, *"Pour le président Hô Chi Minh: un triple hourrah,"* and the men responded, *"Hip, Hip, Hip, hourrah!"* three times.[11]

Massu seems to have been caught up in relief that in the agreement Ho had reached with France, the fighting perhaps was over. Shortly after this he would finish his tour of duty and be reassigned to Paris.

An Uncertain Future

As informal discussions were ongoing in the North and only minor incidents were disturbing the outward calm, the Communists in the South took advantage of the lull. *The 30-Year War* reported,

> Various bases were restored and consolidated.... Around Saigon there were a number of small bases linked to the city. Big bases like War Zone D, the Plain of Reeds, the U Minh forest were spread over several provinces.... Vietnamese political and military forces markedly developed in rural and urban areas and in the rubber plantation region.[12]

Leclerc had said, "Without doubt, the [March 6] accords are not perfect."[13] This soon became clear with skirmishes in the North between the French and the Viet Minh as well as Chinese, with significant loss of life. Meanwhile, d'Argenlieu had virtually given up on the possibility of a united Vietnam under French control. In June he established the Cochinchina Republic, a severe slap in the face for Ho who was insisting on unity of the three parts of Vietnam. The admiral's action also caused deep concern in Paris. Who was ultimately in charge of Indochina policy, the High Commissioner of Indochina or the government of France?

The government planned a conference for Fontainebleau.

With the final departure of the Chinese Nationalists from Tonkin in June 1946, and a deep chasm between Leclerc and the High Commissioner, Leclerc's job was over. He flew off to Paris. Promoted to five-star General of the Army, Leclerc prepared a report on the Indochina situation. Although supportive of compromise, he pointed out that "the government in Hanoi was simultaneously negotiating with France and supporting a war against the French in the South."[14]

The Chinese civil war had been going on for years, and in March 1946, pressed by the Nationalists, the Chinese Communist First Regiment near the border withdrew into the safety of extreme northeastern Vietnam. Ho, having received encouragement in his early years from the Chinese Communists, now found himself helping them. He "not only satisfied the Chinese demand for food and other supplies but also provided medicine to treat the Chinese soldiers who were suffering from malaria and dysentery." In turn, Ho saw an opportunity. This regiment was one of Mao Tse-tung's best, and Ho asked this unit—which had years of war experience—to train his troops and help create an intelligence system. "By July 1947, over 830 officers and soldiers from the Viet Minh army had received training in the camp of the First Regiment."[15]

This early circumstance later led to a formal arrangement whereby for the remainder of the wars in Vietnam—French, American, South Vietnamese—Red China would provide fluctuating but significant amounts of military and economic aid to North Vietnam that was crucial for continued conduct of the war.

***

In late 1945 and early 1946, General Leclerc had moved France well ahead in reestablishing French suzerainty in Indochina but was undeceived about winning an all-out war against the Viet Minh, should it eventually come to that. With the 6th of March Accords, Ho had demonstrated consummate skill in diplomacy. Accepting a pittance of French troops to enter Tonkin—only 15,000—and to remain there for just five years—was a small price to pay for what he would gain—time. And, from a beginning that was only a seed—Chinese Communist support for his revolution—a ripe harvest was possible.

CHAPTER 5

Fontainebleau and All-Out War, July 1946–49

With the 6th of March Accords as a basis, a forthcoming conference in France would hold out hope for a more permanent peaceful relationship between Vietnam and France. A new Supreme Commander in Vietnam, though, was to have very different views from Leclerc, and Ho's government would virtually eliminate non-Communist nationalist competition, thus setting the stage for all-out war. Troops and yet more troops would be committed by the French as war spread everywhere.

The Fontainebleau Conference, and Purge in Vietnam

Over d'Argenlieu's strong objections, the conference was called in July at Fontainebleau just south of Paris. Although not the designated negotiator, Ho Chi Minh went to France and pressed the issues of independence and unity.

While Ho was in France, Giap was acting in his place in Vietnam. Giap issued orders for further repressing the non-Communist Vietnamese nationalists, labeling them as traitors to the nation. "He insisted that all parties gather themselves under the … Popular National Front. Most refused, knowing that the Viet Minh held all key posts within that front organization."[1]

> Giap's methods were blunt. In the Red River provinces his forces launched all-out assaults against nationalist bases. At the same time, Viet Minh urban units tightened their security nets in Hanoi and Haiphong. Nationalist party members went underground or tried to escape to China…. Panic struck the parties as Giap's reign of terror swept their ranks with a force that dwarfed previous assassination campaigns.[2]

Giap had a few things other than war on his mind. During that summer of 1946 he went to see his old professor, mentor, and friend, Dang Thai Mai, and was startled to find that the professor's four-year-old daughter of 1932, Dang Bich Ha, was now a beautiful 17-year-old. A widower, he married her, and despite his

Ho welcomed with rendering of honors at Bourget airport on June 22, 1946 by General Paul Legentilhomme, Paris Military Region Commander (saluting on Ho's right) and Marius Moutet, Minister of Overseas France (on Ho's left). (NARA)

lack of a settled home life, between 1951 and 1956 they would have four children, two girls and two boys.[3]

During the Fontainebleau conference, the question of unity was highly charged on both sides. D'Argenlieu had already fractured unity with his establishment of a Cochinchina Republic separate from Annam and Tonkin. Ho was adamant. From a short distance outside the conference, he made his voice heard. He presented in highly emotive terms the case for unification, integrating Cochinchina into Vietnam: "It is Vietnamese land. It is the flesh of our flesh, the blood of our blood.... Even before Corsica became French, Cochinchina was Vietnamese."[4]

The Tiger and the Elephant

David Schoenbrun had been a World War II war correspondent, and post-war was a broadcast journalist. On September 11, just after the conference ended, Ho told Schoenbrun that he would be leaving France soon to return to Vietnam, and "he would shortly be leading his people in a war against the French." Schoenbrun asked Ho to confirm that he "was a Communist and a graduate of the Moscow school of revolution. [Ho] laughed at the question: 'I learned about revolution not in Moscow but right here in Paris, capital of Liberty, Equality, and Fraternity.'"

Ho urged him not to be "blinded by the issue of Communism.... My people hunger for independence and will have it.... Independence is the motivating force, not Communism. On the issue of independence and unity of the North and South, we are all in agreement, Communists, Catholics, Republicans, peasants, workers."

Ho said they would fight. Schoenbrun objected that Ho had no modern army, no modern weapons, and that such a war would be hopeless for him. Ho replied, "We have swamps that are better than antitank guns. We have thick jungles that planes cannot fly through and where the trees are shields against fire bombs. We have mountains and caves where one man can hold off a hundred, and we have millions of straw huts that are ready-made Trojan horses in the rear of any invading army."

"'Then it will be a guerrilla war?' [Schoenbrun] asked. 'A war of harassment and attrition?'"

"It will be a war between an elephant and a tiger," Ho replied. "If the tiger ever stands still the elephant will crush him with his mighty tusks. But the tiger does not stand still. He lurks in the jungle by day and emerges by night. He will leap upon the back of the elephant, tearing huge chunks from his hide, and then he will leap back into the dark jungle. And slowly the elephant will bleed to death. That will be the war of Indochina."[5]

And so it was.

***

Fontainebleau had concluded with no agreement. Ho was later to reflect on this period of 1946 as not being a total loss because negotiations had failed to produce an independent Vietnam. He explained, "Our comrades and compatriots cleverly availed themselves of this opportunity to build up and develop their forces."[6] Indeed, Giap had been busy.

Both Ho and Marius Moutet, the Minister of Overseas France, felt that Ho should not go away empty-handed, and they signed France's proffered *modus vivendi*. One of the articles was a cease fire to take effect October 31, 1946 in Indochina below the 16th Parallel.

Aftermath of Fontainebleau

On October 23, back in Hanoi, Ho issued a statement on the *modus vivendi*: "I came to France ... for the purpose of resolving the problem of Vietnam's independence and of the unity of Central, Southern and Northern Vietnam.... Sooner or later Vietnam will be independent. The Centre, the South, and the North will be reunified."[7]

Ho did not go home with only news of a fragile *modus vivendi*. He had created a legacy which was to pay big dividends. While in France, Uncle had invited Vietnamese students to visit him. "Come, my children," he had said and they all sat down on the steps of the house. One of the young men recalled, "When Ho realized that among our group there were students from the North, South, and Center of the country, he said, 'Voila! the youth of our great family of Vietnam. Our Vietnam is one, our nation is one. You must remember, though the rivers may run dry and the mountains erode, the nation will always be one.'"

A week later he invited two students from the South to pay him a second visit, a young man and a young woman. They talked of heroes and duty to defend the Fatherland. The young man wrote, "From that afternoon I was Ho Chi Minh's fervent partisan. His culture and burning patriotism offered me a model that I could follow in my own life." This young man was Truong Nhu Tang, who would become in 1960 one of the founders of the National Liberation Front of South Vietnam (NLF). In 1946 his dedication to the cause would cost him his young pregnant wife, who was given to another man when his parents and parents-in-law found he could not give up his work for independence.[8] In 1969 he spent much of his time trying to avoid terrifying B-52 strikes, changing locations often in the jungle not far from me near the Michelin plantation and Cambodian border during my command of Task Force QuarterCav.

The cease fire arranged at Fontainebleau in mid-1946 soon collapsed. The Southern Viet Minh had taken advantage of the thin spread of French troops ever since Leclerc had taken the bulk of his main force north. Ambushes, acts of terrorism, and sabotage had increased dramatically.

Jean Leroy, though, was having great success in the Mekong Delta. His isle of An Hoa with 48,000 inhabitants, ten percent of them Catholic, had become his fiefdom, thanks to his close liaison with high-ranking French officers in Saigon who condoned or supported his moves. His original group of 20 partisans had grown considerably, and he was ruthlessly eliminating the Viet Minh. Leroy claimed, "I was the master uncontested and uncontestable of my isle. I had extirpated the Viet Minh down to the last one and I lived with my family outside all those governments and all those accords."[9]

The New French Supreme Commander, and Rising Tensions

Upon Leclerc's departure, General Jean-Ètienne Valluy, formerly commander of Leclerc's 9th Colonial Infantry Division, had been promoted and appointed Supreme Commander. As a close adherent to d'Argenlieu's manner of handling things, he was all for a military solution, advocating—relative to the French Indochina

Administration—the elimination of the "civil element in favor of a purely military command structure." He told the High Commissioner that, "Instead of contenting ourselves with controlling rebel attacks in the South, we should put serious pressure on the rebels by taking large-scale initiatives in Hanoi and Annam."[10]

On November 20, tensions between the French military and Viet Minh were at the boiling point. In Haiphong, the French tried to seize a shipment of fuel oil under a ban imposed by them, and a fierce battle broke out. Within three days, buoyed by Valluy's tough stance, the French had bombarded Vietnamese and Chinese quarters in Haiphong with artillery and naval gunfire, and strafed and shelled nearby villages. The generally accepted figure for the "Haiphong Incident" was 6,000 civilian casualties, dead and wounded.

At this time in Paris, Leclerc reflected on the case for negotiations and advised, "Since we did not have the means at our disposal to break the back of Vietnamese nationalism by force of arms, France was obliged to seek every means to bring about the coincidence of French and Vietnamese interests." A new French government listened, and at the meeting of the Indochina Committee, it was determined: "The problem as a whole cannot be settled by the use of force alone. International political opinion would not allow to take such a step, nor would we have the support of the French nation."

Acknowledging this, it is virtually impossible to comprehend the Committee's next statement except within a pervasive aura of arrogance and macho intransigence—"But we must make it clear that France does not intend to quit Indochina, and she will defend her presence by every possible means."[11]

Prelude to All-out War

By mid-December 1946 the DRV had made substantial progress in organizing itself, forming military units and civilian defense and intelligence networks. The Communist History says, "At the time, there were 30 Vietnamese regiments in the North and 25 in the South. In addition to rifles and grenades, many units had been equipped with submachine guns and bazookas. Vietnam had nearly one million militiamen, guerrillas and self-defence soldiers."[12] These figures may be exaggerated, but unquestionably in the 15 months since the DRV was proclaimed, the Viet Minh had built up significant forces.

Ho Chi Minh had moved out of Hanoi to a Communist-controlled village 12 kilometers north in the Viet Bac in order safely to continue to plan and direct affairs. Here, at this crucial time, Ho's personal popularity soared. Gone was the animosity toward him in some circles of the Party that had been created when he had allowed French troops into Hanoi in exchange for time to prepare for war. The bush and a thatched hut, not the palace of the Résident Supérieur in Hanoi, was just the right place to direct a revolution for a man who came from the people and remained part of them.

Sainteny and Moutet tried to work something out in messages to Ho, to no avail. All-out war seemed imminent. At headquarters, Ho, Giap, and their staffs made careful preparations: "A detailed plan to encircle Hanoi, besiege the enemy during definite period [sic], and make it possible for the rear area to complete the transfer of all forces to wartime conditions was worked out."

On the 16th the "Central Committee sent a message to the [Cochinchina] Party Committee and to all provincial committees in the South: 'In view of the situation in France and the ambitions of the colonialists, the problem of Vietnam's sovereignty can be resolved only by an all out, protracted and hard war.'"[13]

On the morning of the 18th, Major Jean-Julien Fonde, on the general staff in Tonkin, went to Giap's office to protest the Viet Minh's burnt earth policy in which whole villages around Hanoi were being destroyed so the French could not use them or their crops, and the people were being moved to safer areas. After tea and pleasantries, Fonde presented the story, incident by incident. "We must preserve this country," he said.

Giap was no longer smiling, and now lectured the French officer: "That depends on you. Our decision is made. We will yield no longer. The destruction—it doesn't matter. Policy takes precedence over economics. The losses—a million dead Vietnamese. Of no importance. Some French will die also. We are ready. It will last two years, five years, if necessary. We are ready."

Giap went silent and made a move to rise. Fonde was not ready to go. He reminded Giap that negotiations had gone on for a long time, and that a new French government had been constituted. He said that Giap knew the ideas of the new Prime Minister, Léon Blum, who wanted a negotiated settlement. "The Independence of Vietnam," Fonde continued, "often evoked by General Leclerc, is in the offing. The world is changing apace. What will happen in one year, five years—Be patient. Take time. Prevent the irreparable."

Giap answered, "It is up to you." He reeled off a long list of what the Vietnamese took to be French crimes against the people. "*C'est fini*. It's over. We will yield no longer."

Giap rose, and it was over.[14]

Viet Minh Attack in Hanoi

The Central Committee had proposed a signal for the start of the war: On the evening of December 19 the city power plant would be destroyed and electricity cut off.

The morning of that day came on bright and clear, and Hanoi life seemed to be returning to normal. The Viet Minh had said that, beginning the next day, barricades would be taken down, and strict return to order would take place.

Instead, that evening a huge explosion ripped through the Hanoi electrical plant, and electricity went off. Two minutes later Fonde heard machinegun fire and grenade explosions. The writers of *The 30-Year War* said, "At 2003 hours, all electric lights in the city went out. Explosions resounded from the Lang fortress. Rifles were heard everywhere. The national resistance war had begun."[15]

Fonde's telephone rang. He asked the lieutenant on the other end what was going on.

"The huge clash, I think. *Another 9 March!*" [Referring to the Japanese coup that had struck the French throughout Indochina on March 9, 1945.]

Their communication was cut in mid-sentence. The enemy had severed the telephone lines. Sainteny tried to go to the Citadel fortress but his armored vehicle was hit by a command-detonated mine, and he was seriously wounded.

Indeed it was over!

No peace was possible. The war with the French was on, full force, and it would not stop until Dien Bien Phu had fallen and, later, withdrawing French Union troops near Pleiku were decimated in a huge ambush.

The "Start" of the French Indochina War

Many histories, in French and English, date the "start" of the French Indochina War at December 19, 1946 when the power plant was blown up. Much more correctly, the war built up from 1941 throughout the Vichy French administration in Indochina, to Giap's attacks on the French outposts in 1944, to the "August Revolution" of 1945, and especially the chaos in Saigon which prompted Truong Chinh, later head of the Party, to say of September 23, 1945, "from that moment, our heroic resistance began." In October and November 1945, Ponchardier and Massu's men in the Mekong Delta had had no doubt they were at war. Neither did the men with Leclerc who were fired on while attempting to land at Haiphong in March 1946. Nor those who fought at Haiphong in November 1946. In fact, a good case could be made that the French Indochina War actually started in the 1860s with the French takeover of the provinces around Saigon and subsequent Vietnamese armed resistance.

Having been a combat commander, I had held that the most significant date for the post-World War II eruption of the Indochina war was September 23, 1945, as Truong Chinh claimed. Finally, I found Giap's statement which agreed. He said,

> Many people still think that the Indochina war, the longest of the century, broke out on 19 December 1946. In fact it started 15 months earlier, on 23 September 1945 when French troops opened fire in order to recapture Saigon. The war then rapidly spread all over the South and expanded to Northwest Vietnam, Laos, and Cambodia.[16]

Leclerc's Last Try: Make a Deal!

Léon Blum had been Prime Minister for only a week, and the December 19, 1946 crisis was just three days old when he called Leclerc on December 22 and asked him to go to Indochina on an inspection trip and come back with a report and recommendations. Blum had the highest regard for the general, saying that he was the Liberator of Paris and would be Pacifier of Indochina.[17] D'Argenlieu was not pleased, telling Blum by cable that to send Leclerc was unacceptable. The handwriting was on the wall for the admiral. Despite the awe in which those in power still held de Gaulle, and regardless of the admiral's continued strong backing from his mentor, he was on the way out. His ego and the patience of the government were too much at odds.

Leclerc had Massu, now his operations officer, accompany him. They flew in to Tan Son Nhut on December 28 and, without seeing the admiral, on the 31st went on to Hanoi. On January 2, they went to Haiphong to visit Leclerc's son, Henri, who had been gravely wounded. On that day, Ho sent a radio message to Leclerc, praising him as a great general and good friend, and saying,

> "We still want the independence and unity of Viet-nam." He went on, "Supposing that you wish to fight us for a time, that is problematic, for if you are strong materially, we are morally, with the steadfast willpower to fight for our liberty…. We have decided to remain in the French Union, collaborating loyally with France and respecting its economic and cultural interests, but we have also decided to fight for our independence and our national unity."[18]

The Viet Minh commander in the South, Nguyen Binh, sent a message to Leclerc saying much the same thing.

Did Nguyen Binh and Ho Chi Minh really want to stay in the French Union? That is a moot question because Ho and his inner circle were always adaptable. They had long proven adept at saying what was acceptable at the moment but later adjusting or abandoning that position to fit the needs of the present. They always knew that time was on their side. They could wait.

Giap's forces had fought stubbornly for the first few weeks after December 19 but began yielding to French assaults throughout Tonkin. Giap and his military leaders decided that in some areas they had to go back to guerrilla warfare long enough to build their main forces stronger. Leclerc considered the situation in Tonkin and believed that reinforcements were urgently needed from France as an interim move to stabilize the situation, but upon his return to France he again emphasized to Blum that a political solution was what was really required. In his report, he stated,

> In 1947 France will no longer put down by force a grouping of 24,000,000 inhabitants which is assuming unity and in which there exists a xenophobic and perhaps a national ideal…. The capital problem from now on is political. It is a question of coming to terms with an awakening xenophobic nationalism, channeling it in order to safeguard, at least in part, the rights of France.[19]

Moutet had also been sent to Indochina but returned with a very different report: "We can no longer speak of a free agreement between France and Vietnam…. Before any negotiations today, it is necessary to have a military decision. I am sorry, but one cannot commit such madness as the Vietnamese have done with impunity."[20]

A soldier urges peace, and a civilian urges war.

Ho and Commissioner Sainteny had been on friendly terms, and in late January 1947 as the recuperating Sainteny and his wife were about to return to France, Ho sent him a letter with one last appeal: "We have already had enough death and destruction! What are we to do now, you and I? France has only to recognize the independence and unity of Vietnam, and at once hostilities will cease, peace and trust will return, and we shall be able to get down to work and start rebuilding for the common good of our two countries."[21]

In Paris, Prime Minister Blum offered Leclerc his old job back, replacing Valluy as Supreme Commander and then in a short time taking over from d'Argenlieu also as High Commissioner. Within two weeks Blum was replaced by Paul Ramadier who offered Leclerc immediate succession to d'Argenlieu. The general thought about it, laid out a long list of conditions for the government to consider, and sought the advice of others, most notably de Gaulle who advised him to decline the offer, and instead accept the post of Inspector General of French Forces in Africa. And he did.[22]

In March, Fonde, whom Leclerc knew well as one of his former subordinate commanders, had just returned to France. Admiral d'Argenlieu had been replaced as High Commissioner by a civilian, Èmile Bollaert, and the government was still trying to decide what to do about the modus vivendi signed at Fontainebleau. Leclerc called Fonde into his office, and Fonde passionately began telling the general that the whole thing was a mess, that the old colonial days when the French could dictate to the Vietnamese were long gone. "All of Southeast Asia is moving toward independence. I do not think that France is able or willing to make the effort necessary for a reconquest by force. It almost happened, an agreement at Fontainebleau. Now …."

The general, with a deep frown, interrupted: "Yes, my old friend. It must stop. Your conclusions are correct. I reached that conclusion long ago. The new High Commissioner [Bollaert] seemed convinced when he saw me."

Fonde said that at that moment, the general rose from his chair, took a few steps and clenched his teeth, raised his voice louder, and pointed at his door. Leclerc told Fonde that in that doorway, as Bollaert was leaving, Leclerc once again warned:

> *Encore une fois, monsieur Haut-Commissaire—Traitez, traitez, traitez … à tout prix.*
> [Once more, High Commissioner—Make a deal, make a deal, make a deal—At all costs!][23]

There was no deal.

***

Leclerc took up his North Africa duties, and in 1947 his aircraft crashed in Algeria, killing everyone on board. He was 45 years old.

***

1947, Buildup to a Long War

In January 1947, Vincent Auriol was elected president of the new Fourth Republic. In Indochina the hawk, General Valluy, continued as Supreme Commander, with Salan in command in the North and Major General Georges Nyo in the South. The public in France had been shocked by the large-scale uprising of December 1946, and unrest, defiance, and anti-war protests within France were growing. A Communist, François Billous, the Defence Minister, refused to stand in the National Assembly to pay tribute to the Expeditionary Corps.[24] "French liberals were disheartened and embarrassed by [the colonial war]—particularly as Britain was yielding independence to Gandhi in India and the Dutch were giving up the East Indies."[25]

For several months, troops sent by France to Vietnam had been arriving in increasing numbers: armor and armored cavalry units, paratroopers, colonial infantry, artillery, engineers, and support units. The navy and air forces were augmented. The French had recruited Vietnamese and placed them in units under French officers and NCOs. A volunteer Cambodian regiment was a welcome addition, and French Foreign Legion units were being put to immediate work. By 1947 the contribution of Africans and indigenous Indochinese made a big difference: portions of five Moroccan regiments, four Algerian regiments, and a Tunisian regiment landed. Four battalions of T'ai were formed from hill tribes of the High Region of mountains to the west and northwest of Hanoi.[26]

After the December 19, 1946 conflagration in Hanoi, Salan had moved quickly to take Hanoi, important villages and roads, and control the waterways in a large area of the Red River Delta and beyond. Route Coloniale 4 (RC4), a critical road, was reinforced. It stretched for one hundred fifty miles just south of the border with China, all the way from the Gulf of Tonkin, west and northwest through the important border posts of Lang Son, Dong Dang, That Khe, Dong Khe, and Cao Bang.

Giap conceded that, "In January 1947, the French stepped up their military activities in many battlefields.... By mid-February, a new phenomenon had occurred: the breakup of [our] war fronts." The French were successful in Hue, and in both the northwest and northeast areas of Tonkin. However, Giap said, "The one-year resistance in [Cochinchina] proved that the French, in spite of their tremendous strength, could never destroy our armed forces if we strictly observed guerrilla tactics." The Viet Minh had built up to battalions and regiments but were not strong enough for direct confrontations. Therefore, as Giap explained, they resorted to "mobile guerrilla warfare," something in between guerrilla tactics and main force assaults. Once again they had proven capable of adapting well to a situation and patiently doing what they could in attacking the enemy while building their infrastructure and main force strengths. Using the new tactics, "In March there were no more cases of war fronts breaking up."[27]

French forces tried to engage main-force Viet Minh units in battle throughout Tonkin, but Giap refused to engage decisively, his units instead inflicting casualties and melting away when faced with too much force, leaving scorched earth behind in an attempt to deny his enemy any sustenance. Constantly building his strength, Giap merged all types of fighters under a unified command, claiming at this time a strength of one million, everything from local small-unit militias to main-force battalions and regiments. If so, which is questionable, he significantly outnumbered the forces fighting under the French flag although the French armaments and other equipment were far superior. The French had total command of the air, control over the main inland waterways, and less control over coastal waters. The ground was another matter. Where it was not controlled by the Viet Minh it was contested. Giap continued to be patient, biding his time.

In mid-May 1947, with no fanfare, the French tried one more time diplomatically to engage Ho in negotiations. One of the High Commissioner's main assistants, Paul Mus, who had been in Indochina since the 1930s and spoke fluent Vietnamese, was able to arrange a meeting with Ho in the Viet Bac. Their talk was cordial, but fruitless. Before leaving, Mus asked: "'Mr. President, so the war will go on?' Ho replied, 'We desire peace, but not at any price! It must be peace with independence and freedom'.... This was the last contact between Uncle Ho and a representative of the other side during the resistance war."[28]

No More Conferences, Just War

The *30-Year War* history acknowledged that as of May 1947,

> After more than four months of massive counterattacks and fierce offensives in [Tonkin and Annam] the French Army managed, at very high cost, to establish its control over a number of towns and cities, strategic communication axes, mining and coastal areas, and border strong points.
>
> For the Vietnamese side, four months of nationwide resistance had revealed a fact: despite their modern weapons, the enemy was unable to wipe out the Vietnamese main forces and to take by surprise the Vietnamese leadership. Vast areas in the countryside, and even around towns and cities had remained under Vietnamese control.[29]

The fighting in Tonkin, though often fierce, was still mainly on a small-unit scale—a company here, a platoon or squad there. Mostly the Viet Minh responded in its characteristic manner, returning fire, then usually melting quickly into the landscape, reappearing only when the times and circumstances were advantageous for inflicting more casualties.

The violence in the North was the topic of the moment, but the South, though quieter in comparison, still had its share of troubles. Speaking about the war in the South at the beginning of 1947, Jean Leroy sarcastically said,

> Lucienne Bodard [a French journalist] had called the Cochinchina war, "the pleasant war," pleasant for him certainly from his lodgings at the Hotel Continental [in Saigon] but certainly not for others, those who like me fought each day and each night in the mud of rice paddies.... at the end of 1947 not a single Viet Minh—tax collector, propagandist, or liaison agent— penetrated our isle at night without having been signaled and arrested.[30]

Idealism Hardened by Reality

Guy de Chaumont-Guitry was a 23-year-old idealistic, religious soldier who had fought with Leclerc's 2nd Armored in Germany. He stayed in the Army, debarked in Saigon in March 1947, and would soon take possession of an armored scout car with three other men in his crew and five Vietnamese infantrymen. He was told that "one cannot leave Saigon except in a convoy. All the countryside is dangerous if you don't go in a group and armed."

Guy observed that the enemy always seemed to know what the French were doing, and the French seemed not to know much about the enemy. Twenty-nine paratroopers were killed and nine wounded in an ambush which resulted from a boy giving information to the Viets. Also, "The Viet Minh are always in one place.... If ever [the French command] would leave our units in one place then we could be effective, but with perpetual changing about, it is total mismanagement."[31]

Finally, this highly intelligent, analytical young man concluded, "We fight with a regular army and its European methods against bands which employ guerrilla tactics.... We fight the war of Clausewitz and Napoléon."[32]

Operation *Lea*, The New War of "the Big Battalions"

Ever since the December 19, 1946 outbreak, Ho had been heading his government from hideouts in the mountainous forests north and northeast of Hanoi, the Viet Bac. This was a major problem for the French in terms of trying to control Hanoi itself and the Red River Delta, the rice bowl for North Vietnam.

Operation *Lea* had two main objectives: capture Ho Chi Minh and ensure control of the frontier with China. The plan was to encircle a large area with airborne, ground, and waterborne forces and then destroy the enemy inside the noose.

French intelligence had located Ho's current headquarters in the Viet Bac. No more discussions with him over tea. This time they were out to get him. On October 7, Lieutenant Colonel Henri Sauvagnac's paratroopers, 1,100 strong, suddenly dropped on Bac Kan, 60 miles directly north of Hanoi. And they got Ho! For several minutes radio messages excitedly went back and forth to Salan about the old man with the beard they had captured. Alas! It was discovered that Ho had narrowly escaped, and the old man turned out to be only a minor official.

A new stage in the war had been reached: the war of the "big battalions." From now on, operations of battalion, regiment, and larger size on both sides would be frequent in the North.

At the end of the year Ho and Giap sized up 1947 and declared victory, not final, but a major step on the way. Ho had said, "The enemy forces are like the sunset, arrogant but fading. Our forces become stronger and stronger, like water at its source, like a fire kindled, always going forward and not drawing back." Giap, however, acknowledged that the year had been tough. "Everyone had gotten thinner, had not eaten enough, had spent sleepless nights, and had been constantly on the move. Many suffered from fungus diseases from too many rainy days and constantly damp clothes; their feet became ulcerous and painful."[33] Ho himself was ill but Giap jubilantly attended a large victory celebration.

End-of-year statistics to date for the French Union were sobering: 5,345 dead, 9,790 seriously wounded.[34]

1948, A Widening War

The Communist *30-Year War* states, "1948 was to be a year when the war raged everywhere. The French would launch even fiercer mopping up operations in the [Red River] Delta. In [the South] they would ... bring back Bao Dai to set up a national puppet government. Bao Dai would create an army for that government and set up autonomous regions to divide Vietnam."[35]

Indeed, 1948 started reasonably well for the French.

In the South the need for safeguarding routes for convoys and critical locations such as rubber plantations led to the building of many outposts and towers along the axes of supply and communication and within the plantations. My area of responsibility in 1968–69, a large one north of Saigon, contained the ruins of many of these outposts and towers. A stone watchtower at Village 1 in the Michelin plantation at Dau Tieng was still largely intact when I saw it in 2005 and 2010.

The Viet Minh in turn developed a defensive system which served as a base for attacks, first in the South, and then in the North. These were "resistance villages" or "resistance hamlets." Their incredible ability to utilize the local population throughout Vietnam to constantly resist and harass the enemy on a small scale, year after year after year, while main-force units were preparing for or doing their thing was a major reason for their success.

French/South Vietnamese politics took a decisive turn on May 20 with formation of a Provisional Central Government under General Nguyen Van Xuan. Bao Dai was preferred by many of the council members and Xuan acknowledged the importance of the emperor by consulting with him. "It was Bao Dai who picked the flag of the central government—a background of yellow (the imperial color) with three red horizontal stripes across the middle denoting the three areas of Vietnam [a revival of the flag chosen by an emperor in 1890]."[36]

On June 6 in Hanoi a South Vietnamese official announced the establishment of the provisional government. So now in this complex war there were two governments of Vietnam, Bao Dai's and Ho's, which for a brief time were headquartered quite close to one another in Tonkin. Ho's had the allegiance of great numbers of Vietnamese in all three areas of Vietnam. The new Bao Dai government, however, had little following.

Meanwhile the war went on. Northern leaders often held up the guerrilla warfare in the South as an exemplar. Giap said the Southerners had bogged down "nearly half of the French expeditionary corps who had five hundred military posts and carried out sweeps of various scales."[37] Several books by men who were small-unit leaders in the French Union forces point to the futility of these sweeps by large-garrison units or troops within an outpost. Almost always the enemy knew what would happen and where.

One bright spot in pacification efforts in the South, or so it seemed to French authorities, was the area commanded by the rabid Catholic, Jean Leroy. His concept of pacification was simple: elimination. By 1948 he had formed "brigades" of 49 men called Mobile Units for Defense of Christian Communities (UMDC). Their motto: *Pro Deo et Patria*, "For God and Country." Enjoying support from the commanding general, and promoted to lieutenant colonel, Leroy increased the force he commanded to about 12,000 and was responsible for a large part of the Mekong Delta and area south of Saigon comprising a population of around 600,000. In time, his army would be incorporated into the National Army of Vietnam. Leroy was highly successful in killing Viet Minh (along with many innocents, his enemy claimed, probably with justification).[38] His program of "pacification" enabled pulling out some French Union units and sending them where they were much more needed: Tonkin.

1949: A Momentous Year

In the South, things were not going well for the French. The enemy seemed to be everywhere, constantly inflicting casualties. The young idealist Guy de Chaumont-Guitry was gravely wounded on November 6 and soon died of his wounds. He was buried beside other French soldiers in the cemetery at Vinh Long on the Mekong.

In researching for my earlier book, *One Hell of a Ride*, by a stroke of great good fortune I made contact with a retired French general who in 1949–50 served as a young officer in the Michelin plantation. The closest French equivalent of the late 1940s and early 1950s to my 1/4 Cav of 1969 was 5th Cuirassiers. This armored cavalry unit (battalion size) worked the same terrain we covered and more, stretched thin indeed. Jean Delaunay was a 20-year-old lieutenant, first a platoon leader then commander of 1st Escadron, 5th Cuir (company size). Ultimately, he became a five-star General of the Army and was appointed to the highest post, Chief of Staff, 1980–83. In emails to me across several years he described his Vietnam experiences, and he sent me articles which he or other French soldiers had written reflecting experiences in the area north of Saigon, accompanied by pictures, maps, and illustrations. He said:

> At this time, our enemy was not so strong as yours, using principally mines against us and fighting mostly by ambushes against convoys on roads. By this time in the war, the British and American equipment that had been in reasonably good shape right after World War II was now suffering.
>
> My job was to protect the Michelin Plantation, the rubber being evacuated by barges on the Saigon River protected by landing crafts of our navy [leftover LCIs and LSTs from the U.S. Navy]. "Our" war in the South was essentially counter guerrilla, the Viet Minh trying to cut our ways of communications to prevent economic activity in order to take control of the population and prevent the functioning of the young South Vietnamese administration. They were killing the French and Vietnamese civilians responsible for the plantation and threatening Vietnamese workers to force them to join their ranks in the forest.
>
> The plantation director used the two planes of the Michelin Company. One was an old German Fiesler Storch observation plane which I often used as a reconnaissance plane. I had many occasions to fly in this plane for informal observation missions where I couldn't see anything because the Viet Minh used to take cover when they heard our engine. The pilot was kind enough to evacuate me with this very plane under very bad flying conditions to Saigon Hospital in August 1949 when I lost my right hand to a booby trap. I came back to Dau Tieng some weeks later with a wooden homemade hand.
>
> I don't know if these prehistoric details are interesting for you who fought with armor and air support against a regular Communist army with 20 years of war experience.

I assured General Delaunay that not only I but many others were interested in such details. I knew well the locations of several of the places he described in his many correspondences, places in which my task force had similar experiences some twenty years later.

The New Bao Dai Government

Politically, the French had some reason to hope that their position in Vietnam was improving. President Auriol and Bao Dai had come to an agreement, the Elysée Accords, which, to Bao Dai, initially seemed to assure the independence of Vietnam, but of course to the French meant something less than that, even though for the first time the word "independence" was part of the accord. Vietnam was to be an Associated State within the French Union. It was to be unified under Vietnamese administration, but France was to remain in control of its armed forces, primarily the Vietnamese National Army (VNA), created in 1949. In July Bao Dai appointed himself as prime minister, head of the State of Vietnam.

Proclaiming was one thing, achieving was another. Bao Dai had little following among his countrymen, and he was entertaining the idea of reconciliation with the

Communists, even creating positions in his government for them. A countryman said, "Bao Dai is in Dalat not doing anything at all. He has his women there and his hunting."[39]

As Bao Dai diddled, South Vietnam made an abrupt turn away from a potential compromise government. Ngo Dinh Diem, a staunchly Catholic bachelor who had earlier been offered the premiership and declined, set about rallying anti-Communist nationalists. Later he would power his way to the top.

In May the French prime minister sent the Army's chief of staff, General of the Army Georges Revers, to do a thorough investigation of the whole Indochina situation. In five weeks of extensive travels in Indochina, the general did a superb job, talking at length with men from general down to private, and French and Vietnamese civilian government officials from high to low.

He was astonished to discover that a sumptuous Saigon gaming palace, "*Le Grande Monde*," had been inaugurated in the presence of the French High Commissioner and the top military authorities. It belonged to Bay Vien, the head of the notorious Binh Xuyen, a criminal gang that permeated Saigon and much of the area around it. Bay Vien was paying royalties from prostitution, gambling, and illicit activities to Bao Dai.

Revers' report to Paris praised the men and damned the civilian and military leadership.

Ominous Developments in the North

Yet another new command structure was taking place in Tonkin when on September 10 General Marcel Carpentier became supreme commander for Indochina. He had no prior experience in Indochina, but his subordinate, General Marcel Alessandri, had been in Indochina since 1940 and had commanded units escaping into northwest Tonkin and China after the Japanese coup on March 9, 1945. Alessandri would be the commander in the North.

Two of Carpentier's friends had been offered and refused to take the post, telling Carpentier that he was damned unless he could get 500,000 more men. When he arrived in Vietnam he quickly became aware that General Revers had been wise in counseling abandonment of the posts on Route 4 along the Chinese border. Allesandri, however, could not bring himself to that view, giving up vast territory that had been purchased with so much effort and blood. Soon after arrival, Carpentier learned about the cost of holding it when a large ambush inflicted heavy casualties. Fluctuating in uncertainty, he finally gave the order to evacuate Cao Bang. Alessandri was incensed. Carpentier backed down. He apparently took comfort in knowing that he would be getting reinforcements, men and materiel: 125,000 Vietnamese from the National Army and 48,000 French, as well as Hellcat dive bombers, C-47 Dakotas, and landing craft from the United

States. Tonkin grew calmer, and Annam and Cochinchina were still the same: lots of "minor incidents," but nothing major. Carpentier could breathe a little easier.

The stage was set for disaster.

During the Revers investigation, life west of the Iron Curtain had suddenly become much more precarious when on August 29, 1949 the Soviet Union exploded an atomic bomb, launching a nuclear arms race. This, taken with Chinese Communist successes against Chiang Kai-shek's Nationalists, required Washington to consider far more seriously its attitude toward France in Indochina. The French were now perceived to be on the front lines against Communism.

Chinese Communist Victory

For months the Chinese Nationalists had been suffering huge losses, and Mao Tse-tung's political and military entities were consolidating power. Then, with defeat of most of the Nationalist forces, on October 1, 1949 in Tiananmen Square, Mao proclaimed the People's Republic of China (PRC). Again the Western world was electrified. The next day the Soviet Union recognized the new government. By December Chiang Kai-shek had evacuated with significant forces to Taiwan, and Mao's troops were on the northern border of Vietnam.

Giap was elated. He said, "The year 1949 saw the brilliant triumph of the Chinese Revolution and the birth of the People's Republic of China." Recriminations flew in Washington as to who was responsible for the "loss" of China—with the burden falling on Truman—notwithstanding that China had never been Washington's to "lose." Giap continued, "This great historic event, which altered events in Asia and throughout the world, exerted a considerable influence on the war of liberation of the Vietnamese people. Vietnam was no longer in the grip of enemy encirclement, and was henceforth geographically linked to the socialist bloc."[40]

Geographically linked, yes. But the Communism emanating from Moscow was not monolithic. China and North Vietnam were Communist, but never the "puppets" of any other power.

The war in Indochina changed dramatically with the Chinese Communist victory. The situation was grim for the French. Mao's guidance for international revolutionary warfare had prescribed various stages in insurgency, with the creation and employment of conventional armies as the last step. For years Ho and Giap had been progressing in this direction at the same time they were waging guerrilla warfare throughout Vietnam. Without decreasing that kind of local warfare—in fact increasing it—they had been able to build the "big battalions."

CHAPTER 6

Huge Battles and Simultaneous Guerrilla Warfare, 1950–mid-1953

The early months of 1950 were a whirlwind of political activity on both sides of the Iron Curtain. France formally ratified the accords of the Associated States of Indochina. As Vietnamese Communists vociferously rejected the new federation, the United States, Great Britain, and the Vatican officially recognized it. Britain and Israel, however, recognized Communist China, and the USSR and China recognized Ho Chi Minh's government as the sole legitimate government of Vietnam.

By April, the Chinese had established a Vietnamese military school just across the Vietnam border in China and were training Vietnamese in accordance with Mao's military principles, starting with guerrilla warfare and working up to large regular forces.

This beginning of formal Chinese assistance to Ho's government immensely changed the parameters of the war, especially in terms of weapons, uniforms, medicines, and all kinds of other necessary supplies. Many thousands of tons of equipment captured by Mao's forces from the Kuomintang (much of it U.S.), as well as newly manufactured modern materiel, would now begin flowing to the Viet Minh. This was an enormous step up from clandestine factories in Vietnamese jungles. At the same time, however, U.S. aid to French forces was far more substantial than China's aid to Ho in terms of tonnage, sophistication, and firepower, and it grew from 1951–54. This imbalance continued to be true during the forthcoming war with the Americans. China, the Soviet Union, and the East Bloc countries gave substantial military and economic aid to the North Vietnamese; however, it was dwarfed by the huge American and Allied commitment to South Vietnam.

The Viet Minh Fall Campaign, and War in Korea

The Viet Minh, now officially People's Army of Vietnam (PAVN) but continuing to be called Viet Minh, were planning a 1950 fall campaign which, for the first time in the war, would not only utilize area-wide large attacks by main-force units in the North, but also require simultaneous action in the South, a very significant step for the North: the first coordinated Vietnam-wide major offensive. In Cochinchina, the Viet Minh in Delaunay's area of the Michelin plantation increased their activity in January as preparation for the coming fall offensive, and he was kept busy night and day trying first to protect, and then rebuild, bridges and culverts the Viets had blown.

In Tonkin, emboldened by the Chinese Communist victory, and having built up its main forces, in February the Viet Minh launched an offensive against the Colonial Route 4 garrisons along the border with China. Despite severe losses, the French units were able to hang onto or recover lost posts, but the fighting drew attention to the deficiencies in the French posture—garrisons and outposts that were far out from Hanoi and difficult to support.

Elsewhere, catastrophe. On June 25, 1950, North Korean troops poured across the border into South Korea. The United States was at war. Two days later President Truman stated,

> The attack upon Korea makes it plain beyond all doubt that Communism has passed beyond the use of subversion to conquer independent nations and will now use armed invasion and war.... Accordingly, I have directed acceleration in the furnishing of military assistance to the forces of France and the Associated States in Indochina and the dispatch of a military mission to provide close working relations with those forces.[1]

This was fulfillment of the 1947 Truman Doctrine: the United States would provide political, military, and economic assistance to all democratic nations under threat from external or internal authoritarian sources. It was a stretch, indeed, to consider South Vietnam as a democratic nation, but from a meager beginning in 1945 when the French Expeditionary Corps entered Vietnam, the United States was opting to expand U.S. commitment to the French and the State of Vietnam.

In September 1950 the U.S. formed and sent Military Assistance Advisory Group (MAAG) to Vietnam. With its 35 men America began the long formal relationship between U.S. and South Vietnamese armed forces. Soon, more advanced U.S. aircraft were sent. Ho Chi Minh was now claiming that the Americans, not the French, were the ultimate and most dangerous enemy:

> The U.S. imperialists have of late openly interfered in Indochina's affairs. It is with their money and their weapons and their instructions that the French colonialists have been waging war in Viet-Nam, Cambodia, and Laos. However, the U.S. imperialists are intensifying their plot to discard the French colonialists so as to gain complete control over Indochina.[2]

Mao had beaten the U.S. by a few months in July 1950 by formalizing an earlier advisory arrangement as the Chinese Military Advisory Group (CMAG) in North Vietnam. Later, in 1951, China would provide a Chinese Political Advisory Group in keeping with their doctrine of combining military with political action and ensuring that within military units there was always a political commissar who not only provided Party doctrine and encouragement but shared in combat decisions. From these beginnings, the Chinese Communist Party leadership would develop its position that later played such a dominant role in the Vietnamese war against the Americans: "They would not hesitate to send troops into Vietnam to restore peace and order if the authority of an existing tributary ruler there [Ho Chi Minh] was endangered by either domestic uprisings or foreign invasion."[3] That this threat was real became dramatically apparent when the Chinese stormed across the Manchurian border with North Korea to drive UN forces back south in the Korean War.

The Route 4 Disaster for the French

In Tonkin during the summer of 1950, along Route 4 close to the Chinese border was an unusual calm. Suddenly on September 16, the Viet Minh attacked. They demonstrated that they not only could fight a guerrilla war, but they could field units in a coordinated war of "big battalions."

Orders went out for French Union units to evacuate from Cao Bang to Dong Khe, and this was the beginning of a rout. Giap blocked the way and trapped the French forces in a gorge where by October 8 many were slaughtered.

There was more to come on Route 4. The post of Lang Son had been occupied since the 19th century and was the anchor of the whole Route 4 defensive system. On the night of October 17/18, "it was abandoned intact, with its enormous stocks of supplies, munitions, and materiel, with its hospital and its 150 tons of pharmaceuticals, with its electric plant, its public works shop." That was "enough to equip eight regiments," according to the official Communist history, *The 30-Year War*. A contagious panic set in. Giap could freely arrange the avenues of penetration from China to the [Red River] Delta.... Tomorrow Hanoi?"[4]

On November 29, an elated Ho Chi Minh came to congratulate his victorious three divisions of the Route 4 campaign—now not just guerrilla units, not just companies, battalions, or regiments, but *divisions!*—the 304, 308 and 312. "You have left the mountains to descend toward the fertile rice fields of the Red River.... In a few weeks ... we will march on Hanoi. I promise you, comrades, by next Tet [February 6, 1951] we will enter Hanoi."[5]

Colonel Bui Tin, an early Ho adherent, asserted, "The situation started to change towards the end of 1950 after we forced the French to abandon their garrisons along the northern border, and the Resistance was able to link up with the People's Republic of China.... China was the immense rear area for the Vietnamese Revolution."[6]

America would now be of immense help to the French after some years of, first, its condemnation of colonial reconquest, then an ambivalent stance of modest assistance tempered by indifference, then significant help. On December 23, America weighed in heavily when President Truman signed an agreement with France for aid to Indochina.

During these somber days General Salan tallied the enormous loss of men in the French Union forces from September 23, 1945 to November 1950. Not counting officers from major general down to lieutenant, many of whom were killed or missing, it was 2,900 non-commissioned officers killed, of whom 2,700 were French Union or legionnaires, and 11,500 lower ranks killed, of whom 9,300 were French Union or legionnaires. Adding those missing in action and seriously wounded, evacuated, brought the total to 36,000.[7]

1951, The "Year of de Lattre": A Year of Hope

The people in France had gotten reports that the war was proceeding quite well, with a lasting political solution possible. Light at the end of the tunnel? Then the Route 4 disaster. And now, crowds rallying for an end to the war included outraged mothers, fathers, brothers, sisters, wives from across the political spectrum. A search was on for a savior.

The government had found their man in the immensely respected General of the Army Jean de Lattre de Tassigny. This time there would be no disagreement between the Supreme Commander and the High Commissioner. In early December de Lattre was appointed to both posts, and hopes rode high that he could get the war and peace process back on track.

De Lattre was a "general's general," no-nonsense, no excuses regardless of rank. On December 17, 1950 he and his entourage of generals and top civilian officials, to include those of the Associated State of Vietnam, landed at Tan Son Nhut. Following protocol, Special Minister Jean Letourneau descended first from the airliner. Then followed an interminable wait, designed to set the stage appropriately. Finally, the general appeared in the door, stepped out and paused, regally. He slowly descended, followed by his deputy Salan and the rest of his entourage, all in crisp white dress military uniforms or civilian suits.

This grand entry was de Lattre's style. Long ago he had been dubbed *"Le Roi Jean,"* King Jean, by admirers and detractors alike, each holding to different meanings of the term. He coldly received his predecessors, Messieur Léon Pignon and General Carpentier—two of them for one of him—and upon arrival at his new headquarters began relieving some heads of staff sections, replacing them with men he had brought with him. And he sent the ship *Pasteur* back with no civilians aboard, only wounded French Union soldiers. The civilians were to stay, he said, and contribute to the war effort. He ordered able-bodied French civilians in Vietnam to be put to work as guards.[8] Four days later he flew from Saigon to Dalat, the seat of the new Bao Dai government. But shortly he left, aggravated. He had been unsuccessful in persuading Bao Dai to accompany him to Hanoi.

General of the Army Jean de Lattre de Tassigny, 1946. (By Willem van de Poll, Wikimedia, CC-BY-SA-3.0)

When de Lattre arrived in Hanoi he was taken immediately to a reviewing stand. His new commander in the North, Major General Gonzales de Linarès, greeted him. De Lattre had given orders for all available battalions to be assembled, some of them coming straight from combat. He looked at them and exclaimed to General Salan, "They are scruffy!" It seemed to have been meant in profound admiration, not condemnation. Only hours earlier they had been fighting. Their combat uniforms were torn, stained with mud, some with blood. Their faces, needing shaves, bore traces of dried sweat, but as they passed in review they were in step with the music. De Lattre felt great pride in being their commander.

The colonel in charge of supply for the disheveled troops did not get away easily. De Lattre turned to him and said, "Disappear, colonel!"[9] Then he had the lieutenants and captains assembled, and proclaimed, "I am here. I swear to you that you will now be *commanded!* We will not yield a centimeter of terrain. I bring you war, but also the pride of this war." Later he sat in front of assembled military and civilian officers, French and Vietnamese, and said, "Our combat is selfless; it is all of civilization that we defend in Tonkin. We do not fight for domination, but for liberation. Never has a war been more noble."[10]

Well—

One may cringe. Nevertheless, a great many French volunteers in Vietnam believed with him that it was a civil war, and France was helping the non-Communist populace to establish their own country. For many profoundly distressed soldiers and civilians in Hanoi—French and Vietnamese—the general had come just in time, and he was setting exactly the right tone. With an ear to Ho's boast of being in Hanoi for Tet, de Lattre had found the city in a state of near-panic. Civil servants were evacuating their families, and businessmen were selling their factories and stores at fire sale prices. To show that normalcy would return, De Lattre stated he would be joined shortly in Hanoi by his wife. When she landed, the couple set out visiting wounded troops in the hospitals. The general made it clear to staff that those who were enjoying comfortable sinecures while the fighters did without had better begin producing or pack up and get out.

De Lattre was tough on subordinates and would not abide slackers, but he was benevolent among the lower-ranked men who could see the results of his efforts on their behalf. The headquarters for the supreme commander/high commissioner were in Saigon, but de Lattre had always marched to the sound of the guns, and it was near Hanoi that guns were sounding, so he would spend most of his time in Hanoi close to the fighting. When he had arrived in Hanoi, some of the combat was just 18 miles to the west of the city. The rumble of explosions could be heard. And Ho was not far away. His main headquarters was at Thai Nguyen, only 30 miles north of Hanoi in the Viet Bac.

De Lattre was the finest general since Leclerc. For several days he flew in a light observation plane all over Tonkin, maps on his knees, looking down, studying the maps and terrain, getting to know it. Soon he was devising a plan.[11]

Giap, in writing his memoirs, believed that de Lattre had global strategic considerations in mind as he developed that plan. Giap said, "If the Red River Delta, the rice granary of the North, with its 8 million inhabitants, was re-conquered by the Viet Minh, armed by China and the Soviet Union, this would threaten the whole of Southeast Asia. This delta was [the crucial area] in preventing the 'red waves' from flooding down from the north."[12]

In short order de Lattre unveiled the plan with two components. One was a 350-mile defensive line around the Delta featuring redoubts of concrete blockhouses protected by mines, barbed wire, programmed artillery fires, air strikes, and where possible from the rivers and the Gulf of Tonkin, naval gunfire. It protected Haiphong and Hanoi, the mainstays of the French position in the North. If either fell, the whole French effort in the North would fail, five years of sacrifice of men and money would be for naught, and the ambition to bring all of Indochina into a functioning French Union would end as a fizzled pipedream.

The defensive line was quickly dubbed "The de Lattre Line." Some existing outposts were eliminated and others strengthened. The line formed a wedge which anchored in the north on the Gulf of Tonkin and border of China at Mong Cai, dropped down to north of Haiphong and included other Haiphong defenses, went west past Mao Khe and Vinh Yen to Viet Tri, then curved southeast, enclosing Hanoi, and south to Nam Dinh, continuing south to anchor once again on the Gulf at Sam Son.

This sounded like the Maginot Line which in 1940 failed so spectacularly to keep the German blitzkrieg out of France. However, it was no static barrier. As the second component in his plan, the general ordered a mobile defense: every available unit which could be equipped for mobile warfare was to be positioned in critical locations within this perimeter. These regimental-size strike forces were the best, most combat-tested troops he had. The line was intended to hold any Viet Minh main-force advance in place long enough for the strike forces to react. Upon order the mobile units were to rush to the location and counterattack, assisted by all available ground, air, and naval support, and crush the enemy.

General Pierre Boyer de Latour had moved from command in the South to command in the North. He evacuated a post, which angered de Lattre. "Not a centimeter, general!" De Lattre relieved him and told his deputy, Salan, to take command.

De Lattre was making a strong push with the Vietnamese national government to raise and strengthen Vietnamese forces to take over the war. He told them that France would help them, but ultimately it was up to them to defend their country against the Communists. Also, the general went around to the various military schools where, with largely French officers as the leaders and teachers, young Vietnamese were learning to become soldiers and officers. At these schools, in government assemblies, and in youth groups he called upon Vietnamese young people to defend their freedom, telling them that the fate of their country was in their hands. On one occasion in a Saigon lyceé he urged them to make a commitment: "'Be men! If you are Communists, then join the Viet Minh—there are some good people there, fighting well for a bad cause. But if you are patriots, then fight for your country, because this is *your* war … France can only fight it for you if you fight with her.' His uneasy audience responded with only polite applause."[13]

For many young Vietnamese, there was not much sense of "country" for them to defend. With France still so obviously the leader in the fight against Ho's DRV and the Viet Minh, it was difficult for that idea to take hold. De Lattre early on found that Ho was giving the Vietnamese something to die for—independence and unity—whereas it was difficult for France to motivate Vietnamese into something to live for—an Associated State within the French Union.

The First Major Tests of the de Lattre Line

Mindful of Ho's promise to enter Hanoi by February 6 in time for Tet celebrations, Giap's first objective was to overrun fortified Vinh Yen, which would crack the de

Lattre Line. He had his forward command post installed in the nearby remains of bombed-out cellars of mountain summer houses formerly used by Bao Dai and the French governor general. On the night of January 12/13, 1951, Giap's main forces attacked. De Lattre ordered his mobile strike forces into the fierce battle, and by the night of January 16/17, Giap's troops were in retreat, having lost many dead, wounded, and captured. De Lattre's men had also suffered severe casualties, but they had stopped Giap's thrust.

The French and the Vietnamese loyalists in Hanoi were ecstatic. International television, radio, and newspaper journalists clamored for stories. Ho's boast that he would make it into Hanoi for Tet was fodder for jokes. De Lattre was riding high. "At his arrival everything bad.... A month later everything had changed.... Confidence, resolution, audacity animated the same men.... The expeditionary corps reached its apogee.... The French had feared a new disaster; suddenly they believed in victory. It was a resurrection."[14]

Ho had not made it into Hanoi by Tet in February, but he was busy with an important political development. In order to attract a broader spectrum of people to his cause, since November 1946 Vietnam had not had an official Communist Party. But in February 1951 in the far northwestern reaches of the Viet Bac, just south of the Chinese border, Ho convened what came to be called the Resistance Congress. "The Dang Lao Dong Vietnam, or Vietnamese Workers Party, was inaugurated with Ho as chairman.... It made respectable, at least legal, that which had been secret and, in a sense, illegitimate.... It helped internationalize the Party and integrate it into the worldwide Communist movement as an orthodox element."[15]

With a division, Giap next struck hard at Mao Khe. The defending Vietnamese partisan unit had their wives and children to protect, and they fought like demons to hold on. Paratroopers, legionnaires, and marines reinforced the partisans, and despite continued vicious attacks they punished the enemy with their strong stand and heavy supporting fires. Giap's two-division attack at nearby Dong Trieu likewise failed. After 12 days of bitter fighting, night and day, Giap withdrew.

De Lattre's Personal Disasters

The Viet Minh divisions, as was their custom, had pulled back to reorganize, reequip, and retrain for the next main thrust. Meanwhile, guerrilla activity went on unabated, always pressuring the French and gaining recruits.

De Lattre was now in a position to attempt pacification of the Delta, and he ordered several relatively small operations. In one of them his son Bernard distinguished himself at the head of a company of Vietnamese infantrymen during two weeks of tough fighting. Some days after the operation ended on May 2, a very proud father pinned the Croix de Guerre on his son.

At about this time de Lattre discovered he had liver cancer, but he kept working. Giap's third attack was to test de Lattre as never before. Ninh Binh was the most advanced position in the de Lattre line. Two of Giap's divisions struck on the night of May 28/29. Bernard's unit was one of the first to respond, assaulting and gaining a rocky point during the night. One of the enemy's first mortar rounds killed him.

The general got the terrible news. He was struck to the core of his being. His only son, the young man he so deeply loved, the young fellow who was well on his way to carrying on the proud de Lattre tradition, was dead. In a dreadful telegram to his wife, now in Paris, he asked forgiveness for not being able to save their son. "The next day he confided to some intimates in a sob, 'Bernard, he did not die for France. They can write that on his cross, but it is not true. Bernard, at Ninh Binh, he died for Viet Nam.'"[16]

In this battle of Day River, de Lattre had again stopped Giap. After that terrible summer of 1951 for the Viets, they never again would pose a serious threat to Hanoi and the fertile delta area. Viet Minh desertions were at an alarming rate, and Giap would have to review his strategy of attacks by main-force divisions. Ho even called a meeting of the Central Military Committee and he proposed relieving Giap of his position of Commander in Chief of the Army. Ho seemed to have done this pro forma because the motion was defeated mainly because Ho opposed his own proposal. It may have been put on the agenda just to clear the air or perhaps, as Bernard Fall pointed out, "Giap was retained because the erroneous decision to launch the offensive had been made collectively by the whole senior Party hierarchy."[17]

For de Lattre, grieving, there was no feeling of personal accomplishment. He had fallen in love with Vietnam. He thought the people were courageous, industrious, proud. He had faith in their future, and he had gone a long way toward "Vietnamization," more politically than militarily. Later in Paris at the funeral of Bernard and two of Bernard's men who had been killed beside him, struggling with deep sorrow and suppressed passion, the general told the mourners, "For many years the best blood of France was being spilled in Indochina and the people of France did not acknowledge it. With Lieutenant Bernard de Lattre and his companions, the anonymous dead of the rice paddies have the right to the tears of France."[18]

The End of "The Year of de Lattre"

The general and his wife returned to Hanoi, and he continued with his duties, devastated, desperately ill, but resolute. Giap's setbacks convinced the Chinese advisors that "it was premature for the Viet Minh to achieve a decisive victory through big offensives in a region where the colonial army, close to its base [Hanoi and the Delta] could utilize its superior firepower."[19] (General Westmoreland, 14 years later, before ordering search and destroy in jungles, might well have reviewed de Lattre's tactics of mobile defense of critical areas to protect significant populations of civilians. But he apparently did not.)

Ho and Giap acknowledged that their forces had been insufficiently prepared, and there were to be no more division-size attacks by the Viet Minh for months. They had been severely hurt and needed time to recover. Instead of big unit battles, while they were recuperating and preparing once again for major combat, they shifted for a time to assassinations and guerrilla warfare throughout Vietnam and in northern Laos.

De Lattre's efforts at urging the Vietnamese to take charge of their own future took a step forward on July 14 when the Bao Dai government announced the official birth of the Vietnamese National Amy and decreed general mobilization.

On November 20 the general, gravely ill with cancer, sorrowfully bade goodbye to his staff, and he and his wife lifted off for Paris. Somewhat like the regal MacArthur ten years earlier, he left, promising that he would return. Unlike MacArthur, that was not to be.

***

In 1951, the obvious strength of the Viet Minh and recognition of this internationally, and the rising success of Red China in gaining influence among global Communist powers had led to official reestablishment of the Communist Party in Vietnam (now Lao Dong) in hopes it could take a greater part on the world stage. Ho was named Chairman and Truong Chinh was selected Secretary General in what was the beginning of Ho's somewhat diminishing influence, serving more as elder statesman, diplomat and advisor while Truong Chinh and others took on Central Committee duties of establishing policy and seeing that it was carried out.

Le Duan and Continued Guerrilla Warfare in the South

A rising star in the South was Le Duan. Born in north Annam in 1907 to a poor family, as a young man he moved to Tonkin, worked as a railroad clerk and became caught up in anticolonial activities during which he recruited railway workers. He appeared later as a Viet Minh commander in the Mekong Delta. Le Duan was a very different kind of leader from Ho and Giap, both of whom had been well educated in the Mandarin or French traditions. Slight in stature, speaking like the country people he came from, he was basically self-educated and had good common sense and a keen mind. His documents reveal a prodigious intellect, impressive analytic skills, and mastery of language. An early 1930s Party member, he was imprisoned twice for five years each time, first in 1931–36 like his friend and later right-hand man Le Duc Tho, and again in 1940–45. Le Duan

Le Duan. (TopFoto)

rose to prominence in the Party due to his courage, patriotic fervor, competence, overall administrative skills, and burning desire to be the top man. His guerrilla strategy made life miserable for the French in parts of the South. By 1951 he was directing political and military operations throughout the South.

A Légionnaire in the South

French Légionnaire lore includes the story of General François de Negrier who in 1893 had addressed legionnaires on their way to Tonkin to fight Chinese marauders, and many legionnaires took to heart his famous saying: "You, you Legionnaires are soldiers in order to die, and I am sending you where one dies." In 1951 a Brit who had been in the Royal Navy enlisted in the French Foreign Legion and served in Vietnam for two years of a four-year enlistment. He had been well indoctrinated. He said in his excellent 1955 book, *In Order to Die*, "It was part of the Legion's job to get killed."[20]

By strict custom, in telling of adventures, no legionnaire must ever divulge the true names of himself, his comrades, or dates, times, or places of events which could result in retribution on the participants—in many cases, severe, even mortal. To write his compelling book this young man used the pseudonym Henry Ainley.

Soon after arrival at regimental headquarters northwest of Saigon, Ainley heard gory tales of legionnaires who had been captured and hideously tortured during slow, agonizing deaths. Soon he learned that this happened on both sides. He said,

> The next two years were to confirm what I sensed the first day. Torture and brutality were routine matters in the questioning of suspects, and frequently I was obliged to be an unwilling and disgusted witness, powerless to intervene. Unfortunately, brutality and bestiality were not exclusively reserved for official suspects. Rape, beating, burning, torturing of entirely harmless peasants and villagers were of common occurrence in the course of punitive patrols and operations by French troops, throughout the length and breadth of Indochina.[21]

Although assigned as secretary to a battalion commander because he could read, write, and speak French, which few men in the Legion could do proficiently, he also was posted to guard duty and patrols. On one of the latter which was led by an Armenian sergeant, the sergeant methodically robbed some peasant women and children of whatever little money they had:

> The last ... was a girl of about sixteen, who had been trying to hide in a corner... [He] stretched out his hand and with a violent downward wrench ripped open her jacket and tore down her trousers .... Without thinking, I grabbed him by the shoulder, pulled him off the girl and told him he couldn't do that ... I realized that I had laid my hands on a superior and the consequence could be terrible. [The sergeant] was so amazed that he finally burst out laughing and in the friendliest way told me that I would soon get used to a little friendly rape.[22]

Soon the sergeant and others were busy burning down the hamlet and stealing chickens and pigs. Ainley took no comfort in such behavior. His unit moved on and came upon a horrible massacre at one of the French Union posts:

> The NCO and the two Légionnaires, who had been in command of the native auxiliaries, were dead and had been beheaded by machetes, a dozen of the auxiliaries dead and a score wounded.... Several of the auxiliaries' womenfolk had been scalped or ripped open or both, and three were dead, as well as two small children.... One of the women who had been ripped open was pregnant; she was not dead, and in her arms she held a small child half of whose scalp was missing.[23]

The war in the North was having a serious effect on Ainley's battalion:

> We still hadn't received the reinforcements we had hoped for.... The new troops arriving from Africa were all vitally needed for the Regiment's two battalions in Tonkin. The rare driblets effected to our battalion were those too old or too untried to be of any use for the heavy fighting up North.[24]

After two years, Ainley was hospitalized with physical and mental fatigue, and eventually evacuated back to France. He reflected on why he had joined the Legion:

> I had fondly imagined that the Indochinese war was an all-out effort to protect an innocent people against the unwelcome attentions of the communists.... Not even in my wildest dreams had I realized that I was to become part of a mercenary army deliberately trained to devastate. The men of the Foreign Legion were first-class soldiers, but they had nothing whatsoever to do with a mission of pacification and political re-education. The Foreign Legion was brilliant

at two things—killing and dying well, both of which the Légionnaires did frequently and with *éclat*. But that had little to do with protecting the quiet little yellow men who surrounded us, hated us cordially and occasionally got around to murdering us when they saw the chance.[25]

***

In 1951, helicopters played an increasing role. Drawing on American and their own seminal experiences in Korea, the French in Indochina found air medevac much in demand. Captain Valérie André, a former member of the French Resistance, was not only a neurosurgeon but parachutist and helicopter pilot, the first woman to fly a helicopter in combat. To have such high-level skills as hers available on the spot where a soldier had been seriously wounded was very special to the troops. After many hazardous missions in War Zone D, she traveled to the Central Highlands far to the north. One of her missions there took her to the northern Laotian boondocks where at a tiny post a man was gravely ill and could not be moved by road. If she had had a helicopter available, she could have flown in, but there was none, so she got a ride out on a cargo plane and parachuted down alone, landing in the small drop zone only a few meters from a sergeant. A lieutenant trotted up and scolded the sergeant,

> "What are you waiting for to help the doctor?"
> Bewilderment paralyzed the sergeant.
> "But lieutenant," he stammered, "I expected a different kind."[26]

Serving two tours in Indochina, Captain André was acclaimed for her courageous rescues under fire and surgical skills in several parts of Vietnam, Laos, and Cambodia and went on to become modern France's first female general.

***

In December 1951, as the end of the year approached, Giap attacked the Hoa Binh area southwest of Hanoi with two divisions in an attempt to open a major route to the South. Salan, now both interim high commissioner and supreme commander, reinforced his defending units by dropping paratroopers. Among them was the 1st Vietnamese Parachute Battalion which got its baptism under fire fighting other Vietnamese. So the year ended in Tonkin much as it had begun, with Salan conducting sweeps inside the de Lattre line, Giap attacking with main forces while guerrilla war was ongoing everywhere, and the French defending and consolidating their positions through "pacification."

1952: U.S. Raises Its Ante

The new year in France opened in the National Assembly with an address by the prime minister indicating that "the French Government has no present intention of abandoning Indochina and that it considers that Indochina must stay in the French Union. They reject, although not categorically so, any idea of negotiation with Ho Chi-Minh."[27]

On January 12, 1952 France's defense minister shocked a country which had been ill-prepared to receive the news. De Lattre was dead. "General de Lattre de Tassigny has given everything to his country—his victories, his son, and his life."[28]

On the day de Lattre died, the Viet Minh cut the supply lines to the French forces in Hoa Binh despite the French command's earlier insistence they could hold that position indefinitely. French evacuation of their untenable position at Hoa Binh was a strong indication that 1952 was not going to be "*l'année du Salan*" as the previous year had been "The Year of de Lattre."

Despite some decent performances by units of the Vietnamese National Army, the government could not excite the admiration or support of the people to any degree approaching that of Ho's DRV. In France, anti-war sentiment was hot.

The Nature of the Soldier and Citizen, North and South

A view of ARVN General Tran Van Don may be appropriate at this point, given that a Vietnamese national government of sorts and a Vietnamese national army had been in existence for a few years, both of which had been receiving increasing U.S. aid. General Don had grown up in Saigon and the Mekong Delta where the year-around favorable climate made production of food easy. Virtually no one went hungry. On his first trip to the North as a boy with his father in 1935 he saw how different were the conditions.

> Instead of the gentle monsoon, which gives a warm "tropical paradise" feeling to life for southern rich and poor alike, the northern wind produces cold and highly disagreeable weather. I have seen peasant girls standing up to their bare knees in rice paddies in January planting rice, bravely suffering the effects of both low temperature and chilling winds. Their more frugal existence and more difficult life make the northern people "harder." Used to the perversity of nature and frequent privation of insufficient food, the North Vietnamese have a quite different attitude toward life than we do in the South. They work harder, endure more, and know less of creature comfort. It is no wonder that they were able to fight so courageously and continuously over so many years while living an austere and cheerless existence.[29]

Self-criticism and the Three-man Cell

Colonel Bui Tin explained a development in the Viet Minh that, despite aspects which many of its practitioners quietly despised, nevertheless seemed to enhance their fighting capabilities:

From the beginning of 1952, every unit had to set up three-man cells. Each evening after they had eaten, these cells had to examine together their actions during the day. Every member … had to reveal his fears of hunger, hardship and death as well as his thoughts of envy, lust or enjoyment. This system was said to be necessary to maintain discipline, but it weighed heavily on human dignity and the personality of the individual who was always forced into repentance.[30]

Criticism and self-criticism was just something we had to cope with. There was no sincerity involved. You criticize me so I criticize you as strongly; you forgive me so I do the same.[31]

This technique of self-criticism was the last point in the ten-point pledge that Giap's first 34 fighters took in 1944: "To use self-criticism for personal improvement."[32]

The three-man cell was the lowest unit in the Viet Minh's tripartite arrangement for its combat units—three regiments to a division, three battalions to a regiment, and so on down the chain. At the lowest level the closeness of three men, forced or not, paid off in combat. One took care of another both during heavy fighting and in periods of rest and recuperation. This is well documented in prisoner-of-war accounts: "From induction, each soldier was taught that his three-man collective team was more important than his individual rights or desires … the three-man cell forced a bonding akin to brotherhood, which was essential for coping with fear in battle and boredom in camp." An NVA private first class said, "The three-man cell was very helpful to me. For example, during the infiltration south, the other men in the cell gave me a lot of assistance such as carrying my gun and ammunition and other items for me when I was tired or sick. The attitude of the other men in the cell was so encouraging that I was even more determined to endure the hardships in order to arrive in the South." A three-year veteran said, "When I was wounded the first time on an operation, the other two men helped me to get out from the battlefield."[33]

This system endured to the end of the war.

Late 1952–Early 1953, A New Front in the High Region

Ho and Giap changed strategy, and this was to have profound effect on the course of the war. Despite what seemed like insurmountable hardships, Ho's government had strengthened its support among the populace from north to south. It also had been able to improve the training and equipping of all aspects of the military—main force, regional and local units, and guerrillas. Now was the time, they believed, to open a new front. It would be in the High Region of Tonkin, the Tay Bac, that rugged mountainous area that stretched from southwest of Hanoi north to the Chinese border and west to Laos.

In 1944 French special forces detachments had parachuted into the High Region to recruit Montagnard tribes to fight the Japanese, and they had landed aircraft at the

Giap briefs Ho (center) on his plan to lure French Union forces into the High Region for destruction, culminating in Dien Bien Phu. (TopFoto)

rudimentary Dien Bien Phu airstrip. After the Japanese surrender, these detachments continued to make headway in recruiting Montagnards, mainly T'ai, and forming them into meagerly armed units. Many of the hill people in this vicinity blamed Vietnamese for racial discrimination that forced them out of the fertile valleys into the hills.

In 1953, while Viet Minh guerrilla and main force actions were making headlines elsewhere, many small French posts, supplied almost entirely by air, remained operating in the High Region despite Viet Minh harassment. Dien Bien Phu was not one of them. Salan had withdrawn its French outpost, and the village was soon occupied by his enemy.

Not all High Region indigenous people supported the French. In September 1952 while Ho had attended a meeting at military headquarters in the Viet Bac, he met with his commanders and staff as they prepared for the campaign which would take them through Montagnard tribal country to the west toward Laos. Historically, the Viet Minh had been highly successful in recruiting tribal groups in the Viet Bac; now they had to turn their attention westward. Ho spoke to the group of the critical nature of behavior among the minority people:

The Government has issued policies concerning the national minorities; you and the troops must implement them correctly. This is a measure to win over the people, frustrating the enemy's scheme of "using Vietnamese to harm Vietnamese." We must so do that each fighter becomes a propagandist. You must behave in such a way that the people welcome you on your arrival and give you willing aid during your stay and miss you on your departure.[34]

Several signs were good for Giap. In France, the financial and human toll after more than seven years of war, and strong anti-war sentiments, resulted in the government's decision in May to *decrease* the effective strength of its Indochina force by 15,000 men.[35] Then too, Giap's forces had been able to feed, clothe, and equip themselves on the periphery of the de Lattre Line in the Delta even though the French controlled the richest rice land. Could they not do the same if a large part of its main forces were to move west?

Such a move would have three main advantages. First, it would "liberate" the region and threaten Laos, which hopefully would lead to a much easier route for supplying the South, down along the Mekong River through rich Laotian rice lands instead of south through the rugged central mountains of Annam while trying to evade French blocking forces.

Second, it could require the French to commit large mobile forces far from their bases near Hanoi and Haiphong. The French would have to move them into mountainous terrain which highly favored the Viet Minh. If that happened, those French units would have to be supplied from a great distance by air and could be isolated and destroyed.

Third, by sucking out French strength from the Delta, the local Viet Minh there would be able to build strength internally and supply more clandestine rice to main-force units and the people whose support was so necessary.

A major Viet Minh move to the High Region, though, would be daunting. Giap said, "The way of overcoming this difficulty was to repair the roads in order to use motorized vehicles. And we had to mobilize a large number of *dan cong* (the people who voluntarily took part in the supply to the front). But if the number of *dan cong* increased, the need for food also increased."[36]

That the Viet Minh were able to accomplish their moves is one of the greatest achievements of the war. They repaired roads, especially the one from the China border south to Lai Chau, just north of Dien Bien Phu. It became capable of supporting heavily laden Chinese trucks. Also, they replaced the earlier backpacks of coolies with sturdy pack-bicycles that could be pushed, each carrying up to ten times as much as a backpack.

In addition, a strategic deception plan worked well. Suddenly, on September 20, around Hanoi main-force divisions started using different call signs, their old ones still operating in the same places with dummy staff. This deception would enable regiments of the 308th and 312th Divisions to begin a move west and position themselves for battle, with elements of the 316th and 351st Divisions soon to follow. Separately, for a period, Giap's 149th Independent Regiment garrisoned Dien Bien Phu.

Salan and the *base aéroterrestre*

To counter the threat,

> Salan initiated the concept of the *base aéroterrestre*, a distant air-ground base with a usable landing strip that could be improved. The base would be a logistics center and was placed in a strategic location out of which his forces could reconnoiter and attack enemy units, diminishing the threat of a move on Laos. The base would be resupplied by air, to support attacks from it against the enemy's lines of communication. [In November 1952] he put the first such base at Na San in a small valley opening, some 150 air miles west of Hanoi.[37]

Salan also reinforced the position at Lai Chau, 20 miles north of Dien Bien Phu.

There was no French general who knew Indochina and the Viet Minh better than Salan. In 1924 he was in Tonkin as a lieutenant and set about learning at least the rudiments of the languages of the local tribes. Within weeks Salan had been asked if he would volunteer for a post in northwest Laos, and his eager response was "*oui!*"[38] For the next 13 years Salan was in colonial administration.

Additionally, Salan had medium- and high-level command experience in World War II. He had been back in Indochina almost continuously since October 1945 when Leclerc sent him north to command French Forces in Tonkin and southern China. Later, de Lattre had put him in command of the counterattack at Vinh Yen using two mobile groups and the air force, and Salan had stopped Giap's advance. So by 1952 this general was well experienced in high-level command, and he had had many face-to-face meetings with Giap, and some with Ho. He well knew the terrain and the ways of the Indochinese. When he came up with the concept of the *base aéroterrestre* he had reason to believe that Giap would emerge from the jungle with an attack by a division or two, and thus, in the open, enemy forces could be severely mauled by French artillery, air strikes, and counterattack.

Salan sent several battalions of infantry, some engineers, and artillery units to Na San under a gritty commander, Colonel Jean Gilles. They dug in and erected formidable defenses, inviting a set-piece battle in which the French could bring enormous firepower and counterattack to bear on an exposed enemy. The base, though, turned out to be not much of a threat to Giap's forces. With some difficulty the Viet divisions could bypass it on their way to Laos. Also, the French had a tough time reconnoitering around it in the mountainous terrain, and they suffered casualties from main forces outside which invested the distant fortress.

Fortunately for Salan, U.S. aircraft had arrived in increasing numbers. C-119 "flying boxcars" and C-47 Dakotas for supply and paradrop missions, and B-26

Invaders for bombing were replacing the aged JU-52s. F-6 Hellcats and F-8 Bearcats for dive-bombing and strafing were welcome improvements.

It seemed Salan had been right about this concept of attracting large enemy formations to attack, then annihilating them. The French at Na San, using heavy air support, beginning at the end of November repelled a two-division Viet Minh attack after four days of bitter fighting, causing heavy Viet Minh casualties while incurring only moderate losses themselves.

***

After being repulsed at Na San, Giap replenished his units and began to move on Laos with three divisions. The French position at Sam Neua in Laos near the northeastern border with Tonkin had been garrisoned with 1,700 men. A division was now threatening it, and in mid-April 1953 the post commander received orders to destroy what he could and evacuate to the south. The column was ambushed, and its Laotian partisans deserted and fled in panic. The French commander had to give the remnants the order to disperse, essentially "every man for himself." Salan countered by applying pressure in the Delta, and Giap, considering his rear and how far he was moving from his support base, halted further advance into Laos. But northeastern Laos was now largely in the hands of the Viet Minh and their Pathet Lao allies.

CHAPTER 7

Dien Bien Phu and the End, mid-1953–54

Leclerc, de Lattre, Salan—they were France's best generals. Given their meager resources to commit to such a war and the terrible conditions in which they had to fight it, they did what they could, and generally did it well. After eight dreadful years, the French government, the French people wanted the horror to end. No one could know in early 1953 that the end was approaching.

But not as the French hoped.

Geneviève

On May 5, 1953 a young woman, Geneviève de Galard, arrived in Hanoi during her first tour of duty in Indochina. She was born in 1925 into a family that traced its roots back to Clovis in the 6th century. One of her ancestors had ridden in the Crusades and another had fought with Jeanne d'Arc. After the terrible period of German occupation in World War II she could have had an easy life. Instead, she wanted to find some meaningful way to serve others. She said, "I was proud and at the same time eager to prove myself worthy of these famous [ancestors] who had proved their loyalty to their Christian faith, to their native soil, to a spirit of service and honor."[1] She became a nurse and joined *les Convoyeuses de l'air*, the French military flight nurses service.

Geneviève had experienced a few days of heat and humidity in Saigon, then flown north. She said, "The climate of Hanoi felt delicious. But I was mostly happy to be sent to Tonkin so soon, where the heaviest fighting was taking place." Her first mission was to Luang Prabang in northern Laos to evacuate survivors of the Sam Neua disaster in Laos. Then she flew missions to Lai Chau, capital of the T'ai tribes of the area north of Dien Bien Phu deep in the High Region. Landing, she admired "T'ai women walking in single file at their graceful pace, so elegant in their traditional costume, a white top held close by silver hooks, a long skirt of dark fabric, a wide, flat straw hat."[2]

Geneviève also made several trips into Na San evacuating casualties, and one night after a serious battle stayed to help treat the wounded. "That night I had a foretaste of what I would experience, though far more dramatically, ten months later in Dien Bien Phu."[3] She had no idea that her service would require such extreme courage, skill, and devotion.

The Penultimate General

Two days after Geneviève first landed in Hanoi, Prime Minister René Mayer announced the appointment of the new supreme commander to replace Salan, General Henri Navarre. "Mayer's charge to Navarre seems to have been vague, essentially to go [to Indochina] and create conditions of strength from which France could negotiate an end to this endless war. And by the way, don't expect any reinforcements or increase in budget."[4] The next prime minister, Pierre Mendes-France, stated that the only possible outcome would be by negotiation—a faint echo of General Leclerc's point some seven years earlier.

Navarre had no Indochina experience. Arriving in Vietnam, he soon proclaimed that he saw "light at the end of the tunnel."

Navarre, a cavalryman, selected for his commander in the North an artilleryman, General René Cogny, a huge man who had been captured by the Germans at the Maginot Line. Cogny escaped, joined the Resistance, was recaptured and tortured by the Gestapo and sent to Buchenwald from which he barely emerged, virtually a skeleton, and with a severe limp that required him to use a cane for the rest of his life. He was one of de Lattre's men and had commanded a division in Tonkin. In a bitter exchange of recriminations after Dien Bien Phu, the volatile "Cogny would … refer to [Navarre] as a freezing, 'air conditioned general' and as a disconcerting 'electronic computer.'" Cogny accused Navarre "of approaching military operations as an intellectual exercise, and of calculating acceptable levels of casualties with cold logic. This quality is certainly unattractive; but it has been shared by many of history's most successful generals, including Napoleon."[5]

One might add, and Giap.

A plan for Dien Bien Phu

Salan had left behind a plan for a *base aéroterrestre* at Dien Bien Phu, and in July Navarre ordered that it be executed. For his base commander Navarre chose another cavalryman, Colonel Christian de Castries, who had previous Vietnam tours of duty in 1946 and then in 1951 when he led a mobile group under de Lattre in the fighting at Vinh Yen and was wounded. "The combination of Cogny and de Castries seemed ideal—firepower of artillery, mobility of cavalry.

Dien Bien Phu, about eleven miles long and five miles wide, was one of the very few valleys—indeed the largest one—in northwest Tonkin that was open enough to accommodate a large force. An added benefit to the French was that it produced much of the rice that supported the Viet Minh troops in the High Region. Additionally, its opium bought Chinese weapons."[6]

The village was a strategic intersection of three roads, one north 50 miles to China, another west 30 miles to Laos, and the third east 220 winding road miles to Hanoi. All were in poor condition almost all the way, but passable with difficulty.

Navarre's plan for establishing a base at Dien Bien Phu provoked strong objections among some of his staff and commanders. Colonel Dominique Bastiani, a tough paratrooper, warned that "In this country you cannot bar [the enemy] from taking a direction. The Viet goes where he likes—he's proved that well enough in the Delta."[7] The air force pointed out its limited capacity to support an operation 180 air miles from Hanoi. It would need to expend enormous air strike, para-drop, and supply lift resources in weather that was often terrible. Cogny, after the war, adamantly insisted that he had counseled Navarre against such a move, but there is scant evidence of this assertion.

In answering his post-battle detractors, Navarre pointed to Na San's successful defense. The losses of the defenders had been relatively small weighed against the hundreds of enemy bodies found on the barbed wire encircling the position. But the brash Colonel Gilles, who had commanded at Na Son during the battle, stated he had been lucky. Good French soldiering, he said, was only part of the reason for the good results. The rest was due to the bad mistakes made by his enemy.

The upshot was, "when in August 1953 Na San was successfully evacuated under pressure in order to concentrate the reserves, this seemed to the Navarre air-conditioned headquarters in far away Saigon assurance that [Dien Bien Phu] would succeed in putting a huge dent in Giap's plans."[8] After all, Navarre would have his air force overhead and his artillery inside Dien Bien Phu. And he was planning for some light tanks to be air-lifted, and aircraft to be based at the airstrip. He would have an excellent mobile strike force capability. The enemy would be punished even more than at Na San. And, if necessary, Dien Bien Phu could be evacuated, like Na San.

> Navarre did not envision that "Giap could move five divisions into position around the DBP defenders, little damaged by the many airstrikes directed against them; or that they could be supported by masses of laborers building roads and trails for artillery and supplies; or that when French battalions moved out of DBP on reconnaissance in force missions they would encounter inordinately tough going in the difficult terrain and incur heavy casualties; or that antiaircraft fire from hidden positions would prove deadly against planes trying to drop men and supplies; or that the Viet artillery could be dug into the forward slopes of the hills surrounding DBP to provide heavy direct fire onto the airfield; or, incredibly, that this enemy artillery could survive massive counter battery fire and air strikes and itself become dominant."[9]

Prelude to Ferocious Battle

This part of the French Indochina War—basically from the French point of view—has been treated in depth by historians in French, English, Vietnamese and other languages. An excellent place to start is Martin Windrow's book, *The Last Valley: Dien Bien Phu and the French Defeat in Vietnam*. Windrow says his book is a "synthesis of secondary sources." Most of those sources, though, are in French and, as he says, "may therefore not be familiar to Anglo Saxons."[10]

Only an outline of major actions, incorporating testimony of combatants on both sides, should be necessary. It is powerful affirmation of incredible courage, endurance, and care for one's comrades during miserable, cold, muddy, wet weather. No person should ever have had to face such conditions, but tens of thousands did—the defenders in mud and icy water-filled dugouts on the inner lines of defenses, the attackers in equally horrible dugouts and assault trenches.

American concern over the consequences of a Communist victory were reflected in the September 1953 presidential approval of additional aid for France. President Eisenhower was somewhat optimistic that the Navarre Plan might work. "Admiral Arthur W. Radford, Chairman of the Joint Chiefs of Staff ... [said] 'this was the first time that the [French] political climate had improved to a point where military success could actually be achieved.'"[11]

Major Marcel Bigeard commanded 6th Colonial Parachute Battalion. He had been in the High Region earlier, leading the 3rd T'ai Battalion, and had parachuted into "The Street Without Joy," as well as several other such exotic places. He was renowned as a tough fighter in World War II, coming up the ranks from private to major, and everyone knew him by his World War II radio call sign, "Bruno." On the evening of November 19, 1953, as he recalled in his memoirs, "Officers, NCOs, men were proud and happy. A fine new mission. For me to see again that picturesque village so calm and welcoming where I had landed in a Dakota seven years ago. What would we find for our reception committee?"[12] Major Bigeard was thinking of the Viet Minh who had taken over when the French closed down that small outpost some time earlier. The intelligence was fuzzy.

At daylight on November 20, 1953, a command and control C-47 Dakota bearing three generals—two army, one air force—circled over the village of Muong Thanh, the T'ai name for Dien Bien Phu. They were concerned about the *crachin*, the persistent ground fog and drizzle of the High Region that on the best of days did not begin to burn off until about an hour after dawn, often much later or not at all on some days. In Hanoi, 65 C-47s had sat for almost two hours, loaded with paratroopers burdened with the backpack of their main chute and the reserve pack on their chest, below which was strapped a knapsack to which was attached their personal weapon, ready pockets of ammunition, some changes of clothes and personal items. At 0815 hours the command aircraft over Dien Bien Phu radioed the go-ahead, and the planes back at Hanoi began trundling down the runway, one after another. In the air they took assault formation. As they flew over the High Region, Bigeard looked down. "Viewed from on high, it was beautiful with all those mountains so green. If we could remain up here, us, we paratroopers, life would be much simpler."

They had been flying for almost two hours, much of it in the windy conditions that prevailed over the mountains. Bigeard said, "Crammed into the Dakotas, flying three by three, the wingtips some 30 meters from one another, some men were pale, others vomiting."[13]

Those of us who were paratroopers well know this experience as the plane bounces through rough winds. You are desperate to get out and get the firm earth under your feet again no matter who might be down there to greet you.

Finally, the commands: Stand up—Hook up—Check your equipment—Shuffle to the door—(LOUD BUZZER)—GO!

Suddenly dozens, then several dozens, then hundreds of parachutes descended. As they neared the ground Bigeard's troopers began receiving fire. He heard rounds zipping by him. His battalion medical officer was shot dead in his harness before he landed. Bréche, as he was called—Major Jean Bréchignac—with his 2nd Battalion, 1st Parachute Light Infantry Regiment, close behind Bigeard, was dropping on a nearby landing zone, encountering no enemy resistance. When the empty Dakotas returned to Hanoi they loaded up with 1st Colonial Parachute Battalion and dropped them at about 1600 hours into an unopposed landing zone. By nightfall about 2,700 men, French and their Vietnamese comrades, were on the ground, and the initial objectives were secure.

The units that had jumped that day were the headquarters of 1st Airborne Group, its three parachute battalions, a company of engineers, and two batteries of artillery. Casualties on the French side were 15 killed, 34 wounded, 13 jump injuries. The enemy had lost 115 uniformed dead and four prisoners.[14]

When the first paratroopers were jumping to reestablish Dien Bien Phu, this time as a major French fortified position, a poll in France was showing that only 15 percent of the people favored prosecuting the war toward military victory.[15]

On the second and third day, three more paratroop battalions dropped, along with their headquarters and other units. Sufficient repairs had been made to the landing strip so that General Cogny could land for an inspection visit. About 4,650 troops were now present, and reconnaissance-in-force units began thrusting out into the surrounding hills. On the next day, the 1st T'ai Partisan Mobil Group marched into the garrison, and the first bulldozer arrived by parachute. On the sixth day the first DC-47 Skytrain landed and the airbase became operational with a control headquarters. On that same day, two Viet Minh divisions were identified moving toward DBP. It appeared that the *base aéroterrestre* concept was proving successful in attracting enemy main forces into a classic open pitched battle which would give the French a decided advantage.

Paratroopers descending to establish Dien Bien Phu, November 20, 1953. (NARA)

The base was now beginning to take the shape it would finally reach. The central position was in the village itself on the western bank of a small river, the Nam Youm, and on that side and across the river, atop small hills were strongpoints. To the south by three and a half miles was Isabelle, a second smaller, virtually independent position with its own small airstrip. In a few weeks, joining the infantry and artillery in that position, would be a company of ten light tanks which were flown in disassembled, then reassembled.

On November 29, Navarre and Cogny landed along with U.S. Major General Thomas Trapnell, the third commander of Military Assistance Advisory Group (MAAG). All of them liked what they saw, an increasingly impregnable position. High-level government and military visits would continue for the next four months.

While DBP continued to build, Giap kept the French occupied elsewhere. Viet Minh units pressed the French in both the Delta and in central Annam with regional units and guerrilla forces. Pressure in Cochinchina by guerrilla actions continued. Elements of two Viet Minh divisions struck west from Annam into Laos and by December 26 had captured Tha Ket on the Mekong. Navarre had to withdraw Bigeard's and Bréchignac's parachute battalions from DBP plus three parachute battalions from the Delta and commit them to Laos. Tha Ket was retaken in January but French casualties were high, and significant French Union forces were tied down far from either DBP or the Delta.

On January 5, 1954, Giap arrived at a forest headquarters 9 miles north of Dien Bien Phu to take personal command. His cave bunker would be expanded until it comprised a large complex of underground tunnels with several feet of overhead rock cover. At this time, two ominous developments were reported by French intelligence. One was that 37mm antiaircraft guns were arriving around DBP, and they would put airstrip use and parachute drops in considerable jeopardy. The other was the phenomenal success in the face of enormous obstacles that the enemy engineers (Vietnamese and Chinese) were having in improving roads for use by Chinese-supplied trucks.

Of the U.S. visitors and short-term advisors to the French at DBP, to include Lieutenant General John W. O'Daniel, the new head of MAAG, none is recorded to have expressed strong pessimism as to whether DBP could be successfully defended.

A diplomatic development would have major impact on the coming battle. On January 25, the Big Four (U.S., Britain, France, Soviet Union) met in Berlin to discuss Korea and Indochina. They agreed to meet again in April to begin a wider conference at Geneva. This dramatically raised the DBP stakes. A military victory before Geneva, after nine exhausting years of war, would give the winning side enormous bargaining power. This meant that Giap would have to attack so fiercely he would overrun the position whereas Navarre would have to defend so successfully that the five Viet Minh divisions would be *hors de combat* and the Communists might be inclined to settle on terms more favorable to France. Thus the Navarre Plan would have succeeded.

By late February, although adjustments would be made as the battle progressed, Dien Bien Phu had taken essentially its final shape with strongpoints on the small hills surrounding the central position and airstrip, and a heavily fortified Isabelle position to the south. Before the battle was over, the main position in the north and Isabelle together would be defended by seven parachute battalions, ten infantry battalions, an armored cavalry detachment, all or elements of seven mortar/artillery battalions, all or elements of two engineer battalions, three commando groups, several medical teams, and three communication companies from the army. From the air force there were an airbase control detachment, a fighter group, two artillery observation groups, and a signal company. Supporting units included maintenance, supply, transportation, traffic and provost, and postal personnel. Bernard Fall put the total French Union strength as of March 13 at 10,814, and subsequent airborne reinforcements at 4,291 to total 15,105 plus 2,440 Viet Minh prisoners, men who had been kept for long periods for menial and medical duties. Many of them performed faithfully and heroically for their French captors.[16] Other sources put the total at somewhat over 16,000.

Farther out from the French Union positions, overlooking the valley, were numerous larger hills, and dug into their forward slopes with camouflaged openings were Viet Minh artillery positions. Many of these had direct line of sight to the two airfields. The gunners could look through the cannon bores and see the airstrips beyond. They had put out aiming stakes and plotted data for their targets, from which they would make adjustments after the command to fire. Near the French positions were four enemy divisions and one independent regiment, dug in and camouflaged as they were digging trenches, meter by meter, for their advance closer to the French positions. Giap confirmed that these trenches came within 10–15 meters of the French defenses. Combatants from both sides could and did lob grenades at one another. In support was Giap's reinforced 351st Heavy Division consisting of an engineer regiment, a heavy weapons regiment, two artillery regiments, an antiaircraft regiment, and a field rocket unit. The planning and effort it took to emplace and support all of this, so far from populated centers, across such poor roads and trails, across rivers and streams through such difficult, forested mountain terrain, is one of the greatest feats of modern warfare. Each of Giap's divisions had about 5,000–6,000 men at full strength, supported by impressed or volunteer civilian labor in strength from 100,000 to 300,000 according to times of use and various sources.[17]

Giap Attacks

On March 13, 1954 at 1700 hours, ringing the hills and looking down, were at least 30,000 combatants, probably more. Looking up toward them were about half that number—not bad odds for the dug-in French, considering their powerful artillery and air.

Or so it seemed.

Upon command—FIRE—the Viet lanyards were pulled and some seconds later the ground around the French erupted in a hellish din. A fight to the finish had begun.

That night and for several more days and nights the fighting was vicious. Bigeard's men, supported by tanks, were able to open the road to Isabelle in heavy fighting. A Vietnamese parachute battalion was dropped to bolster the defenses. Artillery replacements parachuted into Isabelle. De Castries busied himself keeping in contact with Hanoi, coordinating support while Lieutenant Colonel Pierre Langlais took de facto control of operations. With French positions being overrun, Bigeard was given command of several units and counterattacked. The T'ai battalion at strongpoint Anne-Marie deserted. Early on, the air force had succeeded in landing some C-47s for supply and evacuation of wounded, but the antiaircraft fire was getting more vicious.

Geneviève de Galard's medevac C-47 flew in at night, wounded were quickly loaded, and she was off again. That night and on succeeding days and nights, several aircraft were shot out of the sky. Geneviève came in on another night mission and due to miscommunication, the ambulances were not at the airfield. The enemy shelling became so intense the pilot had to take off without the wounded, and

Geneviève was crushed, knowing the despair those men must have felt. Back in Hanoi she wrote to her mother, hoping that the letter "would help her understand that if I didn't return, I did not die for nothing."[18]

On March 28 at 4:15 a.m. she was off again to Dien Bien Phu. In darkness and terrible visibility the pilot made two approaches but had to pull up both times since the airstrip was not under him. He was able to land on the third attempt, but the plane skidded off the landing strip and into some barbed wire. The wounded were hurriedly loaded, and just as the plane was to take off, the mechanic reported that the oil reservoir had been punctured and the tank was empty. No oil pressure. "There was no way we were going to be leaving," Geneviève recalled. Nothing to do but unload the despondent wounded.

The *crachin* cleared around 1000 hours and the Viet artillery zeroed in, hitting the stationary plane on the fourth round. Hanoi radioed she could fly out on the next aircraft. In the meantime she visited wounded, cheered them up, and took their letters to be posted when she got back to Hanoi. At the command post she met de Castries, who greeted her amicably. She helped out at the underground hospital where desperately wounded men turned to her in their last gasps of breath. Then

Geneviève de Galard atop a berm at Dien Bien Phu, 1954. (Courtesy Geneviève de Heaulme)

days went by and no plane landed. More strongpoints fell, and the flow of wounded and dying at times overwhelmed her and the medical staff. The fighting was fierce and virtually continuous. Finally it became apparent that the airspace and landing strip were so dangerous no more planes would be able to land.

Geneviève was trapped.

***

In June of 2009 I received an email from General Delaunay asking if I would help Geneviève de Galard get her book published in English in America. It had been published in French on the 50th anniversary of the fall of Dien Bien Phu and been awarded the *Grand Prix de l'Académie des sciences morales et politiques*. For decades she had resisted many efforts to get her to tell her story, but finally "her boys," the veterans of Dien Bien Phu, had prevailed upon her.

I knew about Geneviève de Galard. While I was a second-year cadet at West Point in 1954 I had read about her in accounts of the battle. The whole world had known about her. Teletype, radio, and television carried the news daily to masses transfixed on Dien Bien Phu. Everyone wanted to know more about the incredibly heroic little nurse, the only French woman in the battle. A Hollywood studio teletyped an offer to do a movie, with a famous actress in her role. Other offers poured into the command post for rights to her story. Geneviève, trying to save the men who could be saved, and giving the kind of comfort only a woman could give to the dying, ignored these distractions and kept working, sometimes going out with a helmet clapped on her head to positions at strongpoints under fire to do what she could.

Last Throes

From April 1, Dien Bien Phu continued to receive reinforcing paratroopers, with some landing behind the enemy who killed or captured them. Week after week went by in desperate fighting, the Viet Minh capturing the airfield and slowly progressing toward the central position. A strongpoint would fall, and Bigeard would counterattack. Then another, and he would do it again. In the dark, airborne reinforcements continued to trickle in through the antiaircraft fire and shelling. The losses on both sides were appalling. Viet Minh morale had plummeted, and desertion now became a serious problem. The French, with no evacuation possible, could do nothing about their situation other than continue to defend fiercely and keep as many wounded alive as possible.

But Giap could do something. He had freedom to slow the pace of attacks, give some rest to units, and come up with something to buck up spirits. In typical Giap fashion, when things were not going well, there was always "the right-wing" to blame. "*A rightist and negative tendency* appeared among our officers and men, in various forms: fear of casualties, losses, fatigue, difficulties and hardships, underestimation of the enemy, subjectivism and self-conceit."

The Political Bureau of the Party Central Committee came up immediately with a psychological program, and Giap was the target of severe criticism and maneuvering to replace him. He narrowly managed to hang on to his position, and "after this conference, a campaign of ideological education and struggle was launched from the Party committee to the cells, from officers and soldiers and in all combat units." As a result, "all the Party members, officers and men had more confidence in the final victory and an unshakeable will to destroy the enemy completely."[19]

That episode, coming in the midst of this horrendous battle, reflects how well the Communist manifesto of independence and freedom was able to appeal to the most basic instincts of an enormous number of Vietnamese, not just the men on the line in the worst days of DBP, but throughout the country. Victory was so near it must not be allowed to slip out of their hands through lack of understanding of the goal and resolve to reach it. With renewed energy, the Viet Minh divisions at DBP pressed home their attack.

On the day the Geneva Conference opened, April 26, 1954, fifty aircraft were struck and three shot down. Still, a small number of Foreign Legion paratroopers were successfully dropped on Isabelle. Cold monsoon rains left mud and freezing water in the trenches and dugouts up to 3 feet deep.

By May 4, it was patently obvious what would be the fate of the defenders, yet paratroopers were still jumping to reinforce. De Castries reported the circumstances

Wounded soldiers being evacuated to the hospital bunker in one of last photos taken on May 5, 1954, just before the fall of Dien Bien Phu. (TopFoto)

to Hanoi, closing with: "The situation of the wounded is particularly tragic. They are piled on top of each other in holes that are completely filled with mud and devoid of any hygiene."[20]

On May 5, a few qualified paratroopers dropped, and on May 6 some more of 1st Colonial Parachute Battalion, half of whom were Vietnamese. Between 1,800 and 2,600 (depending on the source cited) paratroopers had dropped in the last days, all volunteers. "Of these, about 700 unqualified volunteers would actually be dropped during April and early May, the great majority making their first jump over Dien Bien Phu."[21] All of them most certainly knew what fate awaited them, but they jumped anyhow into the fearsome night.

The CIA, successor to the OSS, had covertly set up a supposedly civilian company to fly C-119 "flying boxcars" for the French. On May 6, James B. McGovern, a World War II American ace fighter pilot called "Earthquake McGoon" because of his huge size and brash personality, was flying his 45th mission over the valley, and his plane was badly hit. A radio transmission from him seemed to say, "Looks like this is it, son," before he crashed, killing all aboard.[22] At noon, Katyusha rockets with their characteristic howl came crashing in, the first use in Vietnam of these weapons which would become so familiar to those of us on the receiving end in the American war.

End of Dien Bien Phu

Finally, on May 7 there was no hope. Hanoi notified de Castries that he should cease firing at 1700 hours and surrender but not raise a white flag. This set about an exhausting scramble to burn money and documents, disable the few remaining howitzers and the one workable tank, and explode the paltry remaining stock of ammunition.

In the last few minutes, Captain Yves Hervouët was in his bunker. He had commanded his ten tanks with both arms in a cast from his wounds, right down to his last battle-scarred tank. One of his men "raised high a bottle spotted with dirt. '*Mon capitaine*, there is no way that the Viets are going to celebrate their victory with our champagne.' Hervouët agreed…. [He said], 'Let us drink to the freedom we are about to lose, to the satisfaction of having done the best we could to avoid getting where we are. You have no reason to blame yourselves. I will do my utmost to see that justice is done to you one day. Good luck!'"[23]

In her book Geneviève tells of her final minutes until the surrender. "We were all close to tears, Langlais and Bigeard hugged me…. Back at the hospital unit I informed my patients that the combat would stop at five. They were greatly relieved. I distributed the last cigarettes. Calm and a strange silence settled over the valley, and we waited."[24]

In his memoirs, Bigeard, "Bruno," tells of his last radio messages to and from his remaining commanders:

> Brèche to Bruno: "They are coming en masse. I'm smashing my radio. Goodbye, Bruno."
> Botella to Bruno: "This time we're fucked. Goodbye, Bruno."
> Bruno to Botella: "Goodbye … I'm wiping tears running down my face. No, it is not possible."

Then—

> Bigeard noted, "A great calm, a silence of death hovered over the citadel, crowned by a clear blue sky. It was indeed the end. Is it possible?"
> He reflected, "Ah, if we had been victors. But we are vanquished, humiliated, diminished, and I am just one poor guy like all the others."

Foreign legionnaires and paratroopers were especially hated by the Viet Minh. Bigeard defiantly propped his red paratroop beret on his head moments before the enemy entered the command post. He was a prisoner, as he said, "of these little Vietnamese who, in our French army we once felt that they were only good for being medics or drivers. These high-spirited men began at zero in 1945 with an ideal, a mishmash of arms, a purpose: drive out the French. In nine years Giap beat—no question about it—our Expeditionary Corps."[25]

I asked Geneviève if she were not terrified, thinking of what the enemy would do to a woman. She said she had been too busy and exhausted to think, and her men still needed her, so she just kept on doing what she could, checking their bandages, passing out the last cigarettes, comforting them. At 1700 hours, May 7, 1954, the Viet Minh entered de Castries' command bunker, marking the beginning of the end for the French Colonial Empire.

The Aftermath

For days Geneviève's captors kept after her to write a letter to Uncle Ho for clemency and to congratulate him on his 64th birthday on May 19. After struggling with the idea she finally decided to do it, "afraid that a refusal might compromise [my patients'] freedom…. As I saw it, the letter had no political import; it was a letter from a nurse whose only concern was to help her patients, for whom evacuation was becoming more critical with each day."[26]

Giap said, "All the enemy troops stationed at Dien Bien Phu … were taken prisoner and were kindly treated."[27] Kindly? Windrow, who carefully studied all available sources, French and Vietnamese, cited what he considered the most authoritative. It concluded that somewhat over 9,000 prisoners, about a third of them wounded or sick, were marched away, and "perhaps half of them would die or disappear."[28] When Giap had set out on his quest with his 34 fighters in 1944, he had heard Ho state that prisoners must be treated well. In his first action Giap had killed them, and

At the White House President Eisenhower awards the Medal of Freedom to Geneviève de Galard, the "Angel of Dien Bien Phu," as French Ambassador to the United States Henri Bonnet and U.S. Congresswoman Frances P. Bolton look on, July 27, 1954. (Courtesy Geneviève de Heaulme)

in the following days and weeks had killed not only more French Union prisoners but those "rightists" from Vietnamese non-Communist groups who could not be made to see the light.

Ho set the policies. He saw the results. To suggest that Uncle Ho, who had such a remarkable sense for being attuned to people, knew nothing of this in nine years of war goes against considerable evidence to the contrary, inferences from his own statements, and common sense.

After the battle and Geneviève's release from captivity and return to France, she was showered with honors. President Eisenhower invited her to the United States, where the American press was calling her "The Angel of Dien Bien Phu." She was welcomed with a tickertape parade up Broadway, then taken to Congress and met with a standing ovation. At the White House the president decorated her with the highest medal awarded to other than U.S. military, the Medal of Freedom. Geneviève was sent off on a tour of major U.S. cities, where she was received with honors and enthusiastic crowds. I had told General Delaunay I would be delighted to do what I could to get her book published in America. For a year and a half Geneviève and I worked to enlarge her short French text. I suggested additions, translated them, added a chapter of pre-DBP history, did the annexes and maps, and edited the book, *The Angel of Dien Bien Phu*. It was a marvelous experience working with this extraordinary woman and her husband.

I cannot let this go without an update on Geneviève and her husband Colonel (Ret) Jean de Heaulme. As of this writing, both are elderly and in ill health. An anecdote will suffice to depict the character of these two people. When my wife Sandra and I decided to go to Paris some years ago, Geneviève emailed to invite us to lunch at their apartment, and set the date and time. We arrived, had a wonderful lunch that she had prepared and only then learned that on that very morning they had buried Jean's beloved younger brother. Sandra and I were shocked that they had not called us to cancel the lunch. Geneviève said, "No, you are our friends and we wanted to see you, and something might come up to make that impossible on your trip."

***

At least two things were made abundantly clear by the French–Vietnamese war. First, if any person had doubted Giap when he told Fonde, just before the December 19, 1946 breakout of total war, that it was of no importance if one million Vietnamese would have to die, that his side would triumph in the end, the outcome proved Giap correct. It is unclear how many Vietnamese had died by the end, but given the violence combined with famine and other disasters aggravated by the war, the one million number is quite certainly too low.

Second, from its early beginnings in 1944, the leadership of the North demonstrated a remarkable cohesiveness in making the big decisions that guided the war on their side. Yes, Ho Chi Minh was the leader, but more as a first among equals than dictator. In fact, often with no input from Ho, many others in the early decades had done the spade work which made the creation of the Democratic Republic of Vietnam possible. The building of the Viet Bac as a sanctuary for the Viet Minh movement is a prime example, having been established by slow, careful work just north of Hanoi by Ho's predecessors in the Communist movement within Vietnam while Ho was out of the country. The Party, and not just one man, usually made the decisions after long discussions, and with input from many subordinate leaders. This resulted in a cohesiveness representing a broad base leading to major actions. When the decisions turned out to be wrong, the causes were debated and corrective measures directed. Political and military action were inextricably linked, and this cohesiveness in leadership and results did the French in and would bode ill for the Americans and the South Vietnamese government in the renewed war to come.

During the eleven years from 1945 to 1956 when France finally withdrew, the North had one president and one general in charge—Ho Chi Minh and Vo Nguyen Giap (Le Duan had become increasingly powerful and since 1959 effectively had taken over). The political and military leadership on the French side, though, was like a revolving door. During that period, France had five presidents, fifteen prime ministers, eight high commissioners of Indochina, and six supreme commanders of French Union forces. Also, the various Vietnamese governments of the South, starting with the Republic of Cochinchina and ending with the Republic of Vietnam, changed eight times. One side was obsessed with independence and unity, the other was bedeviled by an outmoded colonialism that no other country in the world supported and the French themselves vacillated over dumping but could not quite bring themselves to do it.

Bernard Fall was the most insightful of war correspondents and historians to cover both the French and American wars in Vietnam before being killed in 1967 by a mine in "The Street Without Joy," the place about which he had written the book by that name. He thought that de Lattre, if he had lived, like Leclerc, would have strongly pushed the French government to negotiate when he saw that the war "had become hopeless." Whether or not he was correct, in fact General Navarre in his 1956 memoirs, *Agonie de l'Indochine*, stated that "the war simply could not be won in the military sense" and "all that could be hoped for was a draw."

PART TWO

THE AMERICAN WAR—MANY MORE BULLETS

***

General Creighton W. Abrams:

"In the whole picture of the war, the <u>battles</u> don't mean much."

Saigon, August 29, 1969

***

CHAPTER 8

America in Support, Advisory Mission, 1954–64

The fall of Dien Bien Phu had convulsed France. The people's earlier knowledge that things had not been going well did little to soften the impact. An objective military analysis would reveal that about 4 percent of the French Union and Associated States forces had been lost, and there was no reason in terms of battlefield power, main force against main force, that the war was lost. But the resultant psychological shock surging throughout France swamped that kind of reasoning. France got yet one more prime minister, this time Pierre Mendès-France whose goal was to get a Geneva settlement under the best terms possible.

South Vietnam was also profoundly affected by the DBP disaster. South Vietnamese General Lam Quang Thi wrote that as a young officer after the fall of Dien Bien Phu he had observed the hopes of the Vietnamese for independence to soar, not just in the North, but also in the South. "I knew that the fall of Dien Bien Phu was the beginning of the end of the French presence in Indochina.... I hoped that the Americans would step in to stop Communist expansion in Asia in accordance with the U.S. policy of 'containment.'"[1]

America's Increased Role, and the Triumph of Ngo Dinh Diem

President Eisenhower, in a press conference a month before the collapse of Dien Bien Phu, used the term "falling domino principle." He did not invent the domino theory—that a collapse in Vietnam would lead to Communist takeover of the rest of Indochina, Thailand, Malaysia, Burma, and extend potentially to Indonesia and even Australia, New Zealand, and India—but it now was on the front burner.

Ho Chi Minh and some in the inner circle of the Central Committee were fully aware that the Dien Bien Phu victory, crucially important as it was, did not spell the end of the struggle. Ho said, "This victory is big, but it is only the beginning. We must not be self-complacent and subjective and underestimate the enemy. We are determined to fight for independence, national unity, democracy, and peace. A struggle, whether military or diplomatic, must be long and hard before complete victory can be achieved."[2]

Strong voices within the Party had been urging a continuation of the war before the Americans could act to prevent a takeover of the South. But they were being counseled by both the USSR and China to go slowly so as not to provoke the Americans into establishing bases in South Vietnam, Laos, and Cambodia, taking the place of the French.

On June 1, 1954, Colonel Edward G. Lansdale landed in Saigon to set up the Saigon Military Mission. He had been a key figure in the successful neutralization of insurgency in the Philippines and now was tasked with doing everything possible to support the Southern government and weaken the Northern. It was hoped that this new American initiative, added to the already ongoing MAAG efforts, would stiffen the Bao Dai government.

After DBP, in what was to have momentous consequences, the nominal emperor could do little more to shore up the State of Vietnam's shaky government than on June 16 to appoint Ngo Dinh Diem, a long-time thorn in his side, as prime minister.

Diem, a strict Roman Catholic with a bishop for a brother, had a strong constituency among Vietnam's Catholics. He had been maneuvering for power for years, and with this appointment, a whole new era opened. Despite warnings from the French and doubts within the U.S. administration itself, Diem was accepted in Washington as America's best hope for providing a bulwark against a perceived Red Tide from the north.

Geneva, Independence and Unification

There had been no cease fire after DBP, and sporadic small-scale fighting took place throughout most of Vietnam. Late in June, French Groupement Mobile 100 of about regimental size was ambushed and lost hundreds of dead and most of its vehicles and equipment. Between July 27 and August 11, allowing for time to disseminate orders in various parts of Vietnam and Laos, the cease fire agreement reached at Geneva went into effect.

Pham Van Dong, the DVR's lead representative at Geneva, drew up a draft declaration that was deemed unacceptable.

> Although Viet Minh representatives had met with their Chinese and Soviet counterparts before the conference to formulate a common negotiating strategy, it had become clear that neither Moscow nor Beijing was eager to back the Viet Minh in a continuation of the war, nor were they willing to give blanket support for [North] Vietnamese demands. [They] favored a compromise based on the division of Vietnam into two separate regroupment

zones, one occupied by the Viet Minh and the other by the Bao Dai government and its supporters.[3]

As negotiations progressed, the French and DRV negotiators came to a final sticking point: at which parallel should the two countries be temporarily divided until elections to unify North with South, the 16th or 17th? The French proposed the 17th, which would give the South considerably more territory than would be the case if the former dividing line, the 16th were chosen. DRV objected, but the Chinese delegate, (later premier) Zhou Enlai promised, "With the final withdrawal of the French, all of Vietnam will be yours."[4]

The Geneva Conference closed on July 21, 1954 with an agreement signed by France and the DRV. The South Vietnamese government believed it had been sold out by both France and the United States and it refused to sign. The U.S. was wary of some of the provisions and likewise did not sign. The agreement stipulated that Vietnam would be divided at the 17th Parallel, somewhat north of Quang Tri, with Democratic Republic of Vietnam in temporary charge in the North, and State of Vietnam in the South. The only mention in the Accord itself of elections to unify Vietnam was a phrase: "Pending the general elections which will bring about the unification of Viet-Nam." A British "Conference Final Declaration," though, said, "general elections shall be held in July 1956."

The South Vietnamese and United States governments did not approve this declaration of a specific date, believing, with good cause, that given two more years for the Communists to use their methods of recruitment on the populace, the South would be certain to lose. Instead, the U.S. produced a unilateral declaration: "In the case of nations now divided against their will, we shall continue to seek to achieve unity through free elections, supervised by the UN, to ensure that they are conducted fairly."[5]

Regroupment

In the so-called "regroupment" provided for in the Accords, almost a million Vietnamese would be transported from the North to the South, with perhaps 80,000 to 100,000 going the other way. In the latter group would be many who would be militarily and politically trained by the North to be later infiltrated back into the South to support war against the South Vietnamese and Americans.

In some ways the North got the better of the regroupment deal. The U.S. had heavily proselytized the approximately 600,000 Vietnamese Catholics in the North to go south. Beginning in the fall of 1954, hundreds of thousands of North Vietnamese Catholics used the regroupment provision to come to the South, many of them enduring grave hardships to do so, voting against the DRV with their feet. This movement on the one hand strengthened the South, since the Catholics tended to support its government, but it also solved a large problem for the North, largely denuding the Delta area of people who could have been the nucleus of espionage and insurgency.

The move south would soon cause largely unforeseen problems. Diem so heavily favored these Northern and other fellow Catholics that he caused widespread resentment among the majority non-Catholic population of the South. Then too, Ho's assurance to the Catholics carried ominous overtones: "I solemnly promise you, through your determination, the determination of all our people, the Southern land will return to the bosom of the Fatherland."[6]

The DRV's Politburo Differences over Unification

Reunification of Vietnam had long been Ho's goal, and he had spoken often of it. However, the North had suffered greatly in the long war with France—economically, culturally, militarily. After 1954, for some time in the North there were two divergent views of how to proceed with unification. The North-firsters—prominently Ho Chi Minh, Pham Dong (Finance Minister), and Truong Chinh (First Secretary of the Party) wanted to focus resources and energy on building up the North, confident that the South would eventually be united to the North basically by growth of Socialism in the South and widespread dissatisfaction with ineffectual Southern government—if not by that, then later by revolutionary violence led by the North.

A very different view was held by other powerful members of the Politburo, the "South-firsters." Several of them had long grumbled among themselves about what they considered three huge failures of Ho. First, in order to disguise Communist intentions and broaden the base for independence-minded adherents, in 1945 he had officially dissolved the Indochinese Communist Party. Then in 1946 he agreed to let French troops into Tonkin for a period of five years while he was strengthening his DRV government and negotiating to accept a place in the French Union in return for a French pledge of full independence. Then during the 1954 Geneva negotiations, the dissenters thought he had succumbed to Chinese and Soviet pressure to accept a "temporary" division of Vietnam at the 17th Parallel to be followed in 1956 by elections for a permanent government of a unified Vietnam, elections which hardly anyone believed would indeed be held. The "South-firsters," led by Le Duan, wanted to continue the war immediately in the South and win it before the imperialist Americans could become so strongly entrenched they might have to be forced out.

In 1959 Le Duan became First Secretary, thus inaugurating an era in which Ho—still revered but no longer the center of actual political power—was basically relegated to diplomatic issues, and Giap was initially sidelined by Le Duan's enmity toward him. If we are to believe Colonel Bui Tin, several years after the end of the Vietnam War Le Duan compared himself to Ho: "In very elated fashion, Le Duan said, 'As for me, well, I am better than Uncle Ho. Ho opened his mouth and talked along the lines of the Confucian code of morality, like human dignity, loyalty, good manners, wisdom and trustworthiness. What is that? It is outmoded feudalism. As for me, I am for collective mastery by the workers.'"[7]

What is certain is that Ho was revered by many and Le Duan was feared by all.

The U.S. and Diem

By agreement with the French, on October 9, 1954 Viet Minh troops had marched into Hanoi. The DRV was now secure in the knowledge it had really won the war and could claim Hanoi as its capital. Certainly among French officers and men who were present when the tricolor was lowered for the last time in the North were some who wondered what had happened. What in hell happened? We did our best. We won battles. They wore sandals and backpacks. We were strong, a modern army with a navy and air force. But we lost.

The war had inevitably shifted from under the French. The United States was now de facto in charge. On October 24, 1954, President Eisenhower made a strong commitment to South Vietnam when he wrote to President Diem, offering assistance:

> The purpose of this offer is to assist the Government of Viet-Nam in developing and maintaining a strong, viable state, capable of resisting attempted subversion or aggression through military means. The Government of the United States expects that this aid will be met by performance on the part of the Government of Viet-Nam in undertaking needed reforms. It hopes that such aid, combined with your own continuing efforts, will contribute effectively toward an independent Viet-Nam [South Vietnam] endowed with a strong government. Such a government would, I hope, be so responsive to the nationalist aspirations of its people, so enlightened in purpose and effective in performance that it will be respected both at home and abroad and discourage any who might wish to impose a foreign ideology on your free people.[8]

Diem had started late. Ho had been at his business of building an independent Vietnam (all of Vietnam) much longer, and he had constructed a formidable political and military infrastructure tested by years of war against the French. The bulk of the people—virtually all in the North, and many in the South—admired Ho and shared his yearning for independence. Diem had none of the charisma and little of the profound commitment to his people at the lowest levels that so consumed Ho. Diem's government of nine years, 1954–63, in length about equal to the French Indochina war itself, would never be "so enlightened in purpose and effective in performance that it will be respected both at home and abroad." Instead, it caused deep scars and skepticism among the South Vietnamese people that would be a poor base upon which his successors would need to build.

Before the end of 1954, Eisenhower would get bad news from his special emissary, head of Mission to Saigon, General J. Lawton Collins, a much-respected soldier/diplomat. Collins doubted Diem's "capacity to stabilize the government or rally support for his regime. He recommended Bao Dai's return be considered [from

France where he had gone after DBP], but if this were unacceptable, recommended the U.S. withdraw from Vietnam."[9]

That the White House and State Department were pulling the Vietnam strings—or thought they were—is abundantly clear in many executive branch records such as the December 19, 1954 transcript of meeting: "[Secretary of State John Foster] Dulles was sure Diem could succeed with proper direction."[10]

Lecturing to interested groups in the U.S., Diem maintained that an independent Vietnam under his leadership would "satisfy the Vietnamese population that they have something to fight for."[11] That is what, precisely, Diem was never able to do—inspire the bulk of the population to fight the Viet Nam Cong San—(Viet Cong, the successor name to Viet Minh).

Diem had considerable family help. His brother Ngo Dinh Nhu in effect was vice premier, a man so powerful it often was thought that he and not his brother in reality ran the show. Because the celibate Catholic Diem was a bachelor, Nhu's gorgeous wife, Madame Nhu, or "the Dragon Lady," served as "First Lady." Diem's other brothers were an archbishop, a warlord, and an ambassador to the UK. In-laws and other relatives also did well. "U.S. embassy official John Mecklin recalled, 'There probably had never before in American foreign affairs been a phenomenon comparable to our relations with the Ngo family. It was like dealing with a whole platoon of de Gaulles.'"[12]

Diem destroyed the criminal gang Binh Xuyen then went after the anti-Communist leader of the Hoa Hao religious sect who was too powerful and thus a threat, having him guillotined. The Cao Dai—another religious sect with an army—was cowed into submission.

Then there was the matter of elections. With not just Communists but so many others who hated Diem in the South, certainly he was not going to allow a countrywide election. Eisenhower said that if elections were held, possibly 80 percent of the votes would go to Ho instead of Bao Dai. So Diem's next major step was to hold a general election in South Vietnam, ostensibly for the people to choose between him and Bao Dai as head of a new Southern government. Not surprisingly Diem won with a vote of 98.2 percent. He now was president of the First Republic of Vietnam (RVN), with a constitution which he virtually wrote, giving him ultimate power over the executive, legislative, and judicial branches. He also now remodeled his army as the Army of the Republic of Vietnam (ARVN) which discarded French ranks and salutes, adopted their own rank insignia, and now used the U.S. Army's style of saluting and system of organization at about half the U.S. strength.

After Dien Bien Phu the American government had pressed the French to keep their troops in Vietnam as long as possible to give the South Vietnamese time to stabilize. Diem went along at first but later wanted the French army out, and by mid-1955 the Americans were now ready to see them go. In January 1956 Diem turned down a French request to build and man an aero-navale base at Cap St. Jacques (Vung Tau),

President Eisenhower and Secretary of State Dulles greet Ngo Dinh Diem, President of Republic of Vietnam, at National Airport, May 8, 1957. (NARA)

telling them, "The presence of French troops, no matter how friendly they may be, was incompatible with Viet-Nam's concept of full independence."[13]

Diem's statement is a reminder that many Vietnamese in both North and South had long wanted full independence and did not trust words on paper when a French military force was still on the ground. In 1956 the last French combat units left Vietnam, leaving behind them French plantations and other businesses which often had to deal with the Vietnamese governments both in Hanoi and in Saigon.

Counter to detractors, Diem had some strong supporters. General Thi said, "I believed at that time that Diem was the man of the hour. He had rescued South Vietnam from bankruptcy after the 1954 Geneva Accords. He had created a unified national army by defeating the armed religious sects and assimilating various semi-independent paramilitary forces left by the French. He had successfully resettled one million refugees from the north. From the ashes of the 1945–54 war, he had created a strong, prosperous, and internationally recognized Republic."[14]

Despite some doubters in the Eisenhower administration, Diem seemed to be the man of the hour also in the United States. The lobby group American Friends of Vietnam arranged an impressive U.S. tour for Diem for May 1957. President Eisenhower and Secretary of State John Foster Dulles welcomed him to Washington. Diem addressed a full session of Congress, then was welcomed to New York with a tickertape parade up Broadway. He visited the seminary where he had been a resident some years earlier, then toured cities on the West Coast. Eisenhower, Dulles and major U.S. newspapers heaped praise on him as the Iron Man of Vietnam, a courageous savior of his country.

Return to Revolutionary Violence in the South

Everywhere in the South, it seemed, the Communists were a threat, usually not so much militarily as politically and socially. During the French war they had built up a strong Viet Minh presence with significant public support from southern people. Then during the period 1954–59, under direction from Hanoi, the Communist cadre in the South worked diligently at gaining more adherents and supporters, especially among the rural population. In sparsely populated areas they instituted small but effective civic action programs to show the people they were on their side. They subordinated Communist ideology, which could be a hard sell, to nationalism which was easily accepted, and spread their influence across many areas of South Vietnam.

After Dien Bien Phu, the North began working intensively on consolidating its power and developing its economy in anticipation of further efforts to unify the country. While his prestige remained high among the population as the victor at Dien Bien Phu, Giap had used this time to rebuild the army through training, enhancements in weaponry, and most of all, logistics and administration to support a modernized force. With his eye on the South, he believed he needed time, that precious commodity that had served so well in the eventual victory over the French. But by 1959 Diem's campaign to eradicate Communists had caused severe setbacks, and Giap had lost considerable personal power in the often-vicious inner politics of the Communist Party. Although he voiced objections to moving too fast, wanting to keep time on his side, in January 1959 the Central Committee decided they had to end the four-year period of relative quiet before progress in the South was further hindered. By adopting Resolution 15, they proclaimed a return to "revolutionary violence," the Marxist-Leninist term often used by the Vietnamese Communist leaders to describe the war. In a neat bit of double-talk, Le Duan said, "We won't use war to unify the country, but if the United States and its puppets use war, then we have to use war, and the war that the enemy has initiated will be an opportunity for us to unify the country."[15]

For centuries a basic network of trails had existed from north to south, cutting through rugged terrain in Laos and western South Vietnam. Major work was now started to develop this primitive patchwork into a highly effective system which could be used to transport troops, munitions, and supplies to the South, the so-called Ho Chi Minh Trail. Simultaneously, the ability to move men and materiel by water through the South China Sea was improved. The stage was being set for expanded war in the South.

The DRV, Increasingly a Police State

South Vietnamese general Tran Dinh Tho wrote, "Under President Diem's secret directives, province chiefs were allowed to 'dispose of' [Viet Cong infrastructure (VCI)] members in whatever way they deemed appropriate, including murder, without legal justification."[16]

But no matter how well Diem was able to forge a quasi-police state, partly because of American presence and pressure, he and his brother Nhu could never match Le Duan and Le Duc Tho in the North in gaining strict control of their state.

Le Duan recognized that the DRV had to control tightly what went on not only in the South, but within the North itself. He determined that reinforced discipline was necessary to enable a full national commitment to defeating the Americans who were increasing the size and scope of their advisory mission. Ho Chi Minh's manner of conducting affairs, cruel in effect as it often had been during the French war, was not tough enough. Le Duan and his deputy Le Duc Tho created a police state.

Even Giap was not spared from the hunt for "revisionists." Colonel Bui Tin discovered that some of those arrested were asked, "What about Giap? When and where did you meet him? …. Did Giap have anything to say about Le Duan and Le Duc Tho?" Three high-ranking members of Giap's staff were arrested. Bui Tin later asked Giap why he did not intervene. The reply was that Public Security was too powerful, and he was powerless and had to be careful in order that his colleagues not be detained longer.

In an email to me, Merle Pribbenow said, "Everyone was constantly monitored by Public Security officers and their massive network of informers, and anyone who expressed dissatisfaction was instantly the target of suspicion…. What really kept the country together and inspired the troops to fight was the almost universal Vietnamese tradition of fighting against 'foreign aggression' and the desire to reunite Vietnam into a single country."

The Kennedy Administration: Increased Commitment

The Eisenhower administration had cooled considerably in its enthusiasm for Diem, but in January 1961 John F. Kennedy came into office with solid credentials as a Diem supporter, offering expanded U.S. aid. Kennedy had other problems in Indochina, though, that seemed to demand more immediate attention than Vietnam. The Soviet Union and North Vietnam were supporting the Communist Pathet Lao, NVA units, and neutralist allies in Laos against a pro-American government and were gaining the upper hand. Kennedy had said, "Bear any burden, fight any foe." The CIA set out to do this in Laos. The action controlled by them was called the "Secret War" in that details were kept from the American public. The CIA recruited Hmong tribesman to fight an unconventional war, many of them children age fourteen or less,[17] and the U.S. Air Force bombed targets in Laos designated by the CIA.

Hard on the heels of that ill-thought out venture, in April came the deeply embarrassing Bay of Pigs fiasco in Cuba. Kennedy had approved an overthrow of Fidel Castro by invasion conducted by Cuban dissidents, and it failed miserably. On its heels, Kennedy could not afford to show a perceived weakness in Southeast Asia, and in May, Vice President Johnson barnstormed Vietnam. He praised Diem to the world press as "the Winston Churchill of Southeast Asia." Privately, Johnson knew better and confided his reservations in reports to Kennedy. So the question was how much support, and what kind, should the U.S. continue to give Diem.

The growth of U.S. military commitment in Vietnam is reflected in casualties. The first American soldier to die in Vietnam after World War II ended had been OSS Lieutenant Colonel A. Peter Dewey, killed by gunfire in September 1945 while driving to Tan Son Nhut for a flight back to the United States. On October 21, 1957 Special Forces Captain Harry G. Cramer, Jr. was killed by Viet Cong while training South Vietnamese in ambush tactics. The next KIAs in MAAG were in 1959 when the numbers of dead from enemy action began to mount as advisers were allowed to accompany their units in action.[18]

The American military commitment ratcheted up in December 1961 when two army helicopter companies arrived in Vietnam, the first complete U.S. units which would support ARVN soldiers. Then in February 1962, Military Assistance Command Vietnam (MACV) was created as an expansion of MAAG and commanded by a four-star general, Paul D. Harkins. By February of the following year, Department of Defense acknowledged that U.S. pilots were flying Vietnamese operational missions and were authorized to make air strikes.

During the early Kennedy presidency, U.S. civic aid had also increased. Funds for Diem's "rural development-civic action program" were programmed. Diem had instituted his brother Nhu's Strategic Hamlet Program on a nationwide basis: "Designed to transform villages and hamlets into antiguerrilla bastions, the basic idea was to oppose the Communists with a ubiquitous resistance and defense system whose 'main and long front line' was the villages and hamlets themselves… By the end of 1962 statistics showed that, out of a total of 11,864 hamlets [designated to become Strategic Hamlets], 3,235 had been completed and about 34 percent of the total population [in the South] was considered as living under the [government of Vietnam] protection."[19]

The concept sounded good, the statistics impressive. The problem was that those statistics nowhere near matched reality. Also, hamlet residents deeply resented having their hamlet destroyed and being forced to move into a new fortified hamlet built to provide them government security. Instead of "ubiquitous resistance" to Communists, there appeared to be ubiquitous Communists resisting the government, many within the fortified hamlets themselves.

Vice President Lyndon Johnson and President of the Republic of Vietnam Ngo Dinh Diem confer in Independence Palace, May 12, 1961. (NARA)

Upset at the Joint Chiefs of Staff (JCS) for what he considered bad advice during the Cuba venture, Kennedy recalled General Maxwell D. Taylor from retirement to serve as a presidential advisor, and soon Taylor virtually supplanted the Joint Chiefs. In trips to Vietnam Taylor assessed the situation and felt that Diem must be supported, and that up to 8,000 additional U.S. troops might be required in a training mission. He believed that despite Diem's deficiencies he could hold the country together. General Taylor and Secretary of Defense Robert McNamara might reasonably be credited with the original American "light at the end of the tunnel" view.

Southeast Asia matters were soon shoved aside, though, by the developing Cuban missile crisis of August–October 1962, in which the Soviet Union and the United States came close to a nuclear confrontation. After it was resolved, attention swung back to Vietnam, and Taylor became a prominent player in the process of trying to get something done about the deteriorating situation. Assassinations of district and village chiefs were up, and South Vietnamese government and military performance seemed stagnated.

1963: A Terrible Year for ARVN and the South Vietnamese Government

The year was to begin badly and end worse. On January 3, 1963, South Vietnamese forces attacked a Viet Cong battalion at Ap Bac, a hamlet in the Mekong Delta 35 miles southwest of Saigon and 12 miles northwest of My Tho. They quickly found themselves in a hornets' nest and taking heavy casualties. Three Americans advisers were killed and six were wounded. General Harkins, called "General Blimp" by the press for his inflated claims of progress, pronounced the operation a resounding victory.

The summer of 1963 was even worse than Ap Bac for the government of Vietnam (GVN—the term most often used by Americans instead of RVN for Republic of Vietnam). Televised scenes of Buddhist monks immolating themselves in the streets of Saigon and Hue electrified the world. The monks were protesting discriminatory treatment and violence against Buddhists by the largely Roman Catholic Diem regime. Madam Nhu called these immolations "barbecues," offering to give fuel and matches to the Buddhists. The American public, Congress, and the White House were horrified.

Some units of Vietnamese Special Forces attacked pagodas, quite certainly under Nhu's orders, beating monks and nuns. Schools and universities were ordered closed because professors and students supported the monks. General Cao Van Vien, the highest-ranking general in South Vietnam, respected by the Americans, was Diem's chief of staff and a great admirer of Diem. But General Vien said, "This heavy-handed repression … ended support for the Diem regime at home and abroad."[20]

More bad news for South Vietnam during mid-summer was Giap's greatly enhanced weaponry. The RPG-2 and 57mm and 75mm recoilless rifles came into the inventory, deadly weapons against both infantry and armor. Even more noteworthy, he replaced the early mishmash of rifles with Kalashnikov AK-47s supplied by the Soviet Union, and later with knock-offs by China and East Bloc countries. ARVN soldiers found themselves greatly outclassed in firepower by the AK-47.

But the worst was yet to come. In late summer 1963, President Kennedy wrote a long letter to Diem about the necessity to win over his people, sounding much like General de Lattre 12 years earlier. His point was that "It is their war. They are the ones who have to win it or lose it. We can help them, we can give them equipment, we can send our men out there as advisors, but they have to win it, the people of Vietnam."[21]

Diem had survived assassination attempts, but on November 1, 1963 five paratroop battalions seized key locations in Saigon and surrounded the palace. Their demand was that Diem could stay in office if he would institute reforms.

Diem would not capitulate; rather, he stalled while word went out to other ARVN units who might support him, and soon there were battles, ARVN soldier against ARVN soldier. Diem and his brother Nhu escaped from Independence Palace in the dark, but on November 2 they were discovered and picked up in a Cholon church by an armored personnel carrier. Ostensibly they were to be taken to a meeting with coup plotters to work out concessions which would allow Diem to continue in office. On the way they were murdered. The Kennedy administration was complicit.

Diem's assassination was to result in a year and a half of political chaos in South Vietnam. At first General Duong Van Minh ("Big Minh") put together a fractious junta of generals which had no cohesiveness or direction. Then, three weeks after Diem died, Kennedy was assassinated. Within a day, President Johnson announced that U.S. support for South Vietnam would continue. A day later Johnson said, "Failure was not an option against the Viet Cong. Lyndon Johnson is not going to go down as the president who lost Vietnam."[22]

Diem's assassination threatened to collapse the whole South Vietnamese war effort. The military juntas would last for a few days, weeks or months. Then a civilian was chosen to head the government, an arrangement that lasted only half a year before the generals again took charge in an unstable coalition.

1964, a Year of Even Greater Crisis Requires a New General

With Kennedy dead and Lyndon Johnson now the president, the Vietnam situation demanded rethinking and new major players. Late in December 1963, General Earle G. Wheeler, Army Chief of Staff, had told Lieutenant General William C. Westmoreland he would be going to Vietnam as Deputy Commanding General, MACV, and that he would likely take over the top spot in mid-1964 from General Harkins.

Why was Westmoreland chosen for this critical position? There were other generals to consider.

At 49, Westmoreland was the right age, a West Pointer, and an airborne commander with an impeccable record. Most importantly, he had high-level sponsorship. The army of the late 1950s and early 1960s was greatly influenced—some say dominated—by West Pointers who were World War II airborne generals. If Westmoreland programmed his rise, which to a large degree his record and other evidence indicates he did, he could not have done better than to be well regarded by them.

William C. Westmoreland was born to a wealthy Southern family. A decent student, popular among his classmates, he was an Eagle Scout. In 1932 he entered the Military Academy. He achieved the highest cadet rank, First Captain, in his last year just as Robert E. Lee, John J. Pershing, and Douglas MacArthur had done before him. Commissioned in artillery, during World War II he commanded a field artillery battalion of the 9th Infantry Division in North Africa, then as a colonel was with the division in Normandy, the Battle of the Bulge, and the Remagen Bridgehead.

In the post-war army, Westmoreland knew how and where to steer his career. He transferred from artillery to infantry branch, qualified as parachutist—Airborne all the way!—and served as regimental commander and then chief of staff in the elite 82nd Airborne Division.

Late in the Korean War Westmoreland commanded a paratroop regiment that saw little action, and he was never to be wounded or receive any battlefield awards for valor. But he continued to land choice assignments: Secretary of the General Staff in the Pentagon, Commander of 82nd Airborne Division, and Superintendent of West Point, in which role he was again following the illustrious footsteps of Robert E. Lee, Douglas MacArthur, and especially the man who would become his patron, Maxwell Taylor. Just before Westmoreland's Vietnam tour, he was commander of XVIII Airborne Corps.

Westmoreland's Indoctrination

Westmoreland landed in Saigon in late January 1964. The situation that he found would have been ludicrous had it not been so deadly serious. He said, "Life in Saigon in those days was curiously lethargic.... The South Vietnamese simply called off the war—or ignored it—on weekends and holidays and took long siestas at lunch time."[23] The statement reveals the Americans' impatience in fighting a new war that was old for the South Vietnamese—going back 19 years—and was just about to really get going for a gung ho new U.S. advisory group commander. There was a noticeable difference between ARVN's lackadaisical attitude and the Viet Cong's go-go-go offensive spirit. As Westmoreland looked around he found that "The temporary gaiety that had followed Diem's downfall had disappeared. The atmosphere fairly smelled of discontent—workers on strike, students demonstrating, the local press pursuing a persistent campaign of criticism of the new government."[24]

In February the Viet Cong dramatically drew attention to their goal to kill Americans. Only a few days after Westmoreland arrived, enemy attacks in the Mekong Delta, a bomb in Saigon killing five U.S. personnel and wounding four dozen, attacks in Tay Ninh Province in III Corps zone, and an attack on the U.S. advisory compound in Kontum in II Corps served notice that the enemy was serious about the war.

(IV Corps [Four Corps] was the South Vietnamese administrative and military zone south of Saigon all the way to the southern tip of Vietnam at Cau Mau. III Corps [Three Corps] was the zone around Saigon, north to the Central Highlands which was II Corps [Two Corps]. I Corps ["Eye" Corps] was the northernmost zone up to the Demilitarized Zone—DMZ—the divider between South and North Vietnam.)

While the enemy was busy making gains, General Nguyen Khanh and the generals in his junta seemed to be spending more time plotting how to stay in power and in fighting for the top spot than in fighting the enemy. In succeeding months, attacks which continued all over the country brought McNamara and Taylor, now Chairman of the Joint Chiefs of Staff, to Vietnam to assess the situation for the president. McNamara told President Johnson bluntly, "The situation unquestionably has been growing worse.... In terms of government control of the countryside, about 40 percent of the territory is under Viet Cong control or predominant influence. In twenty-two of the forty-three provinces the Viet Cong control 50 percent or more of the land area.... in the last ninety days the weakening of the government's position has been particularly noticeable."[25]

During 1964, the enemy had raised a complete division in the South, the 9th Division, and its units were particularly effective in December. Late in that month, Maxwell Taylor, now the U.S. ambassador to South Vietnam and furious over a serious instance of yet more infighting, insisted on a meeting with Khanh. The GVN general, his hackles raised, instead sent his principal assistants, four generals including Nguyen Van Thieu and Nguyen Cao Ky. Ambassador Taylor began the meeting, "Do you understand English?" he thundered. Then he dressed them down for the abysmal failure to form any kind of stable government. Taylor wrote, "Devoted as we were to the cause of Vietnam, I assured them that we were not prepared to take any more of this suicidal nonsense.... After reporting back to Khanh, and, I suspect, instigated by him, they let it be known publicly that I had insulted them and the armed forces by treating them like American puppets."[26]

This incident, in the North's view, more than justified their perpetual denunciations of the South as a "puppet regime."

The North Sends Units South

Since 1959 Le Duan as First Secretary, the most powerful man in the Politburo, eclipsed both Ho and Giap. He had urged continuation of the war in the South, and he was taking steps to consolidate control over the fighting of it. Colonel Bui Tin said, "The decision to step up the struggle in the South was taken at the 15th Party Plenum held in 1959.... During 1959 and early 1960 we did not send whole units to the south, but instead secretly selected individuals from among those Southerners who had regrouped to the North in 1954."[27] By 1962 Central Office South Vietnam (COSVN) had been created to control the struggle in the South.

In December 1963, the 9th Plenum of the Party Central Committee in Hanoi adopted a resolution which was to have immense consequences in the American war:

> *Efforts to Move Forward to Gain A Great Victory in South Vietnam.* [It] ... laid out ... directions for .... sending main force troops to the South [in 1964], and intensifying massed combat in South Vietnam in order to, shoulder to shoulder with the entire population, defeat the "special war" being conducted by the American imperialists. Besides those cadre and soldiers being sent off to battle in South Vietnam as individual reinforcements and as "framework units," in 1964 our army began to send to the battlefield complete units at their full authorized strength of personnel and equipment.... The 101st, 95th, and 18th Regiments of the 325th Division were the first mobile main force regiments to march south into battle as complete regiments.[28]

By the time of the 9th Plenum, the powerful, militant Le Duan was particularly annoyed with Giap who had long counseled patience in sending units south, very concerned that the time was not yet ripe for such aggressive actions.

During 1963 Giap had been advising caution, taking more time for training and equipping PAVN. Duan allowed him to remain Minister of Defense but secured the appointment of General Nguyen Chi Thanh as commander in the South, working out of COSVN headquarters. Thanh was an early revolutionary.

> When [Thanh] was arrested for "illegal, anti-French activities" in the 1930s, the judge at his hearing asked him why he chose to be a Communist.... [He] responded, "I fight for the people, for democracy, for our livelihood, so what is the sin? I haven't yet understood Communism, so how can I be a Communist? But Communists are patriots and fight for the masses so what is wrong with that?"[29]

Thanh had earlier been promoted to full general, equal in rank to Giap. Similar to Le Duan, Thanh was a Southerner from a lowly background, a peasant. He was very different from Giap who had been raised as an intellectual. Giap's fall from grace was temporary. His devotion to training troops and strengthening their logistics, an enormous task, ensured him a position of formidable power as the war was to take another major turn.

With the assassinations of Diem and Kennedy, and the resolution of the 9th Plenum to send complete main-force regiments, and later, divisions, to the South, America had been thrust into a new era of the Vietnam War. Whereas COSVN always conducted guerrilla war, and in time, so-called "VC" divisions[30] were to launch coordinated attacks in the South, PAVN main force units up to division size would be pitted against South Vietnamese regular forces with their American advisers and support. As a measure of how much the war in the South was not just influenced by the North, but in fact taken over by it, Merle Pribbenow wrote to me, "Every one of the division commanders, including the commanders of the so-called 'VC' 2nd, 3rd, 5th, and 9th Divisions, was a native of North Vietnam."

With the North fully committed, war on a huge scale was soon to follow.

CHAPTER 9

General Westmoreland, Attrition, Search and Destroy, 1964–67

Westmoreland may have been promoted beyond the range of his competence. He had done well at lower levels of command, but now, despite impressing others as being comfortably in control, having received his fourth star and being appointed COMUSMACV (Commander, U.S. MACV), he indeed may have been in over his head. The chaotic situation he inherited, which might be summarized as foreign troop support in a country which abhorred foreign presence and was on the verge of collapse, speaks for itself. But dire situations have sometimes been converted into victory. Much more to the point, consideration of the organization, equipment, and training of the United States Army of that time, coupled with its command culture, handicapped him, just as it would the two generals who succeeded him as COMUSMACV.

Westmoreland, as Shaped by Advice and the Command Culture of the U.S. Army

The American army of 1964 had been organized and trained to fight a conventional war in the manner of World War II and Korea, with front lines protecting extensive logistical rear areas. The so-called triangular division was the norm for infantry and armor—three regiments, generally of three battalions with three companies, and so on down the line in threes. This kind of division, at about half the strength, is what the French, North Vietnamese, South Vietnamese National Army, then ARVN used in Vietnam.

Almost all the senior American generals who shaped policy for the army in the 1950s and 1960s had commanded in World War II, and some of them also in Korea. Post-war, most of them had influenced in one way or another the way the current army was organized, trained, and equipped. Naturally they were part of a command culture, learning from and influencing one another. In 1963, when Westmoreland had received his Vietnam assignment, General MacArthur urged Westmoreland to make sure he always had plenty of artillery because the Oriental greatly fears artillery.[1]

Westmoreland also recounted a visit which President Kennedy made to West Point in June 1962 to deliver the commencement address. "Where there is a visible enemy to fight in open combat … the answer is not so difficult.… But when there is a long, slow struggle, with no immediately visible foe, your choice will seem hard indeed."

Here were two sets of advice for the man who was to conduct America's war in Vietnam—one from the old general who had led America's fight across the Pacific to defeat Japan: "Make sure you have plenty of artillery [a metaphor for massive firepower]." The other, from the young naval hero of that war in the South Pacific: "Yours are not strictly military responsibilities.… This would be another type of war."[2]

Westmoreland chose the old course, almost certainly because that is what he, all of his contemporary generals, and those of us who had been captains, majors, and lieutenant colonels during the Vietnam War had been brought up on: *firepower*.

As cadets at West Point, 1952–56, my class had no instruction in insurgency warfare. Shortly after graduation, as a lieutenant in the armor basic course I learned a great deal about tanks and low-level armor tactics but nothing about using tanks in the jungle. Then in Europe during the Cold War our training and field exercises were designed to fight the World War II kind of war, holding off superior Soviet forces arrayed against us just across the West German border. As a captain in the armor advanced course in 1961–62, there was nothing about the Vietnam-type war beyond a few brief paragraphs in our training brochures. The Army's senior generals, as more junior officers, had commanded in World War II, and America had won that war. So what could be wrong with the choice of making sure you applied massive firepower at the right place and time—that you had "plenty of artillery"?

The Air Force, Navy, and Marines likewise thought in terms of superior firepower. All armed services during the Cold War were focused on first defending against the Soviet Union, then winning a war against them, utilizing the concepts, training and, except for nuclear weapons, much the same type equipment that had brought victory in World War II. We had a command culture fixed on past victories, and it was not well suited to the war we would fight.

MACV Mission and Resources

In July 1964, just after Westmoreland assumed full command of MACV, President Johnson had named Maxwell Taylor as ambassador to Vietnam, with the following charge: "[To] have and exercise full responsibility for the effort of the United States

Government in South Vietnam.... I wish it clearly understood that this overall responsibility includes the whole military effort in South Vietnam and authorizes the degree of command and control that you consider appropriate."[3]

Not only was Taylor a respected military man but he had been a patron of Westmoreland, so the Taylor/Westmoreland relationship would seem to bode well for a unified approach to the military conduct of the war. However, as Westmoreland pointed out,

> MACV was but one component, albeit the largest, of what was known as the "United States Mission" or "Country Team." Under terms of the Mutual Defense Assistance Act of 1949, the U.S. ambassador headed the Mission. Aside from MACV and the Department of State, other organizations involved were the Central Intelligence Agency, the Agency for International Development... the Joint United States Public Affairs Office ... and the Mission Economic Counselor. It was a complex, awkward arrangement.[4]

Also, Westmoreland in Saigon was not the supreme commander of military operations, land, air, and sea, a position held by Admiral Sharp in Honolulu.

Cold War Major Threats

Even had Westmoreland been given a unified combined command, he and any other commanding general would have been subject to the political and military restrictions confining U.S. military action. As enunciated in turn from Truman to Nixon, the biggest threat to America in the Cold War was not North Vietnam but the USSR with nuclear weapons. And China had conducted a nuclear test in 1964.

Chinese intervention in Vietnam was a possibility. Truman had been roundly trashed for "losing" China in 1949, although one could not lose what was never possessed. Eisenhower had China in mind, perhaps even World War III, when he turned down massive bombing or nuclear weapons as an attempt to save the French at Dien Bien Phu. And China had sent massive forces across the Manchurian border into North Korea which drove the Americans and South Koreans back south. With America deeply into its advisory role in 1964, presidential campaign bluster of Goldwater and LeMay—"Bomb them back to the Stone Age"—was hardly the kind of rhetoric for guiding responsible military action.

HOP TAC

We should take Westmoreland's pronouncements in his book, *A Soldier Reports*, with more than a grain of salt. Nevertheless, they reveal major beliefs and events that shaped the war, and thus are valuable in assessing his role and the war as a whole. One of his first actions, surprising in terms of what happened later, was to stress pacification. He takes credit for designing a pacification plan which, he said,

> I code-named HOP TAC ... cooperation.... It was designed to expand security and government control and services— pacification—gradually outward from Saigon into six provinces that form a kind of horse collar about the city.... When I presented this at the Honolulu conference [with President Johnson and Secretary of Defense McNamara] in June 1964, I received authority to conduct HOP TAC, and thus in effect obtained for MACV the role of executive agent for pacification around Saigon, the role that I believed the military should have for the entire country.[5]

Thus Americans, not Vietnamese, were the center for planning and conducting pacification, and this was to have profound consequences.

The *Pentagon Papers* researchers said, "So unsuccessful was [HOP TAC] that during its life span the VC were able to organize a regiment ... in the Gia Dinh area surrounding Saigon."[6]

Commit Ground Combat Units?

In his excellent book, *Choosing War*, Fredrik Logevall uncovers in great detail steps leading to the fateful decision by President Johnson to commit ground combat units. Johnson inherited his top advisers from Kennedy and kept them on, intensively grilling them on why the war was necessary. All, in the beginning, were inveterate hawks. McNamara, though, relatively soon saw that the war would not only be difficult in the extreme, but probably unwinnable, yet he spoke publicly about winning it and forged ahead with fighting it.

Johnson agonized over the war he hated, the war that interfered with his Great Society program. He tried to rationalize a way out, yet he and his advisers kept coming back to the bedrock of prestige: the *prestige* of the United States was on the line, and it was essential in this Cold War to uphold it. Their personal prestige, too, was inextricably wrapped up in the mess, and they could not, or would not, loose themselves from it. Johnson was caught, like Macbeth, III.iv.136–38:

> I am in blood
> Stepp'd in so far, that, should I wade no more,
> Returning were as tedious as go o'er.

The President's Decision

By 1964 it was abundantly clear that our immense American aid program—military, economic, and societal—had failed. South Vietnam was in crisis. In essence, President Johnson had two basic choices: support the South by any and all means necessary, or withdraw. He could make a further enormous military commitment to include inserting ground combat troops in the South, bombing North Vietnam, and blockading its harbors. He could even invade the North, which would require a very large ground force and bombing so intense it would approach the carpet-bombing destruction of World War II. But China might come into the war with ground troops—even atomic weapons. And even if the China concern were set aside, in order to ensure the safety of the South an occupation of the North would be required. For how long? Five years? A decade? A century? Congress, the American people, and allies rightly would never support such a course.

The president's other choice was to withdraw—an enormously difficult task politically—while trying to get the best deal possible for the South Vietnamese. "In late 1964 there was near unanimity among the civilian and military leaders of the Defense Department in favor of doing what was necessary to save the situation."[7]

Johnson's real mark in history could be made, he knew, by the success of his Great Society Program. And this damned Vietnam War was torpedoing it. He was a Texan. How could a *Texan* lose a war to little yellow men in sandals in "that damn little pissant country"? How could *he*, Lyndon Baines Johnson, go down in history as the first American president to *lose* a war?

At the end of 1964 when President Johnson was tussling with the enormous Vietnam problem—should America cast down the gauntlet and commit ground troops to war in South Vietnam?—American military deaths in Vietnam and adjacent countries as a result of the Vietnam War from 1955–64 stood at 416.[8]

It would have taken enormous courage for President Johnson to have acted other than as he did. The true test of presidential character in weighing a war decision should be ultimately a personal, not political one: *Would I subject my son or my daughter to the dangers and sacrifices I will order other people's sons and daughters to face?*

My son!

My daughter!

Luci Baines Johnson?

Lynda Bird Johnson?

If America's core interests unmistakably require the president to answer—*Yes I would, I have to send my son, my daughter*—then fight, and fight fiercely and intelligently America must. If *No, I will not send my son or my daughter*, then an alternative must be found.

But President Johnson did not have that kind of character. Under the circumstances he inherited, would *any* American president have had it?

When the last American death was recorded in the Vietnam War, the number was 58,318. Wounded were over 153,300.

1965: America Goes All In

Two events in particular shaped America's Vietnam decisions in late 1964 and early 1965. The first was the so-called Gulf of Tonkin incident when in August 1964 North Vietnamese patrol boats in the Tonkin Gulf were reported to have attacked a destroyer, the USS *Maddox*.[9] That incident led to the Congressional resolution: "The

Congress approves and supports the determination of the President, as Commander in Chief, to take all necessary measures to repel any armed attack against the forces of the United States and to prevent further aggression." The president ordered retaliatory air strikes on North Vietnam. Then on February 7, 1965 sappers struck the American advisers compound at Pleiku, killing eight U.S. soldiers and wounding another 126.

That did it.

The president ordered increased air strikes against North Vietnam that led to Rolling Thunder and other bombing campaigns against the North which, with some halts, were to continue almost to the end of the American war. Marines landed on March 8, 1965. Marines ashore, along with a soon-approved troop level of 175,000, clearly signaled that the war had changed from one of denying the enemy a victory by defending to—in Westmoreland's words—"taking the war to the enemy." The buildup to over 543,000 troops had started.

By early April 1965, 17 non-aligned nations were calling for negotiations, and, whereas President Johnson welcomed this idea, he also said, "We will not be defeated. We will not grow tired. We will not withdraw, either openly or under the cloak of a meaningless agreement."[10] The president had concisely proclaimed the exact opposite of what would happen.

With American ground combat troops ashore, a major question was how the Americans and South Vietnamese would interact at the highest levels. What missions would the Americans have? Republic of Vietnam Armed Forces (RVNAF)? The South Vietnamese ambassador to the U.S., Bui Diem, wrote:

> At the top levels of the [U.S.] administration there is no evidence to suggest that anyone considered the South Vietnamese as partners in the venture to save South Vietnam. In a mood that seemed mixed of idealism and naïveté, impatience and overconfidence, the Americans simply came in and took over. It was an attitude that would endure throughout the remainder of the conflict. The message seemed to be that this was an American war, and the best thing the South Vietnamese could do was to keep from rocking the boat and let the Americans get on with their business.[11]

Remembering all too well that Chinese forces had poured across the border into North Korea when the Americans had gotten too close, Washington had speculated on a possible Chinese reaction to U.S. troops ashore in Vietnam. The Chinese Central Committee had made plain to the North Vietnamese leadership its intent: "You may wage the boldest struggle against U.S. imperialism. You need not be afraid of the expansion of the war, its expansion into China. If the war expands to China, we will fight shoulder to shoulder with you."[12]

In April 1965, very soon after the first American combat units landed, patriotism in the North reached a fever pitch. "The Party's Three Readiness Campaign ... called for 'readiness to join the army, to partake in battle, to go wherever the fatherland deems necessary.... Mobilization drives more than doubled the ranks of the PAVN in the first few months of [the new] war."[13]

Victory in Vietnam records: "On 25 July 1965 Chairman Ho Chi Minh appealed to the citizens and soldiers of the entire nation: 'No matter if we have to fight for five years, ten years, twenty years, or even longer, we are resolved to fight on until we achieve complete victory."[14]

Search and Destroy

While planning HOP TAC back in 1964, Westmoreland had his staff come up with terminology to describe the initial military actions intended to push government control outward from Saigon. "Search and destroy" was the unfortunate choice. This, he said, "was nothing more than the infantry's traditional attack mission."

Westmoreland went on, "Many people, to my surprise, came to associate it with aimless searches in the jungle and random destroying of villages and other property."[15]

Perhaps because that happened, and the term seemed appropriate?

Soon after he had launched HOP TAC, Westmoreland was to have something more to concern him than a failing pacification operation in the Saigon area. Earlier, North Vietnamese reinforcements had been infiltrated individually and in small groups into the South. But by the fall of 1964, entire regiments were being sent south. As if the very term "search and destroy" had triggered something in Westmoreland in 1964, shortly after he got combat forces ashore in 1965 he would send them on missions to search for enemy main forces and destroy them. This, on the surface, may seem reasonable enough, given the U.S. military's organization and command culture.

What was behind search and destroy? Westmoreland and every American army officer since the end of World War I studied the "Principles of War," the tenets that were intended to guide modern military combat. After World War I, British military strategist B. H. Liddell Hart analyzed the essence of wars and stated what he considered the time-tested principles for conduct of war. Following Hart's lead, the various armies of the world then expressed their principles of war in manners unique to their circumstances. All of them, though, in one way or another gave great weight to the two cardinal principles as later stated in *Department of the Army Field Manual 3-0*, 1965, a basic reference during the Vietnam war:

> *Objective—Direct every military operation toward a clearly defined, decisive, and attainable objective.* The ultimate military purpose of war is the destruction of the enemy's ability to fight and will to fight.
>
> *Offensive—Seize, retain, and exploit the initiative.* Offensive action is the most effective and decisive way to attain a clearly defined common objective. Offensive operations are the means by which a military force seizes and holds the initiative while maintaining freedom of action and achieving decisive results. This is fundamentally true across all levels of war.

As for *objective*, critics at the time and thereafter have pointed out that the U.S. government had trouble devising a statement of objective for Vietnam that satisfied the public and the Congress. What we were doing or trying to do in Vietnam seemed murky and led at first to confusion and distrust, and later to civil disobedience, riots, and demands for withdrawal.

Patton said there are only three principles of war: Audacity, Audacity, *Audacity!* No American military manual or military school taught that wars were won by being on defense. It was indeed important to learn the ingredients of a good defense, and to practice them when necessary. But defense was taught as a temporary means of regaining the offensive. Westmoreland's first combat units ashore initially would be used defensively, to secure critical installations such as airfields and coastal facilities, but as quickly as possible, they would go on the offense.

So where did Westmoreland go wrong? Or did he?

Command Culture and Its Consequences

U.S. soldiers had learned in past wars they must *attack*. By the time of the Vietnam War, commanders well knew they must hit the enemy in the middle, or hit them on the flank, or go around or over them. Go, go GO! The best defense is a good offense. And that was absolutely true, proven time after time in the wars prior to Vietnam. No commander wants to be known as hesitant or weak. As a cadet, then lieutenant, then captain in the 1950s and early 1960s, I immersed myself in the history of World War II. I watched the many movies of that combat, read the books, listened to the veterans, and attended the service schools. We Americans have a *can do* attitude. The offense was how World War II had been won: *Attack!*

But this was Vietnam! It was not World War II or Korea.

In General Bruce Palmer's book, *The 25-Year War*, he revealed how command culture had tragic consequences for America and South Vietnam:

> The JCS seemed to be unable to articulate an effective military strategy that they could persuade the commander-in-chief and secretary of defense to adopt. In the end ... General Westmoreland ... made successive requests for larger and larger force levels without the benefit of an overall concept and plan.... Not once during the war did the JCS advise the commander-in-chief or the secretary of defense that the strategy being pursued most probably would fail and that the United States would be unable to achieve its objectives. The only explanation of this failure is that the chiefs were imbued with the "can do" spirit and could not bring themselves to make such a negative statement or to appear to be disloyal.[16]

Attrition, Search and Destroy, Body Count, Kill Ratio

In *The Pentagon Papers* and other official reports, the terms "attrition," and "search and destroy" as "strategies" are seen over and over—in MACV communications, discussions in Washington circles, and orders conveyed to Westmoreland in Vietnam. Attrition was the "strategy" Westmoreland chose, and search and destroy his tactic for achieving it. Body count and kill ratio evolved naturally out of those concepts. McNamara said,

> Between 1965 and 1967 Westy intensified his pursuit of an attrition strategy aimed at inflicting more casualties on the Viet Cong and North Vietnamese than they could replace…. The body count was a measurement of the adversary's manpower losses; we undertook it because one of Westy's objectives was to reach a so-called crossover point, at which Viet Cong and North Vietnamese casualties would be greater than they could sustain.[17]

In other words we would reach a point at which we would be killing Viet Cong and NVA faster than the enemy could replace them, thus ultimately ensuring our dominance over them. As command policy this concept, coupled with the kill ratio—the ratio of enemy to friendly killed—is appalling. Soldier-scholar Dave R. Palmer wrote, "Attrition is not a strategy. It is, in fact, irrefutable proof of the *absence* of any strategy [Palmer's emphasis]…. [The commander] uses blood in lieu of brains."[18]

When it was certain that American combat units would be sent to Vietnam, Westmoreland seems to have shifted gears from thinking of himself as top American military advisor to the South Vietnamese government—which he was—to that of battlefield commander—which he also was. While minimizing efforts to get pacification moving and building ARVN into a capable army through Vietnamization, he focused on those NVA main-force units, and he would *attack*. As soon as U.S. troops came ashore in 1965 and secured base installations, Westmoreland sent them on search and destroy missions.

Battles of the Ia Drang

The 1st Air Cavalry Division began arriving at An Khe in the Central Highlands in early August 1965 under command of Major General Harry W. O. Kinnard. The 1st Air Cav was the culmination of General Hamilton H. Howze's earlier work on army aviation and air cavalry and was a superb fighting unit. The division had 435 helicopters, enabling it to do wide-range patrolling, intelligence-gathering, and fighting. Hal Moore said, "The helicopter … held the possibility of making the battlefield truly a three-dimensional nightmare for an enemy commander."[19] As it turned out, it also made the battlefield a nightmare for Moore when he was ordered to air assault into deep jungle.

Hal Moore's 1st Battalion, 7th Cavalry arrived at An Khe in mid-September 1965 with the initial mission to build a base camp.

> We stepped off the choppers into a tangle of trees, weeds, and brush, in the middle of what would become our airfield…. The men of the division and some two thousand Vietnamese

laborers cleared the site by hand, with machetes and axes.... They also built a heavily fortified twelve-mile-long and hundred-yard-wide defense perimeter ... around the base.[20]

Moore learned right away that bases ate up combat manpower, not just initially in building them, but also later with guard duty and a multitude of other tasks in maintaining and defending them.

Moore's companies conducted some relatively minor operations out of Plei Me fort, an old French position, "patrolling south and east, finding nothing and growing more frustrated by the hour." The Corps commander paid a visit and said, "Our primary mission was: Find the enemy and go after him."

Find 'em, fix 'em, fight 'em. That's one of the main things an airmobile battalion was designed to do. On the afternoon of November 13, UPI reporter Joe Galloway said he had heard that Moore's battalion would launch into the jungle the next morning. Shortly, Colonel Thomas W. (Tim) Brown, 3rd Brigade Commander, gave Moore his orders: "Here is your area of operations—north of Chu Pong in the Ia Drang Valley. Your mission is the same one you have now: Find and kill the enemy."

Search and destroy!

Brown would provide 16 UH-1D Huey helicopters to move the troops, and would position two 105-millimeter howitzer batteries within range to support them. Major Bruce Crandall would be in charge of the helicopters. Moore said, "We had not yet been in any battalion-size fight in Vietnam, and Bruce Crandall's helicopter pilots were likewise unblooded."

Moore would be going after North Vietnamese units operating in rugged jungle close to the Cambodian border. On the map, he searched for "possible landing zones in that rough scrub-and-jungle region."[21] His main concern was that once he selected a landing zone (LZ) he could insert fewer than 80 men before the Hueys (lift helicopters) would have to return 15 miles to pick up another load, and then continue the shuttle until he could get the 450 men of his three rifle companies, his combat support company, and a slim headquarters command element on the ground. The region had long been a Viet Minh, then Viet Cong base area.

In 1965 Chu Huy Man was a general in command of a large area in Central Vietnam, and Moore was to meet him several years after the war. He told Moore, "I was confident the Americans will use their helicopters to land in our rear, land in the Ia Drang area. It was our intention to draw the Americans out of An Khe. We did not have any plans to liberate the land; only destroy troops." Moore recounts that General Man's three regiments attacked Plei Me and then regrouped in the Ia Drang-Chu Pong base area:

Under the jungle canopy were excellent training areas and wide trails on which troops could move, even during the day, without being detected from the air. Best of all, the Ia Drang Valley was convenient to the inviolable sanctuary across the Cambodian border.... General Man could also call on the local veterans of the H-15 Main Force Viet Cong Battalion, six hundred strong, for duty as porters, guides, and fighters.[22]

Moore would have preferred not to have to make an aerial recon to select a landing zone since the enemy knew there could be a good reason for aircraft over a particular area. But he had no viable alternative, never having seen the terrain. Early on the morning of November 14 he flew high to minimize the chances of alerting the enemy, rejected two possible landing zones as too small, and decided on the third, Landing Zone X-Ray. "It was flat; the trees weren't all that tall; and it looked as though it could take up to eight helicopters at one time."[23]

Moore flew back to Plei Me and "issued orders to the assembled company commanders, liaison officers, pilots, and staff: 'Assault into LZ X-Ray to search for and destroy the enemy.'" Division artillery would fire a twenty-minute preparation, blasting the landing zone. This would be followed immediately by 30 seconds of helicopters firing rockets, then 30 seconds of their machinegun fire, with the lift ships carrying the infantry hard on the gunships' tails. Moore and his small command group loaded with the first flight and they were off. Moore said that on November 14, 1965 at 1048 hours, "as the chopper skids touched the ground I yelled, 'Let's go!' and jumped out, running for the trees on the western side of the clearing, firing my rifle."[24]

The LZ, a semi-clearing no more than a football field in size, was cold. But it was soon to get hot.

On one of his trips to Vietnam after the war, Moore also met Lieutenant General Nguyen Huu An, who as a lieutenant colonel commanded the NVA troops in the battle. Together, Moore and An went to LZ X-Ray and studied the battlefield. General An said, "When you landed here, you landed right in the middle of three of our battalions of the 66th Regiment, our reserve force. It was the strongest we had. [At] full strength the battalions each had about four hundred fifty men. [To include the headquarters units] the regiment's total strength was about sixteen hundred men."[25]

For Moore's men, it was the beginning of three days and two nights of horrific battle. Moore's battalion, soon reinforced by elements of other infantry battalions, was heavily supported by artillery, cav gunships, Air Force flare ships, and fighter bombers. The enemy had been operating in this area for some time and knew it well, helped by the local guides. In most places the jungle was dense, and in the semi-clearings along stream beds and in occasional openings of double and triple canopy trees, heavy growths of elephant grass reached to five feet. With mountain streams to provide water, jungle foliage for concealment, and a Cambodian sanctuary close by to the west, the NVA were in an ideal position for the actions they were good at: concentrating quickly, hitting hard, and then if necessary withdrawing back into the jungle.

Even with all of its mobility and firepower, the 1st Air Cav was at a great disadvantage, so much so that one has to question seriously why Moore's unit was given such a mission in such terrain. Across broad swaths of formidable jungle the cav could not land its helicopters except in some small clearings that were known to the enemy, and then often only one or two ships at a time. Moore said, "This clearing [X-Ray, about a hundred yards long] was the only decent helicopter landing zone between the slopes of Chu Pong and the Ia Drang [River] and for two miles east or west." That in itself spelled danger—the enemy obviously knew where to watch.

The ability to move so that the commander can exercise initiative is key to success or failure. In terrain which allows flexibility of movement, airmobile units can be deadly. In the jungle that all but engulfed LZ X-Ray, though, Moore's unit was quickly pinned into position, and once the firing started, even to get his own men into the LZ, to say nothing of reinforcements, required immense courage, skill, and determination.

General An said,

> When you dropped troops into X-Ray, I was on Chu Pong mountain. We had a very strong position, and a strong, mobile command group. We were ready, had prepared for you and expected you to come. The only question was when. The trees and brush limited our view of the helicopters landing but we had an observation post on the top of the mountain and they reported to us when you dropped troops and when you moved them.[26]

At the time of the assault, back at 3rd Brigade headquarters the assistant division commander was briefing the division commander: "When General Kinnard arrived I showed him a situation map. He took one look and said, 'What the hell are you doing in that area?' I replied, 'Well, General, the object of the exercise is to find the enemy and we sure as hell have.'"[27]

The battle, night and day, was close in and vicious. After having reinforced (necessarily) piecemeal by air, on the third day, after X-Ray had fallen quiet, Colonel Brown finally landed for a brief visit. Moore had gotten no sleep since he had caught a few hours the night before the assault. He said, "I could still think clearly but I had to tell myself what I intended to say before I opened my mouth. It was like speaking a foreign language before you are completely fluent in it. I was translating English into English."

Only soldiers who have gone through battle for two or three days and nights with little or no sleep can truly know that feeling.

For three days the enemy dead had been rotting in the heat. "Now came the body count," Moore said. "Hating it, I asked my company commanders for their best estimates of enemy killed." The men pushed outward from their final line to be greeted by ghastly scenes of carnage. Moore finally gave 634 as body count plus an estimated 1215 killed and wounded by supporting fires, and six prisoners. "We had lost 79 Americans killed in action, 121 wounded, and none missing."

On the morning of November 17, the fourth day, when the sounds of war no longer buffeted X-Ray, Lieutenant Rick Rescorla said, "We were flown away, but the stench of the dead would stay with me for years after the battle."[28] My troops and I well knew the smell of a battlefield in tropical heat, and we will never entirely rid ourselves of it.

LZ Albany

The withdrawal by air of what remained of Moore's battalion was not to be the end of the horror. The LZ X-Ray battle was followed immediately by an even deadlier day and night for 1st Air Cav sister units in the jungle, in and near close-by LZ Albany.

Larry Gwin was a lieutenant, executive officer of Alpha Troop, 2nd Battalion of the 7th Cavalry. In his book, *Baptism: A Vietnam Memoir,* he describes how his battalion in column formation, without sleep for 48 hours, each man carrying a minimum load of 60 pounds in stifling heat, struck out for LZ Albany.

After stressful going, they were less than 500 meters, they thought, from LZ Albany where they would be picked up. No problem.

But there was a huge problem—enemy lying in wait.

By the next morning, "the battalion, roughly four hundred strong when it left X-Ray, had suffered more than seventy percent casualties—155 dead, 124 wounded. Charlie Company was the hardest hit, losing all but 9 of its 110 men." The survivors and reinforcements spent the day policing up the battlefield, evacuating dead and wounded. The stench of American and Vietnamese bodies, Gwin said, was much worse even than at X-Ray. "At Albany it filled your nostrils and permeated your soul."[29]

A few days after the survivors had returned from Ia Drang to their base camp they looked forward to Thanksgiving dinner. General Westmoreland showed up and wanted to address the troops. Gwin relates that his battalion had been on its way to a hot turkey dinner when they were lined up around the general standing on a stump. "It was a nice speech, full of praise for the great job we had done, and the great victory we had won." After the talk, Gwin and his buddies found themselves at the end of the chow line, looking around for "a place to sit and eat their cold and lumpy dinners."[30]

Confirmation of Attrition as a "Strategy"

Moore wrote of the aftermath of the 1st Air Cav Division's Ia Drang campaign:

> In Saigon, General William C. Westmoreland, and his principal deputy, General William DePuy, looked at the statistics of the [entire] thirty-four days of the Ia Drang campaign … and saw a kill ratio of twelve North Vietnamese to one American. What that said to the two officers who had learned their trade in the meat-grinder campaigns in World War II was that they could bleed the enemy to death over the long haul, with a strategy of attrition.[31]

Never mind that body count was always suspect, and never mind that the loss of a single soldier ought to cause a commander to strive for ways of conducting war that would minimize those losses, attrition it was.

When Westmoreland told a senator from South Carolina, "We're killing those people at a ratio of 10 to1," [the senator] responded, "Westy, the American people don't care about the ten. They care about the one."[32]

"The CIA pointed out that Hanoi's available manpower resources were clearly adequate to sustain the war indefinitely."[33]

Dave Palmer's analysis of time and patience is instructive:

> To Americans, raised in a free, competitive, capitalistic society, time is a precious commodity. It is the one thing that cannot be bought or built. We can't bear wasting it. A moment lost is never regained.... To Asians, steeped in Confucian concepts, time is an endless stream flowing from an infinitely regenerating source. It is precious enough, a commodity to be valued, but because it is of unlimited abundance one can hardly use too much of it. Thus, that which we husband the most carefully they expend the most liberally.... A quick victory is strictly a western concept. In war our attitudes and expectations lead us to seek the lightning stroke of victory.[34]

Instead of taking the slow approach of pacification and Vietnamization—improvement of ARVN—so hopefully they could fight their own war, Westmoreland had decided to use his forces in another fashion. He said, "Since the enemy's large units would be met most often in his base areas, the greater mobility of American units would provide them with an advantage."[35]

Where were those base areas to which Westmoreland referred? Most were in deep jungle, carefully selected to provide natural cover, concealment, terrain barriers, and escape routes.

As for "the greater mobility of American units?" In the air, surely—but the enemy's main force units were not in the air. Like the night, the jungle was the enemy's friend. So Westmoreland's strategy was to pit U.S. ground forces against the enemy's main forces where the enemy had the advantage—in the jungle. I had more than a little experience fighting in the enemy's jungle base areas with my armored cavalry, tanks, mechanized infantry, infantry, and air cavalry. We were ordered to go there, to seek out and destroy the enemy. We went and tried to do that. We can attest that the advantage was with the enemy, not with us.

So, search and destroy it was, and would continue to be.

The Marines—A Different Concept

Brigadier General Frederick J. Karch, a Marine who had fought in the South Pacific, had made several visits to Vietnam in the year before he became commander of the 9th Marine Expeditionary Brigade. On those visits, "He did not like what he saw.... If we go into Da Nang we'll disappear into the countryside and never be heard from again.'"[36] He sounded like George Ball speaking to President Kennedy some four years earlier.

Marine Lieutenant General Victor H. Krulak served for two years in the Pentagon, 1962–64, as special assistant for counterinsurgency to the Joint Chiefs of Staff. Then in 1964 he became commander of Fleet Marine Force Pacific with responsibility for all Marines in the Pacific area to include Vietnam. He was certain that Kennedy had been correct in placing great emphasis on counterinsurgency rather than big unit warfare. Krulak said, "I went to Vietnam eight times between 1962 and 1964. In those early years I learned something of the complex nature of the conflict there." Krulak had several meetings with Sir Robert Thompson, acclaimed for his methods of countering insurgency in Malaya, and Krulak was mindful of Thompson's principles: "The people's trust is primary. It will come hard because they are fearful and suspicious. Protection is the most important thing you can bring them."

Krulak asserted:

> The "spreading ink blot formula" [pacification]… should have been at the heart of the battle for freedom in Indochina. General Westmoreland told me, however, that while the ink blot seemed to be effective, we just didn't have time to do it that way. I suggested to him that we didn't have time to do it any other way; if we left the people to the enemy, glorious victories in the hinterland would be little more than blows in the air—and we would end up losing the war. But Defense Secretary Robert S. McNamara expressed the same view as Westmoreland to me in the winter of 1965—"a good idea" he said about the ink blot formula, "but too slow." I had told him in a letter dated 11 November 1965, "In the highly populous areas the battleground is in the people's minds."[37]

This difference in concepts—search and destroy versus pacification with its primary emphasis on security for the people—was to strain Third Marine Amphibious Force relations with MACV throughout the war. By 1968 Krulak had gone to Vietnam 54 times, in periods ranging from five to twenty days, and he saw the country from the DMZ in the north to Ca Mau Peninsula in the south. He met a lot of people, went on operations with the Vietnamese Marines and ARVN, and observed how large enemy forces could melt into the landscape. "Everything I saw kept bringing me back to the basic proposition that the war could only be won when the people were protected. If the people were for you, you would triumph in the end. If they were against you, the war would bleed you dry and you would be defeated."[38]

An official Marine history said:

> [General Krulak] sought to persuade [Admiral Sharp, Commander in Chief, Pacific], that there was no virtue at all in seeking out the NVA in the mountains and jungle; that so long as they stayed there they were a threat to nobody, that our efforts should be addressed to the rich, populous lowlands…. It is our conviction that if we can destroy the guerrilla fabric among the people, we will automatically deny the larger units the food and the intelligence and the taxes, and the other support they need. At the same time if the big [enemy] units want to sortie out of the mountains and come down where they can be cut up by our supporting arms, the Marines are glad to take them on, but the real war is among the people and not among these mountains.
>   Brigadier General William E. DePuy, MACV J-3 [Operations] …. recommended to General Westmoreland that the Marines be directed to launch large-unit offensive operations against VC base areas with two to three battalion forces during at least two weeks out of every month.[39]

And Westmoreland so directed.

A Marine Platoon Leader in Search and Destroy

Second Lieutenant Philip Caputo had landed at Da Nang Airbase on March 8, 1965, the first day ashore for U.S. combat units. He was a rifle platoon leader in Karch's brigade. Caputo was soon caught up in Westmoreland's directive to the Marines to conduct search and destroy operations:

> General Westmoreland's strategy of attrition … had an effect on our behavior. Our mission was not to win terrain or seize positions, but simply to kill: to kill Communists and to kill as many of them as possible. Stack 'em like cordwood. Victory was a high body-count, defeat a low kill-ratio, war a matter of arithmetic. The pressure on unit commanders to produce enemy corpses was intense, and they in turn communicated it to their troops. This led to such practices as counting civilians as Viet Cong. "If it's dead and Vietnamese, it's VC" was a rule of thumb in the bush.

Caputo entered the war with the idealism of youth, wanting to serve his country and do a good job. But "by autumn what had begun as an adventurous expedition had turned into an exhausting, indecisive war of attrition in which we fought for no cause other than our own survival…. Out there, lacking restraints, sanctioned to kill, confronted by a hostile country and relentless enemy, we sank into a brutish state."[40]

"Some line companies did not bother even taking prisoners; they simply killed every VC they saw, and a number of Vietnamese who were only suspects…. 'If he's dead and Vietnamese, he's VC.'"[41]

One mission resulted in killing of two civilians and burning down their village. Caputo was charged with murder and referred to general courts-martial. Instead, he would get a letter of reprimand. The charges against him and the others had resulted from the village chief going to the district chief to report the murders. One can imagine what the villagers thought when they heard the verdicts—letters of reprimand—and how their subsequent attitudes and actions may have contributed to the outcome of the war.

Civil War in the South, For Awhile

General Lewis W. Walt was "a Marine's Marine." He had fought in World War II, Korea, and now Vietnam. Twice wounded, he had received numerous awards for valor to include the Navy Cross, equivalent of the Army's Distinguished Service Cross, our nation's second highest military medal. In Vietnam he was Commanding General, III Marine Amphibious Force, and Senior Advisor, I Corps. By 1966 General Walt had established a close working relationship with General Nguyen Chanh Thi, the Vietnamese I Corps commander. General Thi appreciated Walt and he reciprocated, being highly supportive of Walt's Marines and the program they called the Combined Action Unit. In his book, *Strange War, Strange Strategy*, Walt said,

> We had found the key to our main problem—how to fight the war. The struggle was in the rice paddies, in and among the people, not passing through, but living among them, night

and day, sharing their victories and defeats.... Then suddenly, came a terrible blow—not on the military but on the political front.... Swiftly and unexpectedly, our hopes were collapsed. Not by the Viet Cong, but even more tragically by our friends and allies, the South Vietnamese themselves.[42]

Concerned with General Thi's popularity and power in I Corps, and fearing a coup, when Ky was prime minister and Thieu a figurehead, Ky summarily relieved Thi. Thi's units, as well as the predominant Buddhist leadership around Da Nang, supported Thi against Ky, and fighting and riots broke out. Caputo said, "South Vietnamese soldiers were fighting street battles with other South Vietnamese soldiers as the two mandarin warlords contended for power. And while the South Vietnamese fought their intramural feud, we were left to fight the Viet Cong."[43]

The infighting spread. Ky's Saigon troops were seizing critical locations in Da Nang while Thi's opposing troops, including an armored force, were moving on the city. For several days and weeks the situation went back and forth, with General Walt trying to placate the contending parties and dampen a civil war. Exchanges of gunfire killed and wounded military on both sides, South Vietnamese against South Vietnamese. When Ky's planes fired rockets that fell into the U.S. Marine compound and wounded several Marines, though, a fed-up Walt launched his own jets with orders to shoot down the Vietnamese aircraft if there was any further attack. Now it was U.S. against South Vietnamese.

Caputo was at his division's command post on a hill "which gave us a ringside seat. Looking to the west we could see [U.S.] Marines fighting the VC; to the east, the South Vietnamese Army fighting itself.... I knew then that we could never win. With a government and an army like that in South Vietnam, we could never hope to win the war."

The insurrection ended on May 25. Caputo said, "General Walt sent a message to all Marine units in I Corps: ... the 'rebellion' had been crushed and that we could 'look forward to an era of good relations with our South Vietnamese comrades-in arms.' The message shocked me. Even Lew Walt, my old hero, was blind to the truth. The war was to go on, senselessly on."[44]

All sides went back to the war against the VC and NVA, but the problems of civil unrest and military favoritism, corruption, and political appointments of generals, province and district chiefs rather than appointments based on merit, continued to plague the South Vietnamese conduct of the war.

The Marines' Combined Action Program (CAP)

General Walt pointed out to Westmoreland that the huge proportion of inhabitants in the large I Corps area lived in hamlets and villages along the coast and on streams that reached back toward the mountains to the west. Walt was not in favor of chasing the enemy in its own lair, that difficult jungle terrain to the west; rather, through his pacification program he would cut them off from the support they found and very much needed in the populated areas. He was not successful in dissuading Westmoreland, who thought the Marines were dragging their feet on search and destroy, but nevertheless Walt was able to devote significant resources to pacification while, following MACV orders, he committed the rest to search and destroy. He recognized that it made little sense to sweep through a village, taking and inflicting casualties, then go on to some other place and have to come back and do it all over again. He wanted his teams to have a continuing presence in the hamlets and villages.

The CAP program put small Marine units down to squad size in hamlets, along with local self-defense forces supplied by the village or hamlet chief. Their mission was to stay in place for long periods and get to know and serve the people while placing out ambushes to provide security.

The schizophrenic contrasts between Marine search and destroy missions and Marine CAP missions reveal much of why the war could not be won. Lieutenant Caputo and his men during search and destroy showed the terrible, dark side of military operations which may exist at one level simultaneous with CAP operations at another level within a single command.

The Marines' Combined Action Program came reasonably close to being effective, at least for a while. With the minimal resources which Westmoreland's directed search and destroy operations left them, General Walt and his Marines did as much as could be done to make their pacification concept a reality. In some areas, for some periods, they succeeded in establishing relatively secure hamlets and villages and gaining the loyalty of the people—loyalty, it unfortunately turned out, more to the Marines than to the government of South Vietnam.

The Allure of the Big Unit War

Westmoreland seemed to discount the kind of war the enemy had been conducting. South Vietnamese General Tran Dinh Tho wrote,

> American military policy sought to train and equip the [South] Vietnamese military as a conventional force to face an eventual conventional invasion. However, this invasion first materialized under the unconventional form of subversion, sustained by guerrilla warfare. The Republic of Vietnam Armed Forces (RVNAF), tailored to the U.S. Army image, were hard-pressed to fight this kind of war, for which they were ill-prepared. Increased U.S. military aid and the availability of U.S. combat support assets failed to solve the basic problem of the long-term conflict.[45]

Big unit battles, not combatting subversion and guerrilla warfare, were Westmoreland's priority. During his four years in command, 1964–68, and especially after ground combat units arrived in 1965, he could have devised ways to use his U.S. units around selected villages and cities to provide security and other assistance for pacification efforts that might have reduced subversion and guerrilla attacks. Simultaneously he might have strengthened ARVN, Regional Forces (RFs), and local Popular Forces (PFs) through Vietnamization. Instead, Westmoreland rejected the Marines' clear and hold tactics which fought subversion and local guerrillas. His mantra was search and destroy. He would fight the big unit war, going after the enemy where they had the advantage and were most likely to hurt his troops.

CHAPTER 10

The Big, Big Unit War, 1967–mid-1968

In 1967 came the Mother of all search and destroy operations. Actually, Mother One and Mother Two. General Westmoreland was particularly proud of these, especially the second operation. In May 1966 General Westmoreland had directed the II Field Force Vietnam (IIFFV) commander, Lieutenant General Jonathan O. Seaman, to plan an operation in War Zone C, northern Tay Ninh Province, to start at the beginning of 1967. The planning associated with this operation was strange. Normally, the enemy situation causes planners first to select an objective. Next comes consideration of the forces required to attain the objective, and the detailed planning begins. Not so in this case. Westmoreland was envisioning an operation over seven months away, an extraordinary circumstance when division-size operations were usually conceived one day and executed within the next few days. "[Westmoreland] further indicated that it should be a 'big operation.' Over the next several months the operation, to be known as Junction City, was planned. As approved by General Westmoreland it was to start on January 8, 1967, and was to be multidivisional, and was to include a parachute assault."[1]

This has to be one of the weirdest sequences of events in conducting a large-scale operation in any war, getting the cart before the horse. It cries out that a major desire of Westmoreland—who had been an airborne division and airborne corps commander—was to get his U.S. Army parachute forces, two brigades, doing what they were designed to do, and what had not been done since the Korean War, make a big play—a combat jump. However, fate played the general a bad hand. Intelligence events intervened, and *Junction City* was delayed until Operation *Cedar Falls* could be launched in the Iron Triangle north of Saigon, and he ultimately had to settle for a one-brigade jump.

After returning from Vietnam in mid-1968, from then until 1972 Westmoreland served as U.S. Army Chief of Staff. One of his projects was to task senior army officers with producing a series of monographs, *Vietnam Studies*. He chose Lieutenant General Bernard W. Rogers for the Department of the Army study, *Cedar Falls-Junction City: A Turning Point*, written in 1971 and published in 1973 as a book. Rogers as a brigadier general had been assistant division commander of 1st Infantry Division during these two operations.

Rogers said, "Operations Cedar Falls and Junction City took place during the first five months of 1967 and were the first multidivisional operations to be conducted according to a preconceived plan. They were to result in a turning point in the war."

Turning point? That these operations could be considered at any time "a turning point" is astounding. Rogers continued, "They confirmed that such operations do have a place in counterinsurgency warfare today; they brought an end to the enemy's thinking that his third phase of the war—large-scale operations throughout the country— would be successful."[2]

It is profoundly disappointing that this rosy assertion stands as official history of the United States Army.

***

The objective area for *Cedar Falls* was the Iron Triangle, a triangular piece of scrub jungle between the confluence of the Saigon River on the west, the Thi Tinh River on the east, and an imaginary line running from Ben Cat on Route 13 on the east to the Saigon River on the west. (See map, 1st Infantry Division Area of Operations.)

A major objective for the operation was the elimination of the village of Ben Suc which lay just outside the northwestern corner of the Triangle. Ready were 30,000 U.S. ground troops, about 10,000 ARVN, and enormous engineer and air resources. The estimated 1,500–3,000 enemy were outnumbered at least fifteen to one.

During the initial assault, 50 Rome plows with their huge blades went to work. The plan was to scrape the entire Triangle flat, but that proved to be far beyond the capabilities of the engineers during the 19-day operation. They were, however, able to knock down everything above ground in the village of Ben Suc plus the three other villages on the bank of the Saigon. At the end of the operation, four villages ceased to exist, leaving rough scars on the terrain.

Rogers reported, "A total of 5,987 persons was evacuated (582 men, 1651 women, and 3,754 children.) Also moved to the relocation site [Phu Loi] were 247 water buffalo, 225 head of cattle, 158 oxcarts, and 60 tons of rice.)" A reporter who accompanied the operation said that the ARVN battalion killed and roasted many chickens, some of which were shared with American troops.

Rogers continued, "It would be weeks before the [South Vietnamese military and civilian agencies] could restore a sense of normality to the evacuees. Eventually they would have their own village with its school, raise their own crops with access to the Saigon markets, and have much-needed medical assistance available."[3]

Happy, happy villagers? Not so. They continued to be sullen. Their homes, their village had been totally destroyed.

Except for one night battle, Rogers said the assault throughout the Triangle had been met with only light resistance. He also asserted, "From every aspect, the enemy had suffered a great defeat." Great defeat? Rogers reported,

> Only two days after the termination of Cedar Falls, I was checking out the Iron Triangle by helicopter and saw many persons who appeared to be Viet Cong riding bicycles or wandering around on foot.... During the cease-fire for Tet, 8–12 February, the Iron Triangle was again literally crawling with what appeared to be Viet Cong. They could be seen riding into, out of, and within the triangle.

Despite all this, Rogers proclaimed, "In nineteen days, II Field Force, Vietnam, had converted the Iron Triangle from a haven to a sealed battleground, and then to a military no-man's land.... A strategic enemy base had been decisively engaged and destroyed."[4]

Junction City

Cedar Falls was big. *Junction City* was to be bigger, in fact the largest planned U.S./ARVN operation of the Vietnam War. Committed were major elements of two U.S. infantry divisions plus four South Vietnamese battalions and fourteen artillery battalions. *Junction City* would also include the first major U.S. combat parachute assault since the Korean War. The primary stated mission would be "search and destroy to eradicate the Central Office of South Vietnam (COSVN) and Viet Cong and North Vietnamese Army installations." The enemy's base was in what was called the Duong Minh Chau area in Tay Ninh Province. It had been heavily used by the Viet Minh during the French war, and this gave the current occupants plenty of experience operating within it.

Espionage Reveals the Plans

Two aspects of the enemy's *Junction City* resistance in early 1967 are especially instructive. The first, espionage, is one of the factors that greatly contributed to making this war unwinnable. General Bruce Palmer said,

> At times the government had been penetrated all the way from [Thieu's Independence] palace down to small units in the field. When I first visited the 25th ARVN Division headquarters in Duc Hoa, the division commander would discuss only trivial matters in his office; he took me outside well away from any building, with only the two of us present. Here he explained that he strongly suspected that his own division G-2 (intelligence officer) was a Viet Cong agent; thus he did not dare discuss operational matters in his own command post.[5]

That the opposing side had a highly developed intelligence and espionage net is well known. Merle Pribbenow sent me an annotated list of some of the most prominent agents who penetrated the highest French and South Vietnamese government and military offices, to include those of Chairman of the South Vietnamese Joint General Staff and President of the Republic of Vietnam. What is not so well known are the details of their operations. Merle included translations of some of their mind-boggling activities.

Colonel Dinh Thi Van was a spy who received the title of "Hero of the People's Armed Forces," a very high award. Van was born in the North and was active in espionage against the French. Like so many dedicated Communists, she was prepared to sacrifice her family life and her life itself for Uncle Ho. She had a husband and a mother she loved very much, but she urged her husband to find another wife so she could continue her espionage, and her mother told her she indeed had a higher duty to perform: "Leave us and do your duty."

For five years she worked assiduously in the South to establish a growing network of agents who started off in minor civil and military positions and then worked their way up. She traveled from Saigon north to the DMZ and back, ostensibly as a vendor of various goods while recruiting agents and helping to set up the network necessary for communication with first Hanoi, then COSVN. Through her contacts in Central Vietnam she visited several high officials: the province chief of Quang Tri, the commanding general of South Vietnam's 1st Division, an official in the Public Security Ministry, and even President Diem's sister and his brother, Ngo Dinh Can, the powerful warlord.[6]

One of her agents was captured and he, to save himself, informed on her. She was tortured for weeks. Through every horror she said, "I remembered Uncle Ho's words, 'never surrender to violence,' and I mumbled: 'My Uncle, I will hold on to the end, I may die, but I will never surrender to the enemy. I will live up to the honor of being a member of your Party.'"[7] Across many months then years of imprisonment her interrogators inflicted multiple tortures that left her unconscious and in pain, and they tried every conceivable psychological ploy to get her to reveal her contacts. They brought some of those contacts before her, those who had been discovered and given the choice to help reform other cadre or die. Still she refused to admit anything other than being a vendor.

Finally, never having revealed anything, in 1964 she was released in terrible health. She discovered that in the five years of her imprisonment, one of her agents had worked his way up to become Nguyen Khanh's bodyguard. Khanh was the general who overthrew Duong Van Minh, the general who succeeded to power when Diem was assassinated.[8] This agent had bribed Khanh's interrogators of a captured high-ranking intelligence cadre, giving them "a huge sum of money" to secure his release. Two agents who had been recruited by her were officers in the Ministry of Defense.

Another agent was Ha Dang, whom she loved as a son and had informally adopted. He became a company commander in the ARVN 5th Division headquartered on Route 13 at Ben Cat.

He gave her information on the defense system along that main highway which, at that time in 1969, I was tasked to secure. He told her that he and two U.S. officers regularly used a U.S. Army L19 observation plane to reconnoiter the whole route system, and he gave her that information plus operational plans of the 5th Division which led to a "victory" over GVN forces in a battle. She said,

> As a lieutenant and a skillful scout, Dang had won the liking of senior colonel Pham Quoc Thuan, Commander of the division. [Dang] told us that in the office, he was allowed to … hear all the reports. In many of Thuan's visits to examine the units, Ha Dang was chosen to be the liaison officer. It was time for me to assign him a specific duty: … their defense system plans…. [and] the enemy's military activities in the tactical zone …. "Keep track of the [locations] of U.S. units, particularly [those of 1st Division, Big Red One]."

Another of Van's agents, Phiet, as a junior officer had established a close friendship with a lieutenant colonel in the G-3 office of the General Staff. This office was responsible for South Vietnamese military plans and operations throughout South Vietnam and thus was a goldmine of information.

> Phiet grasped all stages of the U.S.-puppet's search and destroy campaign for Junction City. The lieutenant colonel shared with Phiet crucial and secret information concerning the enemy's operation plans and the deliberations between [the colonel] and General Westmoreland and Cao Van Vien, Chairman of the South Vietnamese Joint General Staff.

One evening in the lieutenant colonel's home, he copied a manuscript about launching a huge campaign aimed at destroying COSVN and would require 40,000 soldiers: Operation *Junction City*.

Van said, "One month and two days later, the Janson-City [sic] campaign was launched. Our Command had known about a number of the campaign's battle plans and had been well prepared to strike back."[9] Sometime after the operation ended, Van got news that the Party had awarded a medal to Phiet for his great work in uncovering the American plans for *Junction City*.

COSVN's System of Defense for *Junction City*

The second aspect of *Junction City* that is instructive on why the war was unwinnable militarily flows naturally from the espionage, and that is the system of defense devised by COSVN. Parts of two enemy histories sent to me by Pribbenow treat the 9th Division's defense and COSVN headquarters' role in Operation *Junction City*.

Senior colonel Hoang Cam commanded 9th Infantry Division of about 9,000 men. Having been well briefed on what espionage had uncovered, he said that COSVN stated:

> This will be the largest operation that the Americans and the puppets have ever conducted, and the primary direction for the enemy's first attack prong will be to destroy our base area and to find and destroy the headquarters and leadership agencies of COSVN and the 9th Division in order to win a military victory of decisive importance.[10]

Cam explained that COSVN had only two choices, defend the base area or retreat into Cambodia to "try to create an opportunity to attack them [later]." Believing they could inflict serious damage on the Americans in this jungle arena, they chose the first, defend. In order to unify command and use all troops to the maximum, the base area was divided into "districts" and further into "villages," each with its own commander. Additional weapons were issued, and even headquarters troops trained as infantry squads, platoons, and companies and rehearsed various scenarios. (They had plenty of time to do this, given Westmoreland's seven-month planning stage.)

"The 9th Division's main force troops, who had been issued additional heavy weapons, and especially B-40 anti-tank rockets [RPGs], were stationed at locations from which they could easily move in any direction." Cam briefed his staff and commanders. His concept was "to force the enemy to fight the kind of battle we wanted to fight."[11]

"The kind of battle we wanted to fight" was always the goal which our enemy trained carefully to accomplish.

Rogers said that "On D-Day, eight infantry battalions assaulted by helicopter, and one parachuted into a drop zone." Only one battalion received sporadic small arms fire. The other insertions were unopposed. Rogers said, "Throughout the day enemy contact and casualties remained light." The next day two squadrons of 11th Armored Cavalry Regiment and 2nd Brigade of 25th Division "thrust northward.... Only four minor contacts were made during the day's search."

Phase I lasted for 18 more days. "During this period the action was marked mainly by contacts with small forces (one to ten men) and the continual discovery of more and more base camps." To have 40,000 U.S. and Vietnamese troops engaged in search and destroy within a confined area and not have more than small contacts would have been unusual since a full enemy division plus COSVN headquarters units were thought to have been there. The logical explanation is that Colonel Cam did not see conditions right for fighting the kind of battle he wanted to fight. Additionally, because the key agencies of COSVN headquarters had by this time certainly left the horseshoe area, 9th Division did not have to worry about defending them.

Rogers said: "During the twenty-nine days of Phase II operations in which intensive searching and destruction were performed, there were only three major battles, all initiated by the enemy."[12] Phase III continued for another twenty days, "but the organized enemy units became almost impossible to find. Most of the contacts made were with relatively small Viet Cong groups."[13]

The Admiral Sharp/General Westmoreland official *Report on the War in Vietnam* stated, "Junction City convinced the enemy command that continuing to base main force units in close proximity to the key population areas would be increasingly foolhardy." That statement makes one wonder: Had Westmoreland forgotten that soon after *Junction City* the enemy was able to base his divisions again in War Zone C—the location of *Junction City*—and in War Zone D? Had he forgotten that from those two war zones during Tet '68, enemy divisions had emerged to attack Saigon and the outlying populated areas? It has been claimed many times that American units never lost a battle, that when the firing ended we were always the owner of the battlefield. Almost always true, if we speak of battalion level and above. Our firepower and ability to reinforce assured it. And true if we speak of the hours during and immediately following the battle. But where was the enemy the next day, the next week, the next month, the next year? Often, if he wished, he was back in those same locations, up to strength again, usually performing as before, or better.

The enemy had gotten early warning by espionage and was well prepared. Despite being on the defensive, according to Rogers' report they gained the initiative by attacking where they chose, when they chose. And which is better, to be the force standing on the battleground after the battle, or be the force that returns and retains it until the war is over?

Frustrations of Search and Destroy for Westmoreland

Westmoreland said, "Our strength was too limited to maintain enough troops in War Zone C to prevent the enemy from reentering it later."[14] Rogers had confirmed for *Cedar Falls* that the Iron Triangle was again "literally crawling" with enemy. The problem was the same with *Junction City*: "Reconnaissance flights over War Zone C following *Junction City* revealed that the enemy was returning." In 1969 my task force captured prisoners and documents which made clear that the enemy knew the safest place to be was in the area where American troops had just completed an operation. American troops did not hang around. They were ordered to go on other search and destroy missions.

Despite having an enormous number of troops, many times more than those of the enemy, it is true that Westmoreland did not have enough to enable him to stay in these areas even though in the case of *Junction City* he had wished to do so. But why should he wish to stay in jungle? In almost all cases, it was a mistake to go there in the first place and would have been a bigger mistake to stay. Search and destroy itself was a mistake. The enemy conducted war across the full range of his capabilities—guerrilla, regional, main force—and did so at all times with at least guerrilla forces across much of South Vietnam. A fixation on search and destroy required meeting those challenges, so Westmoreland hopped his divisions and brigades around to meet the trial of the moment.

Regarding jungle-clearing: Rogers wrote, "The success of the jungle-destruction operation using Rome Plows, bulldozers, and tank dozers was particularly impressive.

However, the discouraging aspect of such operations is that it takes but a short time for the jungle to grow again."

The jungle did not cooperate. The enemy was no better. Rogers said, "It was a sheer impossibility to keep him from slipping away if he were in terrain with which he was familiar—generally the case. The jungle is usually just too thick and too widespread to hope ever to keep him from getting away; thus the option to fight was usually his."[15]

Did those generals—Westmoreland and Rogers—have any clue that what they said about their search and destroy operations was so damning to them? They had invested enormous resources in those operations in areas where in most cases the enemy had the distinct advantage, where he could do pretty much what he wanted when he wanted. The generals, fighting with conventional war tactics, claimed victories when hundreds of their soldiers were killed and thousands wounded in areas which the enemy quickly regained. And the generals kept on doing more of the same.

Covert War by MACV's "Studies and Observation Group" (SOG)

As *Junction City* demonstrated, the North Vietnamese and NLF/Viet Cong were highly successful in carrying out covert war against the South. How did the South Vietnamese government and Americans fare in covert war against them?

Although the South Vietnamese were able to place some spies of their own in enemy units in South Vietnam, the results were nowhere near as beneficial to them as was espionage for the North and NLF/VC.

President Kennedy had been enthusiastic about not just special forces operations generally, but conducting covert warfare specifically. At first he relied on the CIA, but by 1962, after the 1961 Bay of Pigs failure, Secretary of Defense McNamara was shepherding a transition of responsibility for covert operations to the Department of Defense, and by July 1962, planning was underway for what in January 1964 became the highly secret MACVSOG—MACV's euphemistically labeled "Studies and Observation Group" (SOG). Their four covert missions were: agent networks and deception programs, maritime raids, psychological warfare, and cross-border operations against the Ho Chi Minh Trail.[16]

The CIA had been virtually unsuccessful in conducting any kind of covert war against North Vietnam. This was hardly surprising in view of that country's reputation as the most difficult to penetrate of what in intelligence circles was called "denied areas"—the other areas being the Soviet Union, countries in the Soviet Bloc, Communist China, and North Korea.[17]

The DRV had highly efficient internal security involving several of its agencies, as well as population control. Ultimately SOG was little more successful than the CIA. Virtually all SOG operatives became highly trained, and teams that were inserted were superbly courageous. However, with the exceptions of operations against the Ho Chi Minh Trail which provided useful intelligence, and against some clandestine radio relay stations, in the long run the rest was almost fruitless. The North quickly caught on to insertion teams and captured, killed or turned virtually all of the SOG covert agents into working for the North.

***

The South Vietnamese election of mid-1967, which critics claimed with more than a little justification was corrupt, saw Thieu now elected as president with full powers of a presidency. The defeated, bitter Ky was vice president, an arrangement not likely to bode well for strengthening the South but which more or less worked until Ky later dropped out of formal politics and reverted to his air force role. With Thieu's

President Nguyen Van Thieu (on President Lyndon Johnson's right) and (then) Premier Nguyen Cao Ky (on left), with Defense Secretary McNamara behind Ky during honors at the Honolulu Conference, February 6, 1966. (NARA)

gain of power, the arrangement provided a measure of stability over the highly volatile politics of the past.

Major General Frederick C. Weyand, commanding general of 25th Infantry Division 1964–67, believed that pacification, providing security for hamlets and villages was the way to success, not Westmoreland's search and destroy. His *New York Times* obituary on February 13, 2010 stated, "At a cocktail party in Saigon in 1967, General Weyand, speaking of Westmoreland, had told Murray Fromson, a CBS news correspondent: 'Westy just doesn't get it. The war is unwinnable. We've reached a stalemate, and we should find a dignified way out.... I've destroyed a single division three times,' General Weyand said. 'I've chased main-force units all over the country, and the impact was zilch. It meant nothing to the people. Unless a more positive and more stirring theme than simple anti-Communism can be found, the war appears likely to go on until someone gets tired and quits, which could take generations.'"

Westmoreland reportedly was furious at this leak. Looking at the overall Vietnam scene he saw much progress. When he went back to the U.S. in November 1967 to meet with President Johnson and address Congress, he used the phrase, "light at the end of the tunnel."

President Johnson and General Westmoreland at the White House, November 16, 1967. (NARA)

1968, the Tet Offensive, a Refutation of Search and Destroy

And then two months later—Tet!

So much has been written and broadcast about the Tet Offensive which erupted on January 30, 1968 that there is no need to detail it here. What is not well known is that planning for it had its genesis in Le Duan's 1959 rise to power. At first, he reluctantly had shelved for the time being his desire to move aggressively on the South, uneasy and inwardly resentful at Ho's and Giap's warnings that the North was not ready to push for a general offensive/general uprising in which main-force units would attack and overrun the major cities of the South, and the Southern people would simultaneously respond in a massive uprising.

Le Duan got his chance in mid-1967 when Senior General Van Tien Dung (the same rank as Giap) maneuvered to remove himself as Giap's deputy and get chosen by Le Duan to plan, together, the 1968 Tet offensive. In mid-1967 Le Duan's internal security forces began purging moderates in the Party who would oppose such a move in what came to be called "The Revisionist Anti-Party Affair." By October some of the highest-ranking members had been placed under house arrest, including generals on Giap's staff.[18] Giap saw the handwriting on the wall and "left for Eastern Europe and did not return until well into 1968, after the Tet offensive. Ho Chi Minh followed suit and left for Beijing [ostensibly] to convalesce [from his illness of 1967]."[19]

The relationship of Le Duan with both Ho and Giap during and shortly after Tet in terms of power seems to have been one of accommodation. What is clear is that Ho returned, still very much revered for his past leadership. Giap returned and resumed his duties as head of the Central Military Committee and as Defense Minister, his talents still much needed in the aftermath of disastrous Tet casualties.

Although Westmoreland was never to acknowledge it, the Tet '68 Offensive starkly revealed the failure of his attrition strategy and its trappings: search and destroy, body count, kill ratio. For the enemy, Tet '68 was a military defeat but a huge psychological and political victory. For the Americans, Tet '68 virtually extinguished the light at the end of the tunnel and soon kicked Westmoreland upstairs, out of Vietnam to become Army Chief of Staff in the Pentagon.

An Alternative Strategy?

The enemy's strategy throughout the war was the offensive, always the offensive. Giap said, "Our military art is permeated with the idea of active attack on the enemy. It is mainly the art of attack. Imbued with the strategic idea of offensive in the revolutionary war, let us in our armed struggle actively attack the enemy in a resolute, continuous and thorough manner with all forces and weapons, in all forms, on all scales, everywhere and at all times."[20] And so it was. For 30 years throughout the country from north to south, in daylight and darkness the French colonialists, American "imperialists," and their "puppets" were subjected to resolute attack.

Tet '68 reveals how an alternative U.S. strategy could have yielded far better results from 1965 through early 1968 during Westmoreland's tenure in Vietnam. He had said he would not sit back and wait for the enemy to come to him. He did not sit back, but in Tet '68 the enemy came to him—in spades. Main and regional forces left their jungle base camps and exposed themselves in fiercely attacking cities and villages, aided by local units and guerrillas who also necessarily revealed themselves in order to accomplish their missions of guiding the main units, and sabotaging and attacking critical installations. The attackers at all levels were hurt badly by a combination of rigorous defense and punishing counterattacks, quickly improvised by American, South Vietnamese, and other Free World military forces.

When American combat units arrived in 1965, a defensive-offensive strategy throughout South Vietnam coupled with pacification and Vietnamization might have been an excellent choice if planned well and executed intelligently and aggressively. When Westmoreland and other generals were junior and mid-level officers they had studied fundamentals of the defense along with other forms of warfare. Army field manuals such as FM 100-5, *Operations* (1965) discuss how valuable a mobile defense can be: "Mobile defense orients on the destruction of the enemy force by employing a combination of fire and maneuver, offense, defense, and delay to defeat the attack.... Defenders place minimum forces forward, forming powerful forces with which to strike the enemy at his most vulnerable time and place." Westmoreland's airmobile infantry, mechanized infantry, armor, armored cavalry, and air cavalry could move, shoot, and communicate better than any other forces in the world. As to fixed defensive positions which could blunt or channel an enemy attack so that mobile units could engage them, his straight-leg infantry and ARVN could have well handled that.

In most cases, in order for the enemy's combat forces to strike populated areas they would have to leave their jungle base areas and expose themselves in open or relatively open terrain. They did this in Tet '68. And they paid a horrible price. The aggressive defensive-offensive actions by American, South Vietnamese, and Allied forces during Tet '68 exacted a terrible toll on them.

Instead of search and destroy—which squandered forces with little gain to show for it, and from which the enemy was always able to recover and reoccupy the ground temporarily lost—American and Allied forces could have worked closely with South Vietnamese in pacification. They could have simultaneously equipped and trained them (Vietnamization) if that had been Westmoreland's intention. He spoke of it, planned it, even tried it, but the reality was that under him the plan did not work well because search and destroy was his priority. Westmoreland's units could have

THE BIG, BIG UNIT WAR, 1967–MID-1968 • 157

been integrated into defensive-offensive configurations around selected cities and villages. They could have patrolled extensively out from them, ambushed, and used special forces in a manner which suited them well: longer range reconnaissance patrols to locate the enemy. One can think of other ways in which, from 1965 when our first ground combat units arrived, they could have been employed other than to pit them against enemy main and regional forces in terrain where the enemy always would have the advantage.

A problem with allowing enemy forces to remove from his bases to attack populated areas was that if he could secretly move and strike, as he did in Tet '68, then civilians and their property would be badly hurt in trying to eject him, and they would lose further faith in the South Vietnamese government. This was a conundrum which persisted throughout the war. It might not have come to this so dramatically as in Tet '68 if, instead of conducting search and destroy operations in deep jungle, troops had patrolled and ambushed aggressively out from the fringes of pacification zones in order to detect and identify enemy units, and as these units tried to move on populated areas, struck them in a mobile defense before they could do so much damage. That is what the Marines wanted to do early on in I Corps, but Westmoreland wanted them out on search and destroy. General Bruce Palmer, briefly commander of IIFFV, later deputy to Westmoreland as essentially the commander of U.S. Army, Vietnam (USARV), said, "Our greatest battle successes occurred when the enemy chose to attack a U.S. unit well dug in and prepared to defend its position. As enemy forces learned about the devastating impact of greatly superior U.S. firepower, both ground and air-delivered, they became less inclined to attack."[21]

In discussing Tet '68, Westmoreland said,

> In the prior months of fighting, I had learned conclusively that it was when the enemy came out of hiding to make some major attack that American firepower could be brought to bear with tremendous effect. Even though we might incur some temporary setbacks if he came out of hiding to make a "maximum effort," it would be the beginning ... "of a great defeat for the enemy."[22]

Yes! Yes, Yes, YES!!

That is exactly what happened during Tet '68 in February, and in much weaker follow-up enemy attacks we called "mini-Tet" in April and May. The enemy was hurt so badly, as admitted in their histories, that the Viet Cong infrastructure took months, in some places years, to recover. The NVA main forces were able to rebuild and retrain fairly quickly, and there was plenty of fighting against NVA main forces later in 1968 and 1969, as I, Colonel Burcham, and our troopers and soldiers can attest. The enemy, however, had been hurt so badly that it was spring of 1972 before they could again muster the kind of main force strength they had had at Tet '68. Since enemy histories loudly proclaim great victories, preposterously inflating the losses they inflicted on their enemy, when they acknowledge weakness, this is noteworthy. Their official history, *Victory in Vietnam*, admitted this, relative to Tet '68:

> Our soldiers' morale had been very high when they set off for battle, but because we had made only one-sided preparations, only looking at the possibilities of victory and failing to prepare for adversity, when the battle did not progress favorably for our side and when we suffered casualties, rightist thoughts, pessimism, and hesitancy appeared among our forces.[23]

Translated into the actual circumstances of the battles of Tet '68, those words are an admission that the counterattacks on their exposed forces of all types—guerrilla, local and regional units, and main force units—were devastating. Some of the division histories are much more honest than the official history, and they describe how difficult were their circumstances and how terrible their losses.

If Westmoreland knew, as he said, that when the enemy exposed himself he was hurt badly, why then from mid-1965 to the end of his command in April 1968—nearly three years—did he persist in sending American troops into the jungle after base camps where we suffered so many casualties? He might have been able with a strong pacification and Vietnamization campaign, using U.S. combat troops in the defensive-offensive manner sketched above, or some such other concept, to have strengthened South Vietnam's chances for survival.

That a defensive-offensive concept had merit at the highest U.S. military level was acknowledged in post-Tet comments made during a Weekly Intelligence Estimate Update (WIEU) briefing by General Abrams, the MACV commander who succeeded Westmoreland. In attendance was General George S. Brown, Deputy COMUSMACV for Air Operations, and Commander, Seventh Air Force (1968–70). Brown replied,

> It's clear that we kill more troops, we kill troops best, when they mass and they're attacking. That's when you can really mow them down. Now, if you adopt an attitude of chase them around in the bush, and keeping them off balance all the time so they never can get massed, and on the other hand you can't find them, you're not killing troops as rapidly as if you did something else for a while, let him mass, and then bashed him.[24]

Khe Sanh, A Different Kind of Battle

Khe Sanh, like Dien Bien Phu, began as a place nobody in the outside world had ever heard of. McNamara's planners of his 1966–67 defensive barrier line—"McNamara's Wall, or Fence, or Jungle Maginot Line"—incorporated this small outpost on Route Coloniale 9 as one of many along the line which lay just south of the demilitarized zone separating North and South Vietnam. Route 9 had been important as a colonial east–west trade route from Savannakhet on the Mekong River in Laos to Quang Tri on the Gulf of Tonkin. As an indigenous outpost with a U.S. Special Forces detachment and a small airstrip, Khe Sanh was intended to interfere with any enemy movement out of Laos toward Quang Tri, a vital city in I Corps in the populous lowlands along the coast. Westmoreland was looking to provide a base of operations for SOG to interdict the Ho Chi Minh Trail. His strong belief in the value of Khe Sanh led to improvement of the airstrip, movement of the main fortification a bit farther west, garrisoning it with Marines and strong artillery support, and outposting the surrounding hills with Marines.

Except for patrolling and jostling back and forth for positioning, for a year not much on a large scale happened. Then during the night of January 20/21, 1968 shells rained down on the camp, and the enemy attacked fiercely behind a massive artillery barrage. Soon two divisions had virtually encircled the position and thus began a 77-day battle and siege, the longest, most discussed battle in a single location of the American war. It has been so much documented that there is no need to detail it.

As the size and ferocity of the battle at this distant, forsaken spot quickly mounted, President Johnson showed his concern. He got assurances from his military men, to include Westmoreland, that the enemy would not take Khe Sanh. Enormous airpower and ground reinforcement capability ensured it. The media and armchair generals around the world were so fascinated with what they saw as parallels to Dien Bien Phu that Americans were glued to the battle in front of their television screens. That is—until the Tet Offensive erupted on January 30, a week after the initial Khe Sanh attack. Then the viewers had two critical situations confronting them.

***

At the time of Tet, I was at Command and General Staff College, Fort Leavenworth, with orders to Vietnam upon completion. My dear friend, Major John Martin, was an engineer in a unit near Hue. On February 7, 1968 I went to teach an evening class for University of Kansas at a branch campus in Leavenworth. When I returned home, an ashen-faced Sandra met me at the door.

"What's wrong?"

She put her hands on my shoulders and said, "John Martin is missing."

Before John had left for Vietnam, Kaki had insisted that the SOB not get killed on her. They had five wonderful children, a marvelous, rambunctious family. All Sandra knew was that an aircraft had been shot down near Hue with John in it and he was missing. We had two weeks of waiting, not knowing. Then on February 21 we got word. All aboard had been killed. The cost of the war came down hard.

***

As the fighting at Khe Sanh dragged on, with the garrison, the nearby Lang Vei strongpoint, and the outposts in the hills absorbing ferocious attacks, and with artillery, tactical air strikes and B-52s pounding the enemy positions, it became apparent that the final casualty figures would be huge, and they were. The accounting was confusing, but for certain the friendly KIAs were in the several hundreds, and enemy dead in the several thousands. In the war there was not another battle on such a scale in which essentially the Americans defended a fortified position while pounding enemy outside it with massive artillery and air strikes. Westmoreland viewed it as a victory: "Khe Sanh," he said, "had evolved as one of the most damaging, one-sided defeats among many that the North Vietnamese incurred, and the myth of General Giap's military genius was discredited."[25] Giap also viewed it as a victory, having successfully drawn significant forces away from cities which were attacked during Tet. Perhaps Khe Sanh can best be described as a bloody draw. In late June, a week after Westmoreland left Vietnam for good, the new MACV commander, General Abrams, ordered the base closed. The NVA had lost interest and, after U.S. forces left, committed only a company to reoccupying it and raising their flag over the razed ground as a psychological statement.

***

The nature of the war had changed dramatically in 1967, but no one outside the most secret inner councils of the Politburo would know it until 1968. The highest levels of political and military leadership in North Vietnam had decided in meetings from June to August 1967 that guerrilla and small-unit warfare would continue, as always, but from Tet '68 forward, the war would essentially turn on the success or failure of "big battalions," "big battles." Americans and South Vietnamese in Tet '68 had opportunity to employ enormous firepower on massed enemy. They would have it again in 1972, and the South Vietnamese would finally have a diminished version of it in 1974–75.

CHAPTER II

General Abrams, "One War," mid-1968 to Early 1969

In the aftermath of the Tet Offensive, President Johnson's address to the nation on March 31, 1968 dramatically launched a new era in the war, one in which the United States offered to stop the bombing of North Vietnam and withdraw troops in exchange for the other side withdrawing forces to the north and entering peace talks. He electrified the world by stating, "I shall not seek, and I will not accept, the nomination of my party for another term as your President." On May 13, representatives of the United States and the Democratic Republic of Vietnam met in Paris for exploratory talks.

After Westmoreland left Vietnam to become Chief of Staff, in early June 1968 General Creighton Abrams officially took command of MACV.

"One War"

Abrams introduced a new strategy. He spoke often and emphatically with commanders and staff about his "one war" concept. He said that pacification was not "the other war" as it had been called, but part of a unified strategy which had security for the people in the hamlets and villages of Vietnam as its centerpiece, thus making it possible for them to be won over to the South Vietnamese government.

"'The enemy's operational pattern is his understanding that this is just one, repeat one war,' stressed Abrams. 'He knows there's no such thing as a war of big battalions, a war of pacification, or a war of territorial security. Friendly forces have got to recognize and understand the one war concept and carry the battle to the enemy, simultaneously in all areas of conflict.'"[1]

Abrams was absolutely correct in that the enemy had always fought one war. Ho Chi Minh had begun the war against the French in late December1944 with Giap's attack by only a platoon with a two-fold mission—fight and proselytize. From then

General Creighton W. Abrams, 1967. (NARA)

on it was fight the French, Americans and South Vietnamese "puppets" using all means. And proselytize. Even during periods of big battles, proselytizing continued, all one war for one goal—to win.

General Weyand, who rose from 25th Division to IIFFV commander, then succeeded Abrams as commander of MACV said, "The tactics changed within fifteen minutes of Abrams' taking command."[2]

The problem with Weyand's statement is that the tactics did not change. If any American general could have "won" the war, Abrams would have been the one to do it. He was the very best that America had to offer—a great soldier, a man of prodigious energy and keen intellect. I, and many others, had then, and have still, the utmost admiration and respect for him. But the fact is that pacification and Vietnamization, two core aspects of the one war concept, continued to be seriously short-changed by the orders and actions of Abrams' subordinate commanders. For reasons I still ponder because of his forthright style of leadership and high standards, they continued with search and destroy. Large numbers of troops were committed to missions in terrain and circumstances which favored the enemy, as during Westmoreland's command.

I can attest to the minimal effect. Since 11th Cav was a IIFFV unit I sometimes got to listen to Abrams and his IIFFV commander, and also to brief Abrams on 11th Cav operations. Then, in 1st Division as a battalion-level commander, because of the helicopter I could be with the division generals doing the directing and, only a few minutes later, be down among my soldiers doing the fighting and dying. Until mid-1969 when I left Vietnam, 1st Division, including my task force, continued essentially as a search and destroy force, as did the other American divisions.

In another division Colonel Burcham had similar experience with the continuation of search and destroy during Abrams' command:

> During my command of an infantry battalion in the 1st Air Cavalry Division in 1969, the Division's primary mission was to block NVA main force movements from their Cambodian sanctuaries towards Saigon. Battalion areas of operation (AOs) and missions were assigned accordingly. My mission, as well as that of my sister battalions, was purely to search for and destroy enemy forces within or attempting to infiltrate through our respective battalion AOs.

11th Armored Cavalry Regiment and "One War"

In July 1968 I joined 11th Armored Cavalry Regiment, the famed Blackhorse regiment. Colonel George S. Patton, who had been my company tactical officer as a captain at West Point, and whom I had not seen or talked to since then, had taken command of 11th ACR only a few days earlier. He had seen my orders and gotten me assigned to his command. Patton was Abrams' protégé.

General Abrams had been one of the elder Patton's battalion commanders, leading the counterattack of Third Army at Bastogne. Abrams was a tough, courageous, highly intelligent fighter. For his valor he was awarded two Distinguished Service Crosses and two Silver Stars. In sending Abrams to Vietnam as Westmoreland's deputy, President Johnson had given him the mission of improving Vietnam's armed forces. During his year with Westmoreland he did what he could for Vietnamization, with the goal of equipping and training Vietnamese forces so they could take over the war.

I was flown to regimental forward headquarters at Lai Khe where a captain met me and took me to see Colonel Patton. "Goddamn, Bill, I've got work for you!" he greeted me, clapping me on the shoulder. This was the energetic, profuse, profane Patton I knew from cadet days twelve years earlier, only with graying hair and lines in his face, son of Old Blood and Guts. "Come on," Patton said, "here's what's going on." He propelled me into what turned out to be the briefing tent and began slapping a pointer onto the operations map. In maybe five minutes of fast talking he covered several weeks of cav affairs in actual time, bringing me up to the present. Then Patton rushed me into his helicopter and we were off to check on units. We overflew some positions as Patton gave me a detailed run-down on our units, the terrain, and enemy. Then we landed at other units where I talked with some of the men. Thus began an unforgettable tour with Colonel George S. Patton in combat.

The highlights of my experiences in Vietnam, I believe, are important as a reflection of the whole war, its instances of what appeared to be American successes, and its failures, which often were not so apparent at the time. In these first hours with Patton I realized that being inserted into a war was not an entry into history; it is a step into the unknown, and you either create everything around you or it is created for you.

I quickly learned the specifics of what was going on and took my place in the action. Each event that cropped up was something new and had to be dealt with in terms of the conditions of the moment, not something that had happened to the Chinese a thousand years ago, or to the French twenty years earlier, or even to our own unit yesterday. And if I, with briefings and maps, felt this immediacy, and my most urgent duty was to grasp the circumstances of the moment, act to meet them, and plan for the next, what was it like for our troopers—a driver in an armored cavalry assault vehicle (ACAV) or a tank who knew only that he was the first vehicle in column on a treacherous dirt road and that his track commander would tell him when to turn left or right into jungle so dense he would often lose sight of an adjacent vehicle?

Letter to Sandra, 21 Jul 68. "I've been at the command post at Lai Khe now for a little over 24 hours and, needless to say, have been very busy. The responsibility is awesome; we have over 4600 men, hundreds of armored vehicles, and thousands of pieces of major equipment. In terms of sheer firepower, the regiment is the most powerful ground combat unit in Vietnam."

An armored cav regiment was a magnificently organized, equipped, and trained instrument of war—for World War II. And for facing the Soviets in Europe during the Cold War. But for Vietnam?

Through necessity and innovation we did things that seemed impossible. But we were indeed very heavy, very loud, we ate up enormous resources, and we damaged the countryside just by our movements, to say nothing of the results of our enormous firepower. That has to be weighed while considering our overall contribution in the very complex Vietnam War.

The regiment never operated as a pure cav regiment. Rather, dependent upon mission, it was divested of some of its elements such as one or more squadrons (battalion-size) or ground troops (company size), and it acquired others—one or more U.S. infantry straight-leg or mechanized battalions and an ARVN Ranger battalion, in a flexible system called operational control, or opcon. Sometimes our organic, attached, and opcon or direct support strength approached 6,000 men.

On July 2, 1968, his second day at 11th Cav, Colonel Patton had exhibited his traditional training. His memo to his staff and subordinate commanders stated, "This is basically a reconnaissance war keyed to the meeting engagement." Soon, though, he learned that this old concept was way off the mark except for our air cavalry troop. The enemy would not cooperate by using outdated conventional methods of warfare, and neither would the jungle or swampy terrain or the villages and hamlets containing enemy who were everywhere. Patton adjusted his thinking.

Our regiment had been in country since September 1966, assigned to II Field Force Vietnam (IIFFV), the corps-size headquarters which was responsible for all American forces in Cochinchina from the northern outskirts of Saigon, north and west to Cambodia, and east to the South China Sea. When I arrived, the regiment was opcon to 1st Infantry Division and remained that way for the six months I was with Patton. Our operations covered a huge area. It went all the way from Xuan Loc (about 50 miles east of Saigon) west to Long Binh/Bien Hoa, north on the western side of critical Highway 13 almost to An Loc (about 60 miles from Saigon), and sometimes included a large portion of War Zone C to the west of Highway 13. Infamous War Zone D was in our area of responsibility, consisting of rugged farmland which turned into dense jungle as it went farther to the east of Highway 13 and Lai Khe.

Assisting the regimental commander in planning and controlling all regimental tactical operations was the tactical operations center (TOC), or Command Post (CP). As Regimental S-3, I was in charge of it. Basically, it was manned by personnel from our staff sections S-2 (Intelligence); S-3 (Plans, Operations, and Training); Communications; and also liaison personnel from 1st Infantry Division, Division Artillery, Air Force, and Vietnamese units. During the day I would have about three dozen or so people in or close around it at any one time, and at night about a dozen, more when we had contact with the enemy. In these early days I flew with Colonel Patton every day and quickly got to know a lot about our units, personnel, area of operations (AO), and enemy.

Clear and Hold?

I had heard that Abrams wanted a change from "search and destroy" to "clear and hold" tactics, and that small-unit ambushes and patrols were preferable to large assaults into deep jungle. Clear meant to drive the enemy out of a certain territory, primarily a village, and then to keep it clear of them indefinitely. In reality there was not a complete switch to clear and hold away from jungle sweeps, at least not in 11th Cav, and, as I was soon to discover, also not in other units of 1st Infantry

Division. When I first met Abrams a week or so into my tour, I agreed with "clear and hold." But I saw that in fact, following Division orders, we were deep into search and destroy, and we continued that way. Patton's motto, known to all troopers, was "Find the bastards and pile on." We were trying to do that even in the jungle, and Abrams knew this and did not correct us. IIFFV, 1st Infantry Division, and other divisions and brigades continued with search and destroy with Abrams' tacit, if not direct, concurrence.

My journal: "22 Jul 68. So many killed and wounded for no visible gain. We go into The Catcher's Mitt, busting jungle and losing men without killing many enemy." "The Catcher's Mitt" was in War Zone D, northeast of Saigon and east of Lai Khe, south of the Song Be River. Busting jungle—crashing through it with our 50-ton tanks and 14-ton ACAVs—was almost always a loser. We all hated jungle busting, and from my earliest days with the Cav I strove for ways to reduce our casualties and yet accomplish our given missions in this terribly hostile territory. The enemy would have to have been stone deaf not to hear us and see the trees shake as we pushed up against them, knocking down upon us nests of red ants that bit like hell and, in jungle defoliated with Agent Orange and other toxins, creating a shower of dust and debris from dead leaves that would choke us and decades later give us the cancers that many of our men and I contracted.

In the jungle the enemy would try to place mines where they thought we would pass, or wait at the edge of small clearings—which we always tried to avoid—to fire RPGs at us. Most often we did not know where the enemy was, but they knew where we were. We were worse than an enormous mass of elephants shoving and trumpeting through dense growth. In such places the advantage was always with the enemy. But those were our orders from 1st Division—sweep—as inept a term as has ever been devised for armor operations in jungle—sweep meant search and destroy. There was no Abrams' clear and hold in the jungle of War Zone D. Little to clear—they heard us coming—and nothing to hold.

Strategic Hamlet

On July 28 I recorded in my journal, "At dawn flew out w/Col. to see how the resettlement operation was progressing. It was pathetic to look at the hamlet and see the kids scurrying around, see the people in their activities, and know that we were going to level the place [by Division orders]."

At the time, I wondered how this Strategic Hamlet policy could possibly result in "winning hearts and minds," a simplistic term I disliked and never used. The policy was a short-range expedient with dramatic long-term negative results. Should we ever have wondered that the displaced people would hate us and the ARVN for doing this to them?

On a visit to National Archives I found a 1st Division memorandum dated July 16, 1968 documenting the plans for resettlement of three hamlets in War Zone D at the edge of the jungle, and thus favorite spots for VC infiltration and logistics operations. As it turned out, we razed the one we had visited that day. The hamlet of Binh Co, though, was left standing, and it would play a profound role in my Vietnam experience and my life.

Briefing Abrams

On July 31, I was in the TOC when Patton thrust his head in and bellowed, "Haponski, get your ass over to the briefing tent! Abrams is landing in zero two [two minutes]. Give him a briefing."

No sweat. With eleven days on the job, I was going to brief the commander of ground forces in Vietnam. Abrams later was to make several visits to us in both our headquarters and wherever we were in field operations.

Actually the briefing should be no sweat, I thought. I had learned our units well from having visited them, studied the maps, talked to the commanders and men, and knew how they fit into the overall mission. By now I had planned some of what they were doing and gone on a couple missions with units.

No sweat. Except that this was an enormously hot day under the canvas, and everyone was sweating profusely. I had grabbed a pointer and barely finished checking the latest grease pencil markings on the acetate overlay of the operations map which showed the current friendly and enemy situations when Patton barked from the briefing tent entrance, "Atten—*shun!*"

A rumpled man with a baseball cap sporting four black stars, and with a fat, half-smoked cigar thrust into the corner of his mouth, clomped in and sat down, then Patton beside him. Abrams physically was a direct opposite of the tall, spiffy Westmoreland. "A reporter once described Abrams as looking like 'an unmade bed smoking a cigar,' a characterization that delighted Abrams."[3]

I started by briefing the general on the enemy situation in our area of operations, normally the S-2's job, but today I was the whole show. At first the general appeared interested enough, but after a couple minutes and no questions from him, just after I had gotten into the friendly situation, his eyes glazed, no longer seeing the map. Then his chin dropped, and his head began bobbing slightly. In another minute, Abrams' chin was on his chest, cigar still clamped in his mouth. I thought he was going to set himself afire.

Patton's steely blue-gray eyes were staring straight into me. Most certainly *he* was wide awake. Nothing to do but to go on with the briefing, making a mental note of where I was when the general nodded off. I toned down and droned on at a decibel level I figured would not awaken the general, believing he probably was awakened in the night more than once to take a call from Washington, or give orders in some critical situation.

I had gotten through perhaps eight or ten minutes of elapsed time when Abrams suddenly looked up squarely at me. I instantly picked up the briefing where he had dropped off into his snooze. He listened briefly, looked at his watch and broke in, "Thanks, but from where you stand, how do you see 11th Cav's operations?"

"We're doing well, and we're going to do better, sir." (A good, safe answer.)

"Is that right, George?" Abrams asked, turning to Patton beside him.

"Damn well is, sir," Patton responded enthusiastically.

Abrams grunted toward me, "Good job," and got up to leave.

Patton saw him off and came back into the briefing tent. His eyes were fixed directly on me as he strode up and stopped, uncomfortably close.

He thrust his head forward and barked out fiercely, "I would have fired your ass if you'd awakened him, you know that?"

"I know, sir."

Patton stared ominously at me, as if he were going to draw his pistol and kill me on the spot. Then he broke into a broad toothy grin, clapped me on the shoulder and said, "Damn good job, Bill. Just don't ever try that shit on me."

Gratuitous Brutality

On the evening of August 8, our 3rd Squadron cordoned the village of Chanh Luu, 8 kilometers southeast of Lai Khe. This village had shown itself to be extremely hostile, so it was no surprise when a battle erupted on the next day. Unlike other contacts we had, this was almost entirely a tunnel fight, with our opcon 36th Vietnamese Ranger Battalion engaging the enemy.

Patton and I were in the village at daybreak. In late afternoon we returned to the TOC to plan follow-up actions. While there, I observed the first prisoners being brought in, and late in the evening of August 9, dead tired though I was from the day's exertions, I recorded events in my journal.

> 9 Aug 68. Fear in a sack: the man was dark and powerfully built. His arms were tightly bound by cords, a burlap sack over his head.... Col. Patton said he had been severely handled by our ARVN Rangers and had refused to talk .... The man was not young, perhaps in his late forties. He was in shock, hardly perceiving what was happening. He was bare except for blue shorts, and he was partly covered with caked mud, whether from the tunnel he hid in or the treatment he received I don't know .... Our Vietnamese interrogator appeared and began to question him. He became desperate, pleading, though never quite losing dignity. Tears welled in his bloodshot eyes, and his face seemed to flatten even more. The interpreter was not satisfied with the response, took his fist and harshly raised the man's chin. Then he stepped down on his knee, and I started to intervene but there was no further mistreatment. The man insisted he was an innocent civilian, that his eldest son had joined the VC four years ago and his second son had been killed by a helicopter gunship. The VC had taken his papers, he said, and he had

gone to province headquarters to get more. The officials, not believing him, had jailed him for fifteen days, then sent him back to Chanh Luu without his papers. When we cordoned the village last night he had gone into hiding, afraid since he had no papers.

[Recorded later] Have now found out how the man was earlier interrogated by our ARVN Rangers: tied down flat on his back in his own yard, gauze mask put over his mouth to hold it open, and water poured into it off and on for two hours ["waterboarded"]—that and beating. Now the ARVN have him again.

This was bad.

Brutality by Americans was worse:

4 Sep 68. A clean-cut American boy brutally beats a scrawny, cleft-lipped, ignorant farmer.

I threatened this American that I would get his ass if he laid so much as a finger on another prisoner. I informed his likewise clean-cut lieutenant, who directed the proceedings, that I'd do the same to him.

The creature was pitiful, his cleft lip showing teeth rotted to the gums. His head bled from a beating he had gotten earlier from ARVN. He hunched, a dwarf-like thing caught in the corner of a tent where men beat him.

I thought that maybe in a few weeks the fair-faced soldier would return to a comely young girlfriend. But he would leave behind him a scarred, ill-begotten cast-off creature, afraid of ARVN, maybe afraid of VC. Perhaps he was VC. If not before, he probably would be now. I directed that his head be stitched, and I watched him being led away, gently this time, by a medic. Nagging me, though, was the suspicion he might soon again be in the hands of ARVN who would resume the beating, only harder because an American lieutenant colonel who understood nothing about war had interfered.

That evening at the briefing, I stood and outlined what had happened and said there would be no more treatment of prisoners like this, and everybody had better get the word. I was only a staff officer, looking squarely at squadron commanders, senior to me. Patton sat there. I didn't know if he concurred, but I didn't care. I was steaming.

Regimental Pacification Operations

Between the edge of the vast jungle that was War Zone D and Colonial Route 13, which ran north out of Saigon to the Cambodian border, was a large stretch of farm land with many farming hamlets and villages. Dirt roads, mined in places the VC and locals knew but we didn't, connected the hamlets. The terrain was gently rolling, containing several small streams and rice paddies. Small and large growths of trees and brush sheltered VC in groups, usually of not more than squad size. As part of our ongoing pacification operations I planned and helped control seal-and-search operations in several of these hamlets and villages, such as the large operation at Chanh Luu.

Armored cavalry was lousy for hamlet pacification. In the first place, just traveling across the farmland and dirt roads to get to a hamlet caused damage even though we tried to minimize it. Then too, commanders of tanks and ACAVs in a contact naturally would spur their drivers to move quickly and make sharp turns with no thought other than to kill the enemy and keep themselves and their crews from becoming casualties. Additionally, for moving between buildings and engaging VC, tankers with 90-millimeter cannons and .50 caliber machine guns were far less useful than grunts with M16 rifles. If a tank gun fired, the damage would be enormous—not the best circumstance in our effort to convince the people to feel good about their government.

Although 11th Cav was a great mobile reserve for protection of Saigon, we were way too bulky and powerful to be a good pacification instrument. But here we were, and we would give pacification our best. With any units not out on search and destroy, we set night defensive positions (NDPs) right up against the edge of several hamlets. During the day, troops would work inside a hamlet and patrol out from it, and at night they would set out listening posts and ambushes to interdict the enemy which depended on the inhabitants to support them with food and information on our activities.

Our regimental efforts at pacification were hindered by the district chief who had no interest in it and would not send his RFs and PFs (Regional forces, and Popular—local—forces) out to secure the hamlets. Also, our ARVN 36th Ranger Battalion commander, Captain Cha, was no help. Mostly, we treated him just like one of our American unit commanders. We gave him orders and he more or less carried them out—not really what Vietnamization was supposed to be all about: training the Vietnamese to conduct their own war. I learned that Cha was more adept at victimizing his countrymen than he was at fighting the enemy. At various places along the roads in his area he set checkpoints to extract a fee from any civilian who wanted to pass. U.S. advisors in all areas and at all levels were constantly working at this problem—without much success. Patton was trying to overcome this coercion—with no discernable effect.

This whole pacification effort in our area was askew. It seemed to us that to be effective, the impetus ought to come from the Vietnamese, not the Americans. But here we were, trying to do what we could whereas the district chief could care less and the Ranger commander profited from the war, no doubt giving the district chief his cut.

A Little Girl in Binh Co

The 1st Division summary of operations of September 16 stated that our 1st Squadron "continued reconnaissance in force operations and night ambush patrol operations" in its area of operations. "Reconnaissance in force" was not a new type of operation, just another way of saying "search and destroy." What was theory and sounded good at MACV headquarters and was received enthusiastically in Washington as a better way of going about business—Abrams' "One War"—was not what was happening in 11th Cav's Tactical Area of Operations (TAO). Yet we did not get corrected by Division, IIFFV, or Abrams himself during his visits. Indeed, we were complying with Division orders.

An event of the night of September 15/16, 1968 would greatly impact our future regimental operations. Alpha Troop sealed the tiny farming hamlet of Binh Co which was right up against the edge of the jungle of War Zone D. During the night the troop received small-arms fire and four RPG rounds which caused minor damage to two ACAVs and wounded six troopers, who were dusted off. I learned there was a little, troubled eleven-year-old girl in Binh Co. When Alpha Troop had received the probe, two houses—huts, really, with baked mud walls and thatched roofs—had caught fire from one of our defective illuminating rounds, and the houses had burned to the ground. One house was that of the little girl. I heard she was huddling away from everyone, in tears.

Having to escape from her burning house, with shooting going on only yards away was not, however, the worst thing that had happened to her. I learned later that the pilot of a helicopter gunship, quite likely from 11th Cav back in April before Patton or I had arrived, had looked down and seen a man on a road. The man was leading his two old oxen from Binh Co to Binh My to try to trade them for a younger pair. It was the middle of the afternoon on a clear day. He was wearing black pajamas—like almost all farmers of the area. The gunship attacked, repeatedly, killing the man and his two oxen. The man's wife was now a widow with four girls, the oldest 18, the next 11, and the two little ones, nine and eight.

That eleven-year-old girl from Binh Co, whose name I found out later to be Nhan, reminded me of my eleven-year-old Maura. The hamlet of Binh Co was to become important in our regimental pacification efforts, and Nhan and her three sisters were to become profoundly important in my life.

The next day, in an audio tape I began telling Sandra and Maura about Binh Co. I explained that it had almost no male population since they were either ARVN or VC, quite certainly mostly the latter. The VC used this hamlet and others like it in the vicinity as supply points, so the people were caught in the fighting between our forces and the VC. Until our units arrived, the VC came in from the jungle any time they wished, collected taxes from the inhabitants, propagandized, sometimes helped them, other times harassed them, and paid or forced them to do labor and otherwise aid them. Binh Co had perhaps seventy-five or so houses and maybe three hundred people, just a farming hamlet. The small houses with hard-packed, immaculately clean earthen floors were furnished with the barest living essentials: board pallets to sleep on, things that looked like sawhorses for seats, a pot for cooking, and a minimum of other household items.

Patton told our S-5 civil affairs officer, Captain Lee Fulmer, to pick out from regimental stocks some canned goods and a few other things we thought might be useful to the family. I added a couple gifts I had my driver pick up in the PX, and we flew to Binh Co. This would be a pathetic offering, but maybe it would be a start.

When we arrived, upon our interpreter's query an old woman motioned toward a girl hugging a wall, trying not to be seen. This, I was to find, was Nhan. I pointed my movie camera and took a few feet of film before she saw me and fled around the corner of the house, terrified. Much later I learned that she had never seen a camera and thought I was pointing a gun at her. Our interpreter finally convinced her to face us and come forward. Trembling, she made a few little steps toward us. When I gave her a doll and a dress she was speechless at the gifts, unlike anything ever seen in Binh Co. That night, in my van I entered in my journal, "I'm sure that the house we'll build for them will be better than the one we destroyed."

The supreme irony of that statement was not to be revealed until decades later.

Within a day or two of the illumination round accident, Binh Co had become the center of our pacification efforts. After a few weeks, during which we built two new wooden houses for those that had burned, added a new school, paid for a schoolteacher, put in a playground, and helped the inhabitants develop other projects, Abrams came to visit and liked what he saw. We quickly expanded our pacification efforts to other hamlets. Unfortunately, the province and district chief visited only for the ceremonial opening of the school and took no action to station permanent RFs or PFs.

I came to love the four Binh Co girls, especially Nhan, the 11-year-old, and they provided considerable relief from many difficult and sordid events. The fact was, though, my visits to them were always fleeting since I had so much to do.

Elsewhere, other aspects of the war continued. We kept on jungle busting toward objectives that 1st Division wanted searched, and we helped select B-52 targets for War Zone D. On several occasions I landed in the strike zone immediately after B-52 strikes to conduct bomb damage assessment (BDA). Infrequently I found pieces of bodies hanging in trees. Mostly, though, there was nothing except evidence we had hit a long-vacated site or nothing at all—just jungle. Meanwhile, a myriad of small engagements continued.

Our engineers had finished their construction projects in Binh Co. The new school was a very plain-looking building, simply boards with an earthen floor and a tin roof. I said in a letter to Sandra and Maura, "It's much better than any of the buildings currently in Binh Co. The old school next to it had so many shell holes in the roof it couldn't keep the rain out, so I hope this one will fare better." I told them that after we visited the school we went to the new house of the mother with the four children. It was a rather large wooden building with a tin roof. We asked her how she liked her new house, and she said she liked it. The earthen floor was

Haponski with Nhan (holding hands) and her younger sisters Tuong (front left) and Luong (right) in Binh Co, October 1968. (Collection of author)

just being put in. She was using a decrepit hoe and leveling the dirt. Inside there were already two bunkers built, that is, holes in the floor which every house in Vietnam had because of the war, and into which the family, as soon as they heard any hostile activity, immediately tumbled. Nhan was suspicious of me and hung back behind her mother.

A week later I wrote of going out to Binh Co again: Colonel Patton and I saw the crippled schoolmaster in the stained white pullover shirt in which I'd seen him every time. Large gaps showed here and there in his mouth, and his few teeth were betel nut stained. He was writing an assignment on the board, which consisted of just that—a board. He had some kind of scratchy chalk and no slate at all.

Colonel Patton had worked hard at getting the Vietnamese government officials interested in this place, but except for the school opening, the district chief hadn't visited the hamlet. He had written it off as totally VC. We looked at Binh Co as one of the marginal hamlets which, if he were to take an interest in it, would perhaps come around. We found that when this district chief spoke at the school opening several days earlier he had told the people they couldn't go to Tan Uyen, the large village to the south. They needed to go there to market their farm products and buy supplies, they protested, but he said no. In a letter, I told my family, "That's the kind of person we have to deal with. He's responsible for this entire district and has very little interest in seeing that anything proper is done about it. This is what's so discouraging. There are many good government officials I am sure. We've met some of them. But there are also many who are interested only in what they can get out of the war. This little bandy-legged bastard is one of those. So that's what the people of Binh Co face."

"Find the Bastards and Pile On"

In September and October I went on as many missions with our aerorifle platoon as I could. First Division expected us to carry out sweeps in the jungle, and Patton's motto was our guide: "Find the Bastards and Pile On." The enemy in the open farmland was so well integrated with the populace that there was no possibility of a big fight there. Both by division orders and Patton's nature we went searching in the jungle of War Zone D. Patton had other business one day, so I had his command and control helicopter. We had flown for some time when we heard that one of our scout helicopters had been shot down in the jungle. Flying quickly to the scene we found the wreckage. Circling, providing covering fire as well as we could, we were shot at. Then another scout chopper was hit and crash landed. We flew immediately toward it.

Major John ("Doc") Bahnsen, the air cavalry troop commander, said, "We had already called a medevac and it was settling down about this time. Gray and the door gunner were still laying down suppressive fire, as was Bill Haponski's aircraft as it orbited overhead. Just a few days earlier, my troopers saved Haponski's life, and he returned that favor by helping save ours while we recovered [the lieutenant] and his crew chief."[4]

The reference was to an incident when I had accompanied Doc with his aerorifle platoon into a wooded area in rough farmland and we engaged a squad of VC in thick undergrowth. I was between two aerial rifle platoon soldiers (ARPs) and filming the action as we advanced on line, engaging the enemy. Suddenly a VC popped up directly in front of me with his AK-47 pointed at me, and the ARP next to me instantly fired and dropped him at my feet. Doc and his ARPs were legendary. They would go anywhere, do anything to fulfill Patton's desire to find them and pile on. I was thankful that day they were such tough, courageous fighters, and quick on the trigger.

Progress in Binh Co

By now in late October Nhan had become my little friend, and she saw me coming, dashed up to me and began smiling, an enormous change from the first fearful looks I had gotten five weeks earlier. She was wearing a new white blouse, perhaps purchased with some of the money I had given the mother. I wrote to my parents, "She put her arm around me and hugged me the whole time I was there. I bent down and kissed her cheek, and we went arm in arm to the school."

I found that the schoolmaster we had hired had a blackboard which Lee Fulmer had gotten for him. He had written lessons on it, so there had been improvement since the last time I had seen the school.

Our PIO (Public Information Officer) lieutenant gave me a note with data I had requested. School enrollment was eighty students, and approximately thirty children from Binh Co did not attend because their families were too poor. The teacher was being paid thirty to forty piasters, or about thirty to forty cents per month per student, so for about twelve dollars a month those thirty children could go to school. There were, in addition to the eighty children from Binh Co, thirty students who walked to school from Binh My each day, three kilometers distant. We intended to build a new school in Binh My as soon as we could get the material, and we would try to fund more children in Binh Co. In the meantime I would pay for the thirty children.

In French times Binh My was known as a Viet Minh headquarters for resistance. Like its nearby sister Binh Co, until a month or so earlier it had been VC controlled. Now the VC mostly, but not entirely, had to bypass it because our troops at our adjacent night defensive position had changed the situation. The villagers of Binh My very much wanted the school we were going to build, and indications were that we would succeed as in Binh Co. The problem, of course, was how long we could remain in the area. We might get a new mission and have to leave.

We were continuing our efforts to get the province and district officials interested enough to position ARVN troops or RF/PFs there. It was crucially important to extend the GVN influence to these places if there was to be any lasting hope for them. We were having great difficulty in getting the lumber and funds for the school projects, but many agencies were now interested (maybe due to Abrams' interest in our project?), and we were determined to succeed. Many of the young men of these hamlets were VC, probably living in the jungle close by, and we hoped that our actions would influence them to rally to GVN. The larger problem was to convince the government officials to do the right things for their people, and even more, to get the inhabitants of the hamlets interested in and capable of doing things for themselves, to include assisting in security.

The Gruesome Costs of War

In my journal I wrote, "Many times I have flown over Binh Co and seen the child's house, but have had no opportunity to stop. Today I went back, being sick of what had happened, and desperately needing solace. I did not find it; my sweet child was ill with a cold. She hugged me, and I patted her cheek, kissed her, and asked a medic to check her."

Very early that day I had been headed to Binh Co and, near the hamlet, we had flown over an ACAV just as it hit a mine. Some munitions inside it exploded. Landing and running toward it I saw two men helping a third who was staggering, groping and moaning, covered with blood. One man was on the ground, dead. Several others were wounded and as I approached, one of them shouted, "We're okay." The man being helped, though, was not okay. He had taken the blast in his face and his eyes were gone, blood and gore running down his face and body.

In my journal I later noted that I grabbed the firstaid kit from my chopper and put a compress on his face, the gore slipping through my hands. I thought at first he was black, but later had doubts—through his ripped trousers I saw that his legs were white. Only the top part of his body was black, charred from the explosion, the skin peeled and bare flesh showing beneath. We loaded him onto my helicopter as he gasped for water. We lifted off and I poured him a cup and put it in his bloody hand. He held it, the gore from his face falling into the cup. Desperately thirsty he sucked at the cup and with the water was drinking his own blood. I tried to comfort him, shouting above the helicopter noise that he would be all right. He spoke, and I had to put my ear close to his mouth to hear him. He was asking me who I was, telling me he could not see me.

I recorded in my journal: "'I'm Colonel Haponski; we're only a few minutes out from the hospital,' and he gasped, 'Thank you, Sir.'"

Sir!—Unthinkable! A man in such shape calling me "Sir."

When we landed and got him onto a stretcher I then saw his arm—a huge slice had been cut above the elbow as neatly as a piece of meat in a butcher shop. After we deposited him on the operating table I left the operating room, the gore clinging to my fingers, burned flesh all over me. I literally tasted the smell and I puked onto the floor. I found the latrine and threw up some more and tried to wash the mess off but it clung and reeked. I gagged and retched and retched until, exhausted, I went out and slumped into a chair. An hour or so later, back at our base camp I was able to wash and change clothes and try to get away from the smell and taste and feel of burned, gory flesh.

Abrams and the Pacification Disconnect

In an early 1968 directive, President Johnson had formalized new arrangements to make pacification a priority for American action. From that time forward, MACV would reassert its responsibility for pacification which it had been given in 1964, marking a significant shift away from the 1965–67 confusing, often haphazard, mixed civilian and military control of those efforts.

A civilian with rank of ambassador was Westmoreland's deputy for pacification. After the Tet '68 offensive, Robert "Blowtorch Bob" Komer had wanted to push pacification out into rural areas where the villages and hamlets were VC or contested. Whereas Komer wanted pacification expanded—now!—President Thieu wanted to wait. Thieu said, "Only after the government consolidated its grip on the cities and their environs and on the areas where South Vietnamese forces were already stationed would he propose moving into contested zones."[5] Abrams was not ready to embrace a U.S. pacification offensive so soon after Tet had significantly set pacification back, and he was not fond of Komer's aggressive style.

Shortly after Abrams took over, two months or so before Patton or I arrived at 11th ACR, Abrams had a meeting of corps and division commanders and high-ranking staffs. A staff group from Washington presented a pacification study which Abrams had earlier approved when he was Vice Chief of Staff at the Pentagon. The group of enthusiastic young officers, all of whom had been province and district advisers, alienated their high-ranking audience. Major General Philip B. Davidson said, "The bulk of the comments of the senior officers was virulently negative. Abrams, now angry, got into the discussion forcefully …. That stifled further dissent, but it left the generals unhappy and unconvinced." Davidson continued, "Even those who disagreed with the concept dutifully, if unenthusiastically, gave it their full support."[6]

There is a serious disconnect between Davidson's statement that Abrams' subordinates "gave it their full support," and what was actually happening in the field, then and later—which was much more American search and destroy by divisions than pacification. In fact, Davidson acknowledged as much. He pointed out:

> Almost immediately the news media began to push the story that Abrams was abandoning Westmoreland's large-unit search and destroy tactics in favor of security operations by smaller forces. This was untrue. Abrams made no abrupt and voluntary change of operational strategy. As Bob Komer said later, "I was there when General Abrams took over… there was no change in strategy whatsoever."

Davidson continued,

> I was J-2 MACV when General Abrams took over and I can confirm what Komer said. I talked daily with Abe about the enemy situation and every Saturday conducted the Weekly Intelligence Estimate Update … a gathering which Abrams used (as Westmoreland had before him) to discuss operations with his principal commanders and staff. In 1968, Abrams never spoke of any new strategy nor did he voice any dissatisfaction with large-unit search and destroy operations. What did happen in mid-1968 was that the war itself changed…. By mid-1968 Truong Chinh had secured Politburo approval for his concept of returning to guerrilla-type small-unit action, and in accordance with Truong's concept, the Communists scaled down their operations. Abrams reacted to the enemy operations with increased small-unit patrols and raids of his own, but

he kept maximum pressure on the VC and NVA in his own war of attrition .... It was not Abrams who changed the American strategy for the ground war, but Giap and Truong Chinh.[7]

"His own war of attrition?" Abrams would not have liked that characterization. He was not a body count man. His corps and division commanders, though, wanted to focus on enemy main and regional forces, which produced body count. That was where the big military plays were to be found, if at all. Armies want to fight other armies. Generals want to defeat other generals. But the situation after Tet had made this almost impossible, at least temporarily, because the bulk of enemy main and regional forces in the South needed recuperation. What was left for Abrams was to use his MACV advisory structure and CORDS (Civil Operations and Development Support) in an innovative, much more vigorous way. After the enemy's Fall Offensive of August and September 1968 petered out, Abrams was now ready to move on pacification. But Thieu still was not, and it took a lot of prodding by Abrams to get him to announce a supposedly Vietnamese initiative which Komer had actually drafted, the Accelerated Pacification Campaign (APC), which would run from November 1 1968 through January 31, 1969.

At 11th ACR we had already heard from Abrams the gist of the upcoming APC and were well into the essential part of it, security for hamlets and villages, before it was officially launched. Following 1st Division's mission guidance, I was still planning and helping to conduct operations according to the "pile on" concept. I was also trying to improve the lot of the people of Binh Co, especially my family. I wanted to get a mechanical sewing machine so the oldest of the four Binh Co girls could learn to sew and the family could make a living. "Somehow or other," I wrote to Sandra, "they have to learn how to do that."

By now the tenuous nature of American attempts at pacification had become clear to me. The local enemy never gave up their efforts to win over the people by persuasion or otherwise. In an audiotape to Sandra, November 5, 1968, I told her, "Something is very definitely wrong in Binh Co. It has changed drastically in the last few days." Nhan, instead of holding my hand and skipping along with me as in the past, wouldn't come anywhere near me as we walked.

I learned that about four or five nights earlier, VC had gotten into the hamlet and informed the people that if they continued to cooperate with the Americans there would be reprisals. Four young women, three of them Binh Co residents and one a prostitute who had drifted in, were abducted, warned not to have anything to do with the Americans, then released. So now my "adopted family" was caught between Americans and VC. We would continue taking military and civic action to try to assure the people of Binh Co they were secure, but the very fact that the VC had eluded the nightly ambush our NDP unit put out demonstrated that absolute security was impossible. Was the mother of the four girls now afraid to accept our help?

Vietnamization in 11th Armored Cavalry Regiment

President Johnson had given Abrams a two-faceted mission, pacification being one part, and Vietnamization the other. The president had "specifically charged him to improve South Vietnam's forces."[8] Patton and I had experience first with the 36th Ranger Battalion, and then when they were replaced, with the 51st Ranger Battalion. For some time Patton engaged in a tugging match with the 51st's commander, Captain Minh. The captain wanted to do what he wanted to do, and Patton of course wanted Minh to do as Patton wanted him to do, so the two of them were at loggerheads. I wrote to Sandra, "Both of them will flatter one another—Patton pats Minh on the back, tells him what to do, and Minh smiles and says, 'Yes sir, Roger, Roger.' He can do anything, and he will do anything that Patton wants, he says, but when it comes to doing it, he doesn't, and he has lots of excuses."

Minh filed a complaint that went all the way up to the Vietnamese III Corps headquarters, then over to IIFFV and back down to us. I invested considerable time and staff resources in preparing a draft response for Colonel Patton. Minh had said that the Americans were ordering him to do things, weren't even informing him of what he was expected to do, and that wasn't the way it was supposed to work. We should have been "cooperating" with him. Minh had come to us with a good reputation for field operations, but we weren't seeing it fulfilled. He also had other reputations, one of which was that he had three wives and many girlfriends. My draft of our reply read, "And of course it's difficult to get him in the field at night with all of this activity going on, with his travels back and forth to Bien Hoa and Saigon." Patton cut that part out.

Minh, however, had a point. We had gotten no guidance from higher headquarters on Vietnamization, and in retrospect it must have been treated by them and by us as an afterthought. The Vietnamization concept required the sponsor unit to provide training, but basically we were using his battalion, or rather, trying to use it, as just another unit in our overall operations. I believe we must have been either too busy with combat operations and didn't want to be slowed down by a recalcitrant Ranger unit commander, or there was not enough U.S. higher command interest in providing anything that could be called training except what they got "on the job."

Then we had more trouble with the battalion. I received a report of a survey of 91 people who lived in the area that the battalion was responsible for pacifying. It was highly negative, relating many instances of thievery and abuse. "Thirty-seven respondents reported that they were afraid to remain in the surveyed area because of the Rangers, but that they had property in their hamlets and could not move.... Respondents noted that the district chief also fears the Rangers and despaired that they [villagers], humble people, could do anything to alleviate the situation."[9] The villagers listed many things the Rangers stole on their periodic sweeps, from chickens, fruits, and vegetables to radios and money. They severely beat one man and stripped his house bare of anything of value.

When we confronted Minh with these and similar accusations he laughed them off as fiction and was offended we would even be interested in such things. "You do not understand," he said. "Vietnam is different from America." When we reported villager grievances through province channels we got assurances that the matters would be looked into, and that was the last we heard of them. Vietnamese Ranger, Marine, and Airborne units were said to be the best forces in GVN, and maybe most were. If so, our two Ranger battalions in 1968 seem to have been the exception. Both had been a trial and, I suppose in retrospect, we were impatient—much like other American units with a lot to do. We had gotten no guidance from higher headquarters on Vietnamization and done little on our own that would enable the Rangers to be more capable within a truly viable South Vietnamese army.

The Accelerated Pacification Campaign

In 11th Cav we were ahead of the game in the Accelerated Pacification Campaign (APC). We had been into pacification from the time Nhan's house had burned down in September. Our campaign goal was to raise the three hamlets in our area of operation from their V (VC) or D, E status (contested) to C, B, or A (GVN controlled), according to the Hamlet Evaluation System (HES) of the APC. By the time I left 11th ACR in January 1969, we rated one of them as C, Binh Co. The other two were still D and E. Patton kept trying to get the province chief interested enough to provide RF/PFs for the hamlets and failed. While I was in Vietnam I had arranged a means of sending money to the Binh Co family after I returned stateside. I failed to get it to them. The 11th ACR had moved, and the hamlets went back to the VC and remained that way until the end of the war.

During my six months in 11th Cav we had done what we could for pacification, both working in the hamlets and trying to secure them. We conducted search and destroy operations into the jungle base camps of the Dong Nai Regiment in War Zone D and had minimal success while taking a lot of casualties. I am not sure whether anything we did improved the fighting qualities of the two Ranger battalions we had under our control. We certainly had a difficult time getting them to do what we wanted done. I do know, however, that the battalions were detrimental instead of helpful to our pacification efforts.

But that was the whole problem. They were *our* pacification efforts, not *theirs*. We tried to get them to do what *we* wanted done. That reflected the overreaching dilemma throughout South Vietnam: the people who presumably were the ones most interested in ensuring civilian loyalty to the government should have been the source of pacification ideas, planning, and implementation—the Vietnamese themselves. Instead, all the way from Westmoreland's 1964 HOP TAC program, which he named and planned, through Abrams' 1968–69 APC program, which Komer planned and which Abrams strongly urged President Thieu into implementing, and beyond, it was the *Americans* who were mostly the inspiration, mostly the planners, and a mainstay of the forces which provided security, such as it was.

CHAPTER 12

Inside a U.S. Unit at Squadron (Battalion) Level, 1969

On January 5, 1969 in Di An (Zee On), 7 miles northeast of the northern edge of Saigon, I took command of 1st Squadron, 4th Cavalry, 1st Infantry Division. Throughout Vietnam, the Accelerated Pacification Campaign still had almost a month to go. Hating war, with years of service in armor and cavalry from platoon through battalion level, and regimental combat experience, I was well trained to wage it, and I would give it my best. My goals in commanding 1/4 Cav were to hurt the enemy as much as possible, save as many of my men as I could, and help the South Vietnamese people.

The squadron was the core of Task Force 1/4 Cavalry, or Task Force Haponski as it was variously called. Depending upon our mission, in addition to my armored cavalry troops, opcon to me I had other armored cavalry troops, straight leg infantry companies, mechanized infantry companies, tank companies, engineers and signal personnel. I will briefly describe only those facets of our actions which show how battalion-level events reflected the whole in conduct of the war. For the entire story, read my book, *One Hell of a Ride: Inside an Armored Cavalry Task Force in Vietnam*.

Early Days in Command

My task force was initially placed under operational control of 2nd Brigade of 1st Division. I was responsible for an area of operations on the northern outskirts of Saigon—all of Di An District and a portion of Lai Thieu (Lie Tyu) District. In an audiotape to Sandra I said, "It's quite a challenge—15 villages including 34 hamlets, and lots of industry, large power plants, sugar factories, many other things I don't even know about yet—a very different area from the totally rural and jungle area in which 11th Cav operates north of Bien Hoa."

I was pleased at the prospect of working with Nguyen Minh Chau, the Di An district chief who had a sterling reputation among Americans. Chau was a Vietnamese Marine Corps major who had been seriously wounded four times and partially paralyzed as a result of the third wound. His fourth wound had occurred only two months earlier, just outside the gate of Di An Base Camp, when he was shot at night riding in his jeep. He barely survived the assassination attempt and carried the bullet in his lung to his grave years later.

The 2nd Brigade's operational report for the period November 1, 1968–January 31, 1969 stated: "Capture of key reconnaissance and high-level staff personnel has compromised existing enemy plans."

The enemy was planning for the 1969 Winter–Spring Offensive with, as always, its ultimate target, Saigon. On the day after my assumption of command, my task force was to play the central role in discovering what these "existing enemy plans" were. It would be a case of astonishing beginner's luck which would resonate all the way to the top, to General Abrams himself.

An informer had told Chau he knew where the VC district chief, Bay Phuong, was going to hold a meeting. The killing or capture of Bay Phuong would be a blow to the VC infrastructure and its operations in Di An district.

Partially paralyzed and not yet fully recovered from the assassination attempt, Chau walked unsteadily with a cane. Nevertheless he went out into his district every day to help his people. Chau and I would conduct a combined operation, with my troops cordoning the hamlet and Chau's RFs/PFs searching it. By long-standing SOP, the American commander was always in charge, which, of course, was a major impediment to Vietnamization.

We captured not Bay Phuong, but a much bigger prize—a lieutenant, as our prisoner claimed. Ultimately, he was revealed to be a lieutenant colonel, a prestigious rank indeed in an army which gave similar responsibilities to officers two or three grades lower than in our army.

Lieutenant Colonel Nguyen Sau Lap[1] was a senior planner for COSVN's military operations. He had been in Saigon for several days, planning the attack on Saigon for the 1969 Winter–Spring Offensive, and was on his way back to COSVN when we captured him. He ultimately revealed details of his plan, to include dropping the massive Newport Bridge connecting Saigon with Bien Hoa. Lap's information was key to Abrams' ability to defeat the enemy's offensive.

Pacification in Di An/Lai Thieu Districts

Our primary mission in the Di An/Lai Thieu area was providing a ready reaction force in case the enemy tried again to take Saigon. We also had a pacification mission which was already progressing well when I arrived, and I shifted it into high gear. I had come from 11th Cav thinking I would never see the equal of its S-5, Captain

Lee Fulmer. I was wrong. Captain Tom Witter, a Pennsylvania National Guard officer, matched Lee in zeal and competence. There was nothing Tom would not do or try in order to make life better for "his" Vietnamese, as he fondly called them.

In Di An District, Chau in fact was the prime mover of the pacification program, unlike in every other district I knew where the American advisor was de facto in charge. Chau and his small staff collected and analyzed the intelligence, did the planning, and executed the plans. His RF and PF, although small in number, were doing a decent job of providing nighttime security in the hamlets. My guys and I were ready to do whatever would help Chau.

Tom Witter worked closely with Captain Steve McGeady, our equally tireless, courageous, and competent doctor. Steve and his medics traveled throughout our area to do what they could about both minor and serious ailments among the Vietnamese. Meanwhile, my Viet Cong Infrastructure (VCI) platoon under highly competent Lieutenant Walt Kurtz kept probing, trying to find the VC who controlled enemy activity within the villages.

In 1969 all Vietnamese Corps areas, I, II, III, and IV, reported gains in pacification, and in reality, overall there were gains. Colonel General Tran Van Tra, the COSVN deputy commander and later commander, said in his unfinished memoirs, "During [early 1969] .... many infrastructures were lost and many comrades were lost, especially in the areas adjacent to cities and the highly populated areas which were important strategically."[2]

Our task force contributed significantly to their loss.

Pacification Problems at Squadron (Battalion) Level

We were trying to assist Chau in making the people healthier, more secure, prosperous, and contented with their lives under the South Vietnamese government. But in doing so, our sweep missions and convoy escort duties were unavoidably causing damage to their crops, roads, and sometimes homes and people, just as in 11th Cav.

Support units in our area of operations (AO) also were causing problems with defoliation agents sprayed from trucks into copses outside hamlets. The spray would drift over onto crops, wilting them. We did not know that the Agent Orange and other toxic sprays were endangering villagers and ourselves, a dreadful fact to become evident both to the Vietnamese and to us years hence. Our very presence and what we deemed were necessary activities often were causing damage and providing the enemy with support and recruits among the population.

The Gathering Storm: Enemy Winter–Spring Offensive, 1969

The enemy main forces were up north, and that is where I believed we should be employed, using our firepower and mobility against them in areas where we could maneuver.

On March 16, 1969, the course of the war changed for my task force in a manner not seen since Tet 1968, over a year earlier. IIFFV intelligence indicated a buildup of NVA main force units taking place about 25 miles north of Di An in the Michelin rubber plantation area, both in the rubber itself and in the jungle surrounding it. MACV and IIFFV had determined that Saigon was under no immediate threat, and here was an opportunity to strike the enemy before they got any closer. I had been in several plantations, though not the Michelin, and I knew that armor could be deadly there because we could maneuver.

Unknown to me at the time, Jerry Burcham's 1st Air Cav battalion was operating to our northwest. Their infantry missions and methods were far different from ours, and his unit was not included in the Michelin operation ahead of me. He recalls:

> I was assigned four successive battalion AOs during the first six months of 1969. Three of the four were in uninhabited jungle areas north of Tay Ninh and the fourth was a flat, treeless area along the Vietnam-Cambodia border in the Angel's Wing west of Saigon. I can recall no instance in which specific intelligence was available from higher headquarters regarding enemy activity within any of the four AOs. I normally employed one rifle company to defend the battalion fire base while the remaining three companies conducted search and destroy operations and night ambushes. My rifle companies each spent three days on the fire base followed by nine days in the outlying areas. The companies were deployed from the battalion fire base by heliborne assault. This was a very noisy and visible process that alerted any enemy in the vicinity. After insertion into its landing zone (LZ) and during a company's time away from the fire base, it moved overland to search for and engage the enemy and establish night ambush positions. The enemy clearly had the advantage in terms of tracking our movements and accepting or declining engagement.

Most of the time in 1st Infantry Division I was given no intelligence from higher headquarters which might have enabled us to find enemy. When I did get information and was directed to have a cav unit bust jungle to locate and destroy the enemy supposedly in that location, usually we found nothing there. This time, though, corps-level intelligence was to pay off, big time.

The corps commander (II FFV) ordered a three-division operation, with the mission to search out and destroy 7th NVA Division forces and supporting units. Operation *Atlas Wedge*, as conceived and executed, would turn out to be the largest and most effective such operation of 1st Infantry Division's post-Tet '68 years. The intelligence was accurate and for once, search and destroy was the right tactic for the occasion. We didn't have to search much—we knew the enemy was there. We had to destroy.

I decided to leave Tom Witter's S-5 civil affairs section in Di An to help Major Chau since there were no hamlets where the squadron task force was headed, just jungle and rubber plantation

For the upcoming mission my command headquarters would be my two ACAVs with me sitting on top of my ACAV, HQ 16. We would have to attack through jungle before we reached the Michelin. On the night of March 17, late in the evening, keyed up from two days of intense planning and preparation, I wrote in my journal, "Tomorrow we go into the dense jungle in search of the enemy. It will be difficult, crashing through with tanks. Supposedly the 7th NVA Division and the 34th Artillery Group are in there."

We had been doing pacification work in the Di An area for the two and a half months I had been in command, and now we were to be employed in the role I had been advocating all along, combat against main force units in terrain favorable to our deployment. At least it should be favorable when we reached the rubber plantation.

My journal continued, "Today as we flew low over the area I could see some evidence of heavy traffic. It will be no picnic. I trust that I will bring out as many as I take in."

This was not to be.

The Long Nguyen Secret Zone

From our line of departure paralleling Route 13, ahead of us looking west were miles of jungle, and beyond that, the huge rubber plantation. It was terrain rich in history, most of it violent. I radioed my TOC at Lai Khe: "Beginning jungle busting move now."

One of my great troopers, Terry Valentine, told what it was like as a crew member on a tank while jungle busting: "Dense jungle, thorny vines, termite mounds that even tanks could not knock down, trees and bamboo that had hives of ants in them (very vicious ants at that). Vines were so intertwined that I was being pulled right off my tank when I got tangled up in them."

From the time we left Route 13, we were in for one hell of a ride.

Operation *Atlas Wedge* was to become a test of our courage and endurance. I learned some things about young men, and about myself, that I could have learned in no way other than to be down there with them in the Long Nguyen Secret Zone and other such exotic places. I am profoundly grateful for having had that privilege. And I learned much more, first-hand, about our enemy too.

The Michelin Rubber Plantation

In the Long Nguyen Secret Zone we had only one contact with an enemy squad at night in dense jungle and found only deserted base camps (small wonder—they heard us coming). On the fifth day my task force entered the rubber. The 11th Cav had had some sharp engagements with elements of 7th NVA Division in the plantation a few days earlier, marked by the stench of rotted corpses.

As we moved north, the plantation floor became overgrown, in some places shoulder-high, evidence of not being recently worked. The overgrowth, however, was no hindrance. We could move quickly down the lanes of the immense plantation, unlike through the jungle.

On March 23, the 11th Cav was ordered to withdraw and resume its former mission far to the southeast. My task force now was left with the entire Michelin responsibility. I received orders to attempt to regain contact with the 7th NVA Division, deny them use of the plantation for base camps, and destroy any units we encountered. To support this action I acquired command of Fire Support Base Doc which 11th Cav had hastily established at the edge of the plantation.

We reconnoitered in the plantation, then were ordered to pull out to allow it to fill up again with enemy. On March 25, before we moved out to Doc, though, an incident occurred which will never leave me. The squadron daily journal entry of 1557 hours recorded my report, "Engaged three VC moving south along stream, and at 1600 hours, 3 VC KIA." Additionally I reported two of my infantrymen wounded, one very seriously. I had spotted three enemy and jumped off the top of my ACAV and run toward them, trying to fire my AR-15 but it jammed. Green tracers from an AK ripped past me just above my shoulder, and I killed one, perhaps all three, of the enemy with grenades. Their clothing and documents revealed them not as VC but as NVA reconnaissance troops.

We had been ordered to pull out. It was long after dark when we carefully made our way into FSB Doc. Earlier in the day I had had little time to feel the effects of killing the man before he killed me. But now, as I sat on top of my ACAV in the night, I felt like hell. Many times previously I had fired on the enemy, but from the air or at a distance on the ground I did not know the results. And I had often ordered fire to be brought on the enemy while directing my troops. But now I myself had killed a man, maybe three. I was miserable. I had learned first-hand what my troops had to endure.

A Mobile Defensive-Offensive Battle

FSB Doc was an open area covered with shoulder-high elephant grass and clumps of dirt left when the village of Thi Tinh had been razed years earlier in Diem's strategic hamlet program. Huge anthills and some copses of brush and trees dotted this wasteland. Only three quarters of a mile to the west, seeming even closer at night, lay the edge of the Michelin plantation. On the night of March 27/28 I knew in my head and could feel in my gut that we were in for an attack.

Like the French years before, American units in Vietnam had given up too much of their mobility in favor of fixed defenses, too much of their offensive power in favor of protecting their logistical assets. But this was not for me to sort out. Especially not that night. My defense of this fire support base would be as mobile as I could make it. One of my cav platoons would be placed outside the base, and as soon as they heard the enemy mortars, they would start engines and wheel the perimeter and cut up any attack as it came in.

Haponski at edge of FSB Doc at noon after the battle. (Collection of author)

At 0210 hours, hell erupted. Fierce mortar, rocket, and RPG bombardment, and machinegun and small-arms fire of a reinforced battalion blasted into our firebase. The first horrendous concussions had been sheer terror. My ears rang so loudly from the instantaneous din that in the flashes of explosions I saw mouths of men near me shouting, but at first I couldn't hear them or the screams of my wounded. My radioman at my shoulder in the open hatch was wounded in the chest, but he shouted he was okay, kept flipping dials and monitoring. Then quickly the powerful ground assault struck. The cav platoon outside the perimeter was soon in among the enemy, attacking. Because of the circling platoon and the return fire from our artillery and tanks, ACAVs, and infantry bunkers inside the base and, a little later, from air cav rockets and Air Force miniguns, the NVA struck hard against but never penetrated our perimeter.

Once again, in a kind of mini-repeat of Tet '68, when the enemy chose to attack, a mobile defensive-offensive tactic in trafficable terrain caused them big trouble.

The 7th NVA Division history says, "On 28 March, 6th Battalion of 65th Regiment, led by Battalion Commander Minh Ho and Political Officer Tran Van Duc, daringly attacked a concentration of American vehicles at Thi Tinh, inflicting heavy damage on troops of armored personnel carriers and killing many soldiers."[3]

Relative to the statement that they daringly attacked us, that is for sure. It took guts beyond imagination to take on an armored unit on the perimeter and an infantry company in bunkers plus artillery tubes available for direct fire if I had called for it. Add the firepower from the mortars within Doc and the artillery from our adjacent artillery fire support bases, and then add the firepower we got from the air, and the result was awesome.

Battalion Commander Minh Ho was a courageous man. He and his men did well indeed. Even after having taken a terrible beating in the initial assault they bravely tried to continue the attack, then covered their withdrawal with one company.

The enemy report of the battle said they killed "many soldiers." We lost six men killed and two dozen wounded and evacuated by dust off. Other wounded, to include Doctor McGeady and my radioman, were treated by our medics on site and returned to duty.

The enemy historian claimed a victory on their "beloved soil of Thi Tinh." In a sense he was right. I was certainly willing to allow that any losses at all of my fine young men was a victory for them.

Attack into the Michelin

On the day after we had pulled out of the rubber to let it fill up again with enemy, the IIFFV commander had said in a memo: The 1st Inf Div and the 25th Inf Div should go back into the Michelin possibly this weekend, timing dependent upon enemy activity.

The attack into the Michelin which I had been planning since we were ordered out of the rubber had been delayed by the enemy's assault on us in Doc, and it needed to be launched, soon. My task force's strike would be a major attack, the only one by any of the *Atlas Wedge* divisions. We would be the whole show.

On the night before the attack, we had an egregious security breach by my S-3 Operations officer who was back at my TOC in Lai Khe. On our command net I suddenly heard him ask me in the clear, "Is our big attack into the Michelin still on for tomorrow?" I grabbed my handset and keyed it, hoping to squelch the rest. I had been patient with him for other mistakes. As soon as I could get through to him on the secure net I told him to pack up and get out.

In addition to spies within ARVN units, the enemy had a highly developed radio intercept capability. The capture of an entire radio traffic monitoring station just outside Saigon in 1969 revealed the sophistication of enemy methods and laxness of American radio discipline. The report resulting from the capture revealed that they had been monitoriong U.S. and South Vietnamese traffic for years. One can only guess how many lives this cost.

Beginning at daylight the next morning, we had a tough, tough fight through a bunkered base camp. We did a lot of killing. How many others were carried off we did not know. I would never know if that radio call alerted our enemy and caused us casualties. We had been fiercely resisted. B Troop had been the hardest hit by RPGs, losing six men killed and several wounded within less than a minute. Among the B Troopers was Platoon Sergeant Chuck McGrath, acting platoon leader, his arm and chest bandaged from his tank getting hit by the initial RPGs, his driver and back deck man killed. His platoon was also the hardest hitting as he led his men in the fighting. Years later he had no recollection of any of his actions which earned him the Silver Star. His men hazily remember some of what happened. They recall taking courage from him. In shock themselves over their terrible losses of friends, responding to his orders, they went about their work, some on the ground, some on their vehicles, taking bunker after bunker.

Just before dark the day-long battle was over. Gene Raynes, an ACAV crewman, came across McGrath, bandages stained with blood, sitting with his back propped against a rubber tree, his hands hanging loosely at his sides, palms up on the ground. Raynes lit a cigarette and stuck it between McGrath's unmoving lips. Raynes said, "I seen him just sitting there and I thought he might need a smoke. At first the cigarette just stuck there, then he moved it with his lips and took a drag, and then he chewed me out, 'Damn it Raynes, I can light my own cigarettes.' I noticed though he smoked it."

At dusk I walked among my C Troopers and talked with them. It's always the eyes that tell you what men have been through. Many young men had become old this day.

The clearing on the stream bank as darkness fell was strangely peaceful, and the C Troopers could bathe. Most, though, were too exhausted, too heartsick at the losses of their buddies. From early in the morning until just before dark we had lost twelve wonderful young men KIA, and about three dozen dusted off. Another three dozen were patched up and continued the fight.

Once again I was impressed with the way our enemy faced the enormous firepower of armored cavalry. As we moved forward firing our 90mm tank canons and .50 caliber machine guns of every armored vehicle, they maintained their positions and launched their RPGs at close range, inflicting casualties on us. They were courageous, highly skilled young fighters.

This was one of those battles which demonstrated that when the enemy left jungle base camps and exposed himself to attack in terrain where a mobile force could maneuver, he was in dire straits, as in Tet '68.

I, as the commander, had caused immense physical destruction of the plantation. Huge swaths had been bombed and burned out from air strikes I had called in. Trees were in shreds. Gaping holes marked where 500- and 750-pound bombs had impacted, scattering body parts. Long, narrow swaths blackened from napalm canisters revealed bunkers into which flaming jelly had penetrated, incinerating everyone inside. The smell of burned and rotting flesh in 100-degree heat was nauseating. My young men and I were exposed to sights, sounds, and smells that will never leave us.

The rubber trees that were still standing were dripping latex from the topmost shredded leaves and broken limbs down the trunks, leaving white trails of tears all the way to the ground where they congealed in dirty gray puddles. It seemed as if every living thing had been scarred, desecrated with the wounds of bullets, grenades, RPGs, rockets, canister, artillery, bombs, napalm. It was as if the whole wretched plantation was weeping at the terrible madness.

Our battle turned out to be not only the single largest battle of *Atlas Wedge* with more enemy KIA than any other, but it was the biggest fight in all of Vietnam on that day and for many days to come. At best, a dubious honor. At worst, an everlasting shame at the folly of men. We all tried to do our best that day. I know that we fought like hell for ourselves and our buddies. They in the NVA 165th and 209th Regiments did the same.

***

To the northwest of us, Colonel Burcham had air assaulted his battalion into deep jungle and established Landing Zone Jess. He recalls:

> After securing the new LZ, I sent a rifle company to reconnoiter a wooded area about a quarter mile from the LZ. As it approached the woodline it came under intense fire, pinning the company down and seriously wounding the company commander. I called in air strike after air strike along the woodline for a distance of approximately a half mile. The following day, I sent a company into the area and they reported that the smell was terrible and that we had decimated a very large bunker complex to the point that the enemy force had been buried in their bunkers by the bombing. Although it was impossible to determine a body count, I was informed by the brigade commander several days later that signals intelligence had completely lost contact with an entire NVA regiment that was thought to have been operating in the area.

Body Count/Kill Ratio

Shortly after *Atlas Wedge*, Lieutenant General Julian J. Ewell succeeded to command of IIFFV. He had the reputation of being a body count man, especially concerned with the kill ratio of units—that is, the number of enemy killed as compared to the number of men lost KIA. He said, "The only way to overcome VC control and terror is by brute force." Burcham recalls:

> In early 1969 the 1st Air Cavalry Division had a change of command. I was informed that the new division commander had been assigned a body count quota by the IIFFV commander, and had been told he would be relieved of command if that quota was not met. I was further informed that my battalion quota was an average of at least one kill per day per rifle company away from my fire base. A "kill" was defined as follows: "If a point man engages an enemy 200 yards down a trail and thinks he may have killed him, that is to be reported as a kill." Since

I habitually had three companies deployed away from the firebase, my assigned body count quota was a minimum of three per day. The unstated implication was that I would be relieved from command if I failed to meet that minimum.

In 1st Infantry Division I was not given a quota but found that this new emphasis on body count and kill ratio was to have a powerful effect on division operations. In order to increase the count, ambushes directed by Division and Brigade became a higher priority, and my armored cavalry task force was not exempt. This ineffective use of our combat power as ambushers handicapped us in doing other things we could do well.

Convoys Ambushed

From my journal, recorded soon after an ambush: "I saw the burning, snarled wreckage of the tanker trucks, ammo trucks, and helicopters, and then I took command of the ambush area."

At that time, Route 13, Thunder Road, was not in my area of responsibility but I had gotten a call from the acting division commander to get there and take charge. This day, April 28, 1969, was the first in a series of four attempted ambushes.

This convoy attack shook Division. As a result, in addition to many other widespread missions I would be responsible for convoy security on Route 13 from Lai Khe north to An Loc and then Route 303 to Quan Loi, a distance of 32 miles. I was also to protect convoys on two other supply routes of 38 miles, a total of 70 miles of dangerous road. The only way to accomplish my road security mission, given the paucity of forces I had to support it, was to "blitzkrieg" both sides of the roads with half of a cav platoon, moving swiftly, hitting into any ambush position before it could cause convoy casualties.

On May 2 the enemy struck again on Route 13, and yet again the next day. We could maneuver along the sides of the road in the wide Rome plow cut along the road, and the enemy took a beating.

Then on May 21 I was alerted that in addition to all other missions, I would send some of my task force into the jungle south of the Michelin as part of a division force reacting to a reported enemy buildup. I had my executive officer take charge of the road security and I would take the attack mission.

The Horrific Ben Chua Mission

Our portion of Operation *Bushwhacker* would be a tough, dangerous mission. The tough part would be the jungle busting to search and destroy and conduct bomb damage assessments (BDAs) from B-52 strikes. The dangerous part was the location. The jungle area we were to penetrate was known for units taking casualties from

VC who knew the extensive trail network, having operated there for years, and who were now guiding NVA units.

As always, we had to fight off the red ants that dropped down from the branches along with the poisonous defoliation dust that we ingested. We were headed for a recently bombed area just north of a village that was anathema to Americans and South Vietnamese, Ben Chua. Years earlier the Ben Chua villagers had fought the French and survived, and they remained bitter about the American/ARVN destruction of their nearby sister village, Ben Suc, in the *Cedar Falls* operation.

My helicopter was shot at in the air every day, and my tanks and ACAVs hit mines, wounding several men. Late one afternoon, Division ordered us to seal Ben Chua for a search by ARVN the next day. As we put in the seal, I heard a horrendous explosion which lifted one of my 50-ton tanks several feet into the air and filled the sky with dirt and debris. The tank commander, his gunner, and his driver were lying on the bank of a stream about 150 feet away where they had been blown out of the tank. Miraculously not dead, but grievously wounded, they were later evacuated to Japan. SFC Merrill Barnes, the tank company mess sergeant who had been riding on the back deck with his marmite cans of hot food for his troops, though, was buried in mud with only his head showing, horribly wounded. One of the tankers in his company and a medic dug the unconscious Barnes out of the muck, and the medic directed artificial respiration until Barnes died. Our engineer search team had not detected the 500-pound bomb dug into the stream bed right where we had put an armored-vehicle-launched bridge across. The bridge above the bomb was blown to bits, the tank destroyed.

During the night we were probed, RPG'd, and mortared. Shortly after daylight the ARVN were landed by cargo helicopters to begin their search. On our seal, there were no kids waiting for handouts. Instead, the few that we saw clung sullenly to their mothers or grandmothers, avoiding looking at us. Old men indifferently looked on. Ben Chua was devoid of young men, unquestionably VC. As Viet Minh, the village had defeated the French; as Viet Cong it was continuing the fight which had caused us several casualties while in return we caused none, and it seemed as if Ben Chua would fight us forever.

Unknown to us and virtually everyone else in the world, as I was directing my unit while trying to save my men, Dr. Henry Kissinger was meeting with Le Duc Tho in Paris about a U.S. offer of total troop withdrawal from Vietnam.

Mother of All Ambushes

For some time, intelligence staffs were reporting an expected Summer Offensive: "The primary objective [is]… to gain a favorable position at the Paris Peace Talks." Division-size attacks were expected in the An Loc and Quan Loi areas, villages on our Thunder Road convoy route.

This was June 6, 1969, 25 years after D-Day Europe, the Normandy invasion.

Earlier in the morning I had explained to Division that I had no available reaction force in case of ambush, and they gave permission to break off just one platoon of cav from its jungle-busting mission and start it toward Route 13.

We learned later that our enemy was the reinforced 101D Regiment with strength in the ambush position of about 800 men. The regiment had set up a kill zone three miles long, on both sides of the road. Eventually I had on the ground my whole B Troop and an 11th Cav troop with their accompanying infantry, around 200 or so men, but with our mobility and firepower from many sources, and especially with room to maneuver—150 yards of Rome-plowed strips on each side of the road to the edges of the jungle—we had an enormous advantage. Again we had surprised them, and we were pounding them hard.

With a raging battle below, things were also hot in the air. I had told my pilot to orbit at 1,000 feet or so, and radar locked on us. After we evaded for a couple more passes, our aero scouts spotted the antiaircraft position in a jungle clearing and their gunships eliminated it. Even more unusual was the next event. Several times I had had AK and machinegun fire directed at my helicopter, as it was during this day, but never RPGs. On one of our orbits I watched in amazement as not just one or two but about two dozen RPG rounds came shooting up at us simultaneously, as if several RPG teams had been coached to attack aircraft en masse. I leaned out and watched the rounds approach from below, shoot on past us, then arc back earthward and explode. It happened again on the next pass, although with fewer rounds this time. Later I learned that although individual RPGs occasionally had hit and brought down helicopters at quite low altitudes, nobody had ever heard of such a salvo. Perhaps the enemy had been experimenting with radar-controlled antiaircraft fire and RPG salvoes. If so, thank God he had negative results to report for this day.

The enemy initially had to fight in position, then tried to flee into the nearby jungle. One of the enduring images I have of Vietnam is looking down from my helicopter just before dark on June 6 and seeing enemy below me crossing jungle clearings, still trying to escape to the west as we pounded them from the air and with artillery.

The enemy evacuated their dead and wounded as well as they could, but they left behind many bodies, and we took two prisoners. The additional dead and wounded carried off must have been frightful. We captured a lot of weapons and ammunition to include mortars and recoilless rifles. The 101D Regiment had not been able to employ many of them because it had been so quickly overrun. One of our prisoners told of utter confusion as his unit was suddenly struck with armored vehicles.

Five of my men and two ARVN were wounded, thankfully not seriously. Once again, a mobile unit had inflicted heavy losses on an enemy against which it could maneuver.

Despite these enemy losses, as after the Michelin battles, they were resilient. The 101D Regiment licked its wounds and within two weeks struck a unit farther north, out of my area. The units we fought in and around the Michelin and on Thunder Road survived severe losses and lived to fight another day. They were extraordinary soldiers, in for the long haul.

The 7th NVA Division history says: "The soldiers of 7th Division can never forget the challenging and brutal year of 1969."[4] Our task force shared a measure of credit for making their lives miserable.

***

I had taken care of my Binh Co family as well as I could back when we had the pacification mission in Di An area, going to Binh Co a few times and having the girls to my base camp. But when we went north to fight main force units, I was unable to visit them. Because of the intense fighting, on only one occasion was I able to return to Di An by invitation of Major Chau to celebrate the opening of a district school and a building for sewing classes. I got an hour to myself to fly over to Binh Co and was terribly disappointed to find that Nhan had left a day earlier to visit her older sister in another village. Her mother said that ever since I had left, after her long day of chores was finished Nhan would go to what had been our landing pad at the edge of the hamlet and look into the sky to see if I was coming.

CHAPTER 13

American Withdrawal and Vietnamization, 1969–72

1969: Setbacks for Our Enemy

Things generally were going well for President Thieu and GVN. The official Communist history *Victory in Vietnam* states: "By the end of 1969 the enemy had retaken almost all of our liberated areas in the rural lowlands of Cochin China. We were only able to hold onto our bases in the U Minh Forest, the Plain of Reeds, and a number of isolated liberated base spots."[1] The decent performance of GVN's armed forces during Tet '68 had given them spirit, and the general mobilization after Tet had seemed to go reasonably well. Also, the enemy's revered Ho Chi Minh died on September 2, 1969. Gone was the hallowed figure who had so inspired generations of Vietnamese, North and South, to fight for independence and unification.

But the North responded to these setbacks as it always had—with greater resolution. The history relates:

> To increase forces available to attack the enemy, the Central Military Party Committee and the High Command sent many units with full TO&E [Table of Organization and Equipment] strength to South Vietnam. At the same time, the main force units on the battlefield were reorganized to conform to our supply situation and to the new situation and responsibilities of each local area, especially in the key theater: eastern Cochin China [IIFFV area].[2]

That the enemy was able to reorganize, recruit replacements, resupply, retrain and be ready to fight again was a testament to how they had been able to modernize their armed forces at all levels yet retain their historic readiness to do battle. Even given how tough 1969 had been for them, they still were able to use main forces to attack us, as evidenced by the wide-spread February attacks and the later large battles my task force and other units fought.

> Reviewing this situation, the 18th Plenum of the Party Central Committee [in January 1970] stated clearly that... in 1969 the enemy made some progress because our efforts to counter

his actions were not timely, the operations of our main force units and our guerrilla warfare actions were not very effective, and we did not devote a sufficient level of attention to the need to attack the enemy's pacification program.

(The history continued with the difficulties of troops stationed along the Ho Chi Minh Trail): "For three solid months, from June through September 1969 ... 6th Engineer Battalion ... ate sycamore berries, roots, and weeds in place of rice, and they were forced to burn straw and eat the ashes in place of salt."[3]

The enemy's main forces and infrastructure alike had been sorely stressed by Tet '68, mini-Tet '68, Fall Offensive '68, Winter–Spring Offensive '69, and the Summer Offensive of 1969. Conditions from late 1969 into early 1972 led some American participants and subsequent historians to claim that victory for the South could have been achieved. Pacification and Vietnamization had made some gains. Tests to determine how sustainable were the gains lay just ahead.

The 1970 Operation in Cambodia

Westmoreland and Abrams had long wanted to interdict the Ho Chi Minh Trail and its Laotian and Cambodian bases with sizable ground forces. The trail—actually now a huge network of roads—went from North Vietnam through Laos and Cambodia, then fed into South Vietnam at multiple points. Also, although only a relatively minor amount of supplies made their way into RVN clandestinely by sea on the eastern coast, much more arrived in the Cambodian port of Sihanoukville, then were trucked eastward. Huge supply and munitions depots lay a tantalizingly short distance across South Vietnam's western border with Cambodia and Laos. Some small cross-border operations had indeed been conducted secretly, such as a brief raid into Laos in late February 1969 by a unit of U.S. Marines in the A Shau Valley. Additionally, MACVSOG sent patrols across the borders both to interdict and report on activities, but with limited success. Continuing air strikes also failed to stop the flow of goods and troops into the South.

In March 1969, with an eye on speeding up the Paris Peace Talks, President Nixon had authorized secret bombing of Cambodian bases near the Vietnam border. But it was not until May 1970 that a cross-border operation big time was ordered by Washington. Nixon was ebullient. "He was, he said again and again, going to 'clean out the sanctuaries. You had to electrify people with bold decisions,' he said. 'Bold decisions make history ... 'like Teddy Roosevelt charging up San Juan Hill.'"[4]

Striking into Cambodia was a "bold decision" indeed, and when it became known, it certainly did electrify people. Congress and the people of the United States were shocked. Universities were rocked with demonstrations, and at Kent State four students were killed by rifle fire of National Guard soldiers. *Why!* many demanded, would Nixon spread a losing war into another country?

The goals of the "incursion" as it was called, were elimination of huge base areas, destruction of COSVN, disruption of the supply operation from the port of Sihanoukville in Cambodia, punishment of enemy main forces, and, importantly, a test of Vietnamization. Could RVNAF plan and conduct a large operation against enemy main forces? Just as pacification was at core an American idea, not Vietnamese, the move into Cambodia was an American test of Nixon's relentless emphasis on Vietnamization as a means of exiting Vietnam "with honor."

President Thieu tasked his two best field commanders with the major RVNAF thrusts. As for the Americans, IIFFV would send a powerful force of ground units and air cavalry.

RVNAF's performance was spotty—very good to very bad—but overall they did reasonably well in encountering and combating NVA formations and completing their missions. However, the Vietnamese units still had U.S. advisors who connected them with heavy American air strikes, airlift, and artillery support, so this was not a true test of Vietnamization which could prove their abilities to fight without that support.

How was the Cambodia incursion viewed by South Vietnamese military leaders? General Tran Dinh Tho wrote: "Despite [the incursion's] spectacular results, and the great contribution it made to the allied effort, it must be recognized that the Cambodian incursion proved, in the long run, to pose little more than a temporary disruption of North Vietnam's march toward domination of all of Laos, Cambodia, and South Vietnam."[5]

In his memoir, *No More Vietnams*, Nixon asserted that Cambodia 1970 was "the most successful military operation of the entire Vietnam War."[6] Lieutenant General Bruce Palmer had a different view. He had been IIFFV commander, then a Westmoreland deputy in Vietnam. Palmer said, "Looking back, the Cambodian incursion of May 1970 was the second major turning point in the war, in my view. Tet 1968 ended any hope of a U.S.-imposed solution to the war, while Cambodia 1970 fatally wounded South Vietnam's chances to survive and remain free." Consider how the gains from Cambodia boomeranged:

> The loss [of Cambodia's Sihanoukville port] forced Hanoi to rely entirely on cross-country routes from the North for maintenance of its forces in the South. In effect the Ho Chi Minh Trail became the jugular vein for the NVA effort in all South Vietnam. As a consequence Hanoi expanded its initially primitive routes into a wide network of all-weather roads and way stations that could handle even tanks and other heavy equipment. In the end, this logistical capability enabled Hanoi to overrun the South with massive conventional assaults....

(Palmer might have added that the enemy also constructed a modern pipeline with branch lines for transporting fuel to the southern battlefield.)

> Although NVA capabilities against the heavily populated areas of [all of the IIFFV zone—the Saigon area, and south to the southernmost tip of Vietnam] were greatly reduced, the nature

of ARVN was such that Saigon could not take advantage of this development by shifting some ARVN troops northward. ARVN was a territorial based and supported army. The families of ARVN soldiers lived near their home stations and were partially sustained by local ARVN resources—housing, for example. Historically ARVN regiments and divisions [except the elite Airborne and Marine divisions based in the Saigon area] had not performed well when deployed any great distance from their families. In the Vietnamese culture, particularly in the South, family ties were stronger than loyalty to ARVN or the government, and if the families needed help when so separated, the soldiers simply deserted.[7]

One of the boomerang effects of increased pacification and Vietnamization efforts in June 1969 was to prompt the National Liberation Front (NLF) into creating the Provisional Revolutionary Government (PRG). Now there was a second national government in the Republic of Vietnam's geographical territory. Truong Nhu Tang, the boy who had been so much influenced by Ho Chi Minh when he met Ho in France so many years ago, became its minister of justice. He said, "The [Thieu] administration's effort to portray the Saigon regime as an autonomous, legitimate government would now be answered by another Southern government fighting hard in every international forum to establish its own claim to legitimacy."[8]

The top civilian and military leaders opposing the South Vietnamese and Americans were Communists, members of the Party, but they were *Vietnamese* Communists, not Soviet- or Chinese-style Communists. Lower, the situation was different. Tang said,

> After the war one American writer declared that the average guerrilla couldn't have told dialectical materialism from a rice bowl. By and large, this was true. As far as most Viet Cong were concerned, they were fighting to achieve a better life for themselves and their families, and to rid the country of foreign domination—simple motives that were uncolored by ideological considerations.[9]

Tang also spoke of espionage: "By this time the shattered Saigon networks [as a result of Tet '68] had been rebuilt, and we had been successful in inserting people into the Thieu administration at all levels and into the Southern army as well."[10]

He told how, in the winter of 1969–70, they solved the problem of transportation other than by foot.

> Quite often the peasants would get their bikes [and motor scooters] from the local Saigon army forces—in our case the ARVN's 5th and 18th Divisions…. Eventually our Finance Department was able to set up regular supply channels directly between these divisions and the Front. From that point on we had a regular supply, not just of Hondas, but of typewriters, radios, cigarettes, and a variety of other goods. Before long, there was a thriving business between senior officers of these ARVN divisions and the Front in weapons and ammunition as well.[11]

Well! The money and military aid the U.S. poured into Vietnam enabled corrupt ARVN officers to funnel it directly to their enemy.

1970: Colby Sees Pacification as a Success

Colby, the head of CORDS (Civil Operations and Revolutionary Development Support), said that by late 1969 basic security for most of the population had been achieved. Now, in 1970, it was time for a new, improved plan. He wrote, "The word went out to the American advisers at the national and local levels that the plan should be written and worked out by the Vietnamese, the Americans to be as helpful as they could but not to dominate the planning process—as they certainly had in the APC and the 1969 phase."[12]

Colby entitled Part Six of his book, "VICTORY WON." President Thieu was enthusiastic about the forthcoming 1971 Plan. Colby said, "The fact that the stated goals were reasonable and real produced confidence that at last, a winning strategy to end the war's agony had been found." He stressed that the 1971 Plan was Thieu's, but in discussing it he revealed how much American influence was still at work. He peppered his discussion with what "I," and "We"—Americans—would do.

On security, Colby tells of a lengthy motorbike ride which he and Deputy for CORDS John Vann planned, going alone, in the Mekong Delta. Then, surprisingly, he undercuts its significance when he adds, "Although we were both sure we would make it, John arranged for a couple of helicopters to be on alert to respond to our radios if trouble did arise."[13]

Helicopters on alert to rescue them? Was this "Security with Fingers Crossed"?

1971: A Semi-Test for Vietnamization, Lam Son 719

Operation Lam Son 719 was the South Vietnamese portion of a combined US/RVNAF operation between early February and late March 1971 to move into a huge base area in Laos and disrupt the North Vietnamese interdiction and supply system, causing as many enemy casualties as possible. A revised congressional Cooper-Church Amendment of January 5, 1971 prohibited U.S. ground forces and advisors from crossing the border but did not ban air support. Abrams determined that the U.S. role would be to secure a staging area up against the border for RVNAF and provide air support over Laos, and artillery support up to the range of the weapons emplaced near the border. U.S. helilift, air cavalry, tactical air, and B-52 support over Laos were crucial elements of the overall plan.

Under a mediocre commander in Vietnamese I Corps area, RVNAF seemed cursed from the beginning. Terrible weather severely curtailed air support and turned roads and trails into a quagmire, and helicopters ran into heavy antiaircraft fire. After early successes, the commander found that the NVA was much stronger in the objective area than anticipated. Instead of melting away, they put up a fierce defense which was soon reinforced. Although some RVNAF units performed well, at least initially, even some of the elite airborne and Marine units ultimately panicked and broke, not having U.S. advisers with them to control air support. According to General Palmer, Abrams was furious at Thieu for not reinforcing, "and never quite forgave him. [Thieu] believed that the heaviest offensives from the north were yet to come, early in 1972, and that he could not afford the severe casualties that were implicit in a prolonged campaign in Laos."[14]

President Thieu declared the operation a resounding success. One of his generals had another view. Major General Nguyen Duy Hinh said,

> The picture of ARVN soldiers hanging on the skids of a helicopter which evacuated them from lower Laos, and other equally dramatic photographs showing battered I Corps troops returning back across the Laotian border, caused grave concern among South Vietnamese, military and civilian alike.... Popular sentiment seemed to be aroused by the dramatic accounts and personal feelings of the I Corps troops who returned from Laos. Almost without exception they did not believe they were victorious.

General Hinh thought that in many respects RVNAF had done well, but pertinent to the question of Vietnamization, he said, "Credit should be duly given to the role performed by U.S. Army aviation, U.S. Air Force, and U.S. Naval air, for without them Lam Son 719 could hardly have been possible."[15]

And that was the problem with Vietnamization: just as during the pacification efforts, in essence American planning and support dominated the Vietnamization process. Colonel Vu Van Uoc, Commander, Air Operations Command VNAF, said after the war that ARVN completely lost the notion of being an independent army.

In a television address to the American people on April 7, after the RVNAF withdrawal, President Nixon proudly proclaimed, "Tonight I can report that Vietnamization has succeeded."

If Lam Son 719 were to be graded as an exercise in Vietnamization, by most standards other than Nixon's, it was a failure.

1972: "Nguyen Hue Campaign," or the Easter Offensive

Thieu's rationale for breaking off battle during Lam Son 719 and withdrawing his battered troops from Laos had been to preserve as many of them as he could for what he foresaw as a much greater trial ahead, a heavy enemy offensive in 1972. He was correct. The Communist official history stated, "In May 1971, the Politburo decided to develop our strategic offensive posture in South Vietnam to defeat the American 'Vietnamization' policy, gain a decisive victory in 1972, and force the U.S. imperialists to negotiate an end to the war from a position of defeat."[16]

Beginning on March 31, 1972, the equivalent of 13 enemy divisions plus several independent regiments and supporting units struck successively on three major fronts in a coordinated assault, assisted as always by regional and local forces, first in Vietnamese I Corps (the far north in South Vietnam), then III Corps (Saigon area north to Central Highlands, then II Corps (Central Highlands). Their armor and heavy, long-range artillery were used to back up the infantry in vicious assaults that overran initial objectives. In I Corps, the enemy battled for a month, captured Quang Tri and then advanced on Hue. In II Corps they tried to split South Vietnam in half by taking Kontum in the west, then advancing east toward the sea. The III Corps critical target was An Loc, which, if taken, would open the gateway for a 60-mile surge down a much upgraded, now-paved Route 13 to the heart of South Vietnam, Saigon.

Because of massive U.S. withdrawal from Vietnam, the South Vietnamese were now fighting without the aid of American ground combat units but still had some advisors who controlled crucial air support. Before the offensive, North Vietnamese forces had been successful in taking and holding the jungle area to the northwest of Loc Ninh, so when the NVA launched its offensive, called the Easter Offensive by the Americans, the village of Loc Ninh northwest of An Loc became an important target.

Two years earlier, 1st Infantry Division had been withdrawn to the States. This left our old Task Force 1/4 Cav area of operations along Route 13 north of Lai Khe to the South Vietnamese, primarily ARVN's 5th Division whose units had sometimes worked with my task force in 1969.

In early 1972, major units of 5th Division and reinforcements from ARVN 18th Division were located at and around Loc Ninh and An Loc as a bulwark against three nearby NVA divisions plus supporting units, numbering ultimately some 35,000 fighters.

In the first few days of April, the NVA stuck hard at Loc Ninh. Most ARVN troops initially defended well, then some units broke and panicked. On April 8 Loc Ninh fell. The NVA 7th Division then pushed south, bypassing An Loc and occupying Route 13 all the way from what had been our June 6, 1969 counter-ambush area, south to our old Thunder III FSB, then farther south to 6 miles north of Lai Khe, headquarters of 5th ARVN Division. The 7th NVA Division's mission was to prevent ground reinforcement from reaching An Loc, the only access road being Route 13. Now the NVA with its Soviet-made T-54 tanks "owned" this area where, only three years earlier, I had been "King of the Road."

In a helicopter above the battles raging below was Major General James F. Hollingsworth. He commanded Third Regional Assistance Command comprising what was left of the former IIFFV after virtually all of its combat units had been withdrawn to the U.S. In this position he was both adviser to the III Corps commander, and commander of the remaining American advisors in III Corps. In World

War II Abe and Holly had been two of the very best tank battalion commanders under Old Blood and Guts. Profane, brash, with numerous valor and Purple Heart awards from three wars, Hollingsworth was a fighter. Abrams told Hollingsworth to give full support to the South Vietnamese defending An Loc. Hollingsworth, being Hollingsworth, took this as a call for him to fight this battle, and fight it he did. Day and night he flew over An Loc, programmed B-52 strikes, brought in tactical air to hit troops and tanks on the ground, constantly encouraged his advisors with the An Loc defenders to hang in there, and helped them coordinate the ground and air support they needed.

Inside An Loc was advisor James H. Willbanks who wrote the definitive book, *The Battle of An Loc*. He coordinated and fought until wounded and evacuated several weeks later. Willbanks quoted Hollingsworth's statements to *Newsweek* reporters:

> "Once the Communists decided to take An Loc, and I could get a handful of soldiers to hold and a lot of American advisors to keep them from running off, that's all I needed." He told the advisors in An Loc, "Hold them and I'll kill them with airpower; give me something to bomb and I'll win." General Abrams chastised Hollingsworth for this statement because he thought Hollingsworth had given the impression he was taking over what should have been a South Vietnamese-run show. In fact he would do just that because the ARVN corps commander was not prepared to handle a battle of this magnitude. It was just what the American general had prepared for his whole life.[17]

The regional and local forces who, until Abrams' times, had been poorly supported by their government and the U.S. aid mission, had by now been equipped and trained to a level that made them credible fighters. These men fought tenaciously to defend their homes and families. With enemy tanks in the streets of An Loc, the defenders used LAWs—light antitank, shoulder-fired weapons—against the unsupported tanks with devastating effect. The American advisors played a heroic and crucial role, providing the necessary ground communication for Hollingsworth's overhead direction of air support.

When the smoke of battle finally lifted over An Loc, the RFs, PFs, PSDF (Popular Self-Defense Force) and ARVN soldiers were standing as victors.

Virtually all RF/PFs and PSDFs in the An Loc battle lived in the An Loc/Quan Loi/Loc Ninh area, and many of the ARVN 5th Division soldiers had their homes just south of it. The ultimately successful defense of An Loc demonstrated that when South Vietnamese were defending their home turf, under command of a few good, heroic leaders such as Colonel Nhut, the province chief, and with the lives of their families at stake, they would fight like tigers.

As a test of Vietnamization, however, there was no reliable gauge since again ARVN had advisors which brought them reinforcement and enormous air support, to include crucial logistic resupply by landing helicopters and C-123s on the small airstrip, and when antiaircraft fire was too intense, by airdropping equipment and supplies from C-130s. A general much respected by Americans, Lieutenant General

Ngo Quang Truong, who commanded I Corps, wrote a treatise about the Easter Offensive in which he praised various forms of U.S. support, obtained through the advisers. He was especially thankful for B-52 support which was used several times as tactical air, striking concentrations of enemy close-in to An Loc as they launched their attacks. After praising the leadership of Colonel Nhut and the resilience and effectiveness of the soldiers on the ground, he wrote, "The enemy's back had been broken and An Loc saved only because of timely B-52 strikes."[18]

By late September 1972 the enemy had been pushed back from their advanced positions in all three Corps zones. However, some terrain in the battlefield areas remained under enemy control. Tang, the PRG's minister of justice, and a perceptive commentator on the war, said "For all the verbiage that has been spent on these events, what had happened was very simple. Practically the entire North Vietnamese army was now inside South Vietnam—to stay."[19]

Of huge significance in terms of the viability of Vietnamization was its present—1972—and its near future. It had been severely tested ever since the 1967 decision of the Politburo to conduct war with "big battalions" in "big battles." With support of the Viet Cong infrastructure, guerrilla activities, and small unit battles continuing as always, the emphasis for the North continued to be on its general offensive/general uprising strategy, the final phase in Mao's "People's War." In the face of this strategy, the question was, could the South go it alone?

President Nixon, in his book *No More Vietnams*, had declared the Cambodian incursion of 1970 a success of Vietnamization, coming on the heels of his declared success of pacification. Carrying this mindset into the 1972 Easter Offensive, he was not going to let Vietnamization now fail.

However, a June 10, 1972 transcript of a briefing by General Abrams and his staff demonstrated then, and in later analyses, that the South could not go it alone. The transcript stated, "A dramatic increase in the Free World Military Forces' tactical air capability has been realized since the enemy offensive began."[20] A significant portion of the U.S. Air Force, Navy, and Marines responded from wherever they were based in the world to answer Nixon's call for maximum effort to defeat the offensive.

General Truong, the South's best field commander, acknowledged this massive U.S. support. He wrote,

> Among other things, the United States substantially increased its air and naval fire support and provided South Vietnam with as much equipment and supplies as were required. Furthermore, this support was coordinated with an increased bombing campaign in South Vietnam, increased interdiction of supply lines in Laos, renewed bombing of North Vietnam, and the blockade of major North Vietnamese ports, all in a remarkably successful effort to reduce the effect of the enemy offensive.... Quang Tri city certainly could not have been retaken, nor could ARVN forces have held at Kontum and An Loc had it not been for the support provided by the U.S. Air Force.[21]

Nixon could not allow himself to realize that if such a U.S. effort were necessary, that in itself would proclaim the failure of Vietnamization. He insisted that because of his intensive bombing of North Vietnam, "We succeeded in crippling North Vietnam's military effort."[22]

Nixon's assessments were—well, Nixon's.

Pacification had taken a severe beating during the enemy's 1972 offensive. South Vietnam's General Tran Dinh Tho wrote,

> For all its efforts, the GVN was still a long way from solving the social and economic problems that plagued Vietnam, especially in the context of a war in which the enemy always held the initiative and had the capability to wreck any achievements any time he chose. This happened in 1968 [Tet Offensive] and again in 1972 [Easter Offensive], when a few months of attacks undid years of hard toil. Unless South Vietnam was free from North Vietnam's military threat, pacification or any nation-building task remained a hopeless proposition.[23]

Situation, late 1972, early 1973

Both sides were exhausted from fighting and needed replenishment in manpower, supplies, and equipment. The South Vietnamese had had the advantage of enormous help of the Americans. But their enemy had made inroads that would take great effort, time, and casualties to try to overcome.

The North had been stopped from attaining their ultimate objectives in all four Corps areas, but they retained important advantages for further action. The bulk of their units, several of them severely battered, were still in South Vietnam or just across the border in Cambodia or Laos. As had been their practice from the earliest times of the French war, while they recuperated, resupplied, re-equipped, took in replacements, and retrained for the next missions, they kept fighting to the best of their ability. The NVA and ARVN sparred to grab land before the anticipated final Paris Peace Talks in order to enhance their positions at the bargaining table. The guerrilla war continued while NVA main force units exerted pressure and in many places scored tactical victories.

Near the end of 1972, from the Demilitarized Zone in the north, NVA offensive actions had opened a corridor relatively free of ARVN interdiction all the way south from I Corps down the western reaches of South Vietnam through II Corps to III Corps north and northwest of Saigon. The danger to the South's capital was palpable. Except for garrisons at An Loc and Chon Thanh on Route 13, the NVA controlled all of crucial Binh Long Province.

Barely northwest of An Loc and its ARVN garrison, which did not patrol much beyond its defensive perimeter wire and bunkers, the PRG headquarters was so secure that in the spring of 1973 Loc Ninh became its temporary capital. The ARVN

5th Division was hard-pressed in trying to keep Route 13 open from Lai Khe for supply of the garrisons, and aerial resupply soon became the only means to enable their existence. In IV Corps south of Saigon to the southern tip of South Vietnam, unlike farther north, enemy units did not focus so much on terrain objectives as on continuing pressure throughout the whole area with guerrilla and small regional force actions.

In their well-used "talk-fight" strategy, North Vietnam stalled on negotiating a final peace agreement, perhaps to buy time for highlighting for the world Thieu's profound intransigence: he adamantly would not sign. In essence the draft agreement included: an in-place cease fire, withdrawal of U.S. forces; exchange of POWs; prohibition of sending additional troops to Vietnam; equipment replacement only on an item-for item basis; international commissions to ensure compliance, and an international agency to organize free elections in South Vietnam.

Ominously for the South, the draft agreement did not require the withdrawal of all of the North's troops from South Vietnam. President Thieu had insisted all along that the agreement must guarantee removal or he would not sign. The spectacle of Nixon bullying Thieu to sign left no doubt in many quarters that America had pulled the strings from the beginning.

Enraged at the North's delaying tactics, to show them he really meant business, in December 1972 Nixon ordered *Linebacker II*, the "Christmas bombing" of North Vietnam. This time the air assault would be primarily with the big stuff: B-52s in concentrated attacks. He told Admiral Moorer, chairman of JCS, "I don't want any more of this crap about the fact we couldn't hit this target or that one. This is your chance to use military power effectively to win this war, and if you don't I'll consider you responsible."[24] The goal of the bombing was to take out the remaining military and other facilities in the Hanoi-Haiphong area which supported the North's war effort—power plants, industrial buildings, electric works, railroads, bridges—a devastating blow not just to the military but to the North's economy. To get the recalcitrant Thieu in line, Nixon sent General Alexander Haig to him with an ultimatum: sign or all aid will be cut off immediately.

Thieu was finally forced into acquiescence by Nixon's threat, and the North quickly resumed talks. Nixon said, in Nixonian reasoning, "Militarily, we had shattered North Vietnam's war-making capacity. Politically, we had shattered Hanoi's will to continue the war."

An agreement was signed.

Nixon proclaimed in his book, *No More Vietnams*, written 10 years after the war had ended when only an alien from Mars would not have known that North Vietnam had won the war, "On January 27, 1973, almost twenty years after the French had lost the first Vietnam War, we had won the second Vietnam War."[25]

Well!

The "Sustainability Quotient"

Nixon's statement deserves the derision which it received, but the circumstances which led up to it went to the very core of American participation in this war.

Mathematicians define "quotient" as the result of dividing one number by another. The term has also come to have much broader meanings. Sociologists, psychologists, and business consultants speak of other quotients such as moral, emotional, adversity. These quotients include the capacity to analyze and to act.

War inevitably damages both sides. I believe that America collectively—its people, its Congress, its president—has what may be called a sustainability quotient in conducting war. It is an ability to sense how long America can engage without further pervasive damage to itself, and an ability to act upon that feeling.

Tet 1968 vividly revealed that America had reached the limits of its sustainability quotient. A sense of what the U.S. could and should do was central in two key addresses by the U.S. presidents who led most of the American effort in the Vietnam War, Lyndon Johnson and Richard Nixon.

Two months after Tet, Johnson said in his March 31, 1968 address to the nation that his administration had offered 30 previous peace initiatives "that we have undertaken and agreed to in recent years." If the war were to continue, he said, "Armies on both sides will take new casualties. And the war will go on. There is no need for this to be so. There is no need to delay the talks that could bring an end to this long and this bloody war."

The war continued.

Nixon began his January 23, 1973 address, "I have asked for this radio and television time tonight for the purpose of announcing that we today have concluded an agreement to end the war and bring peace with honor in Vietnam and in Southeast Asia."

Johnson did not live to hear Nixon's address. He had died on the previous day.

The American war in Vietnam had been building since 1945 when the U.S. supported the French Expeditionary Force. This was nearly 23 years before Johnson spoke, and 28 years when Nixon definitively proclaimed that America was getting out. By contrast, America's World War II had lasted three years and seven months. For America, that global war was far shorter than the "limited" Vietnam War. When faced with the necessity for survival during World War II, the sustainability quotient was simply the duration of the war, whatever that might turn out to be. Americans knew that the war had to be fought until it was won, and fiercely supported the effort. But after many years of war in Vietnam, Americans ultimately concluded that its survival did not depend upon "victory." An acceptable duration had been exceeded.

PART THREE

THE VIETNAMESE WAR—THE RESULT

***

Haponski's question:

"Were you afraid of the VC? of the Americans?"

The answer of the four women from Binh Co—Nghanh, Nhan, Tuong, Luong:

"We were not afraid of them. But we were afraid of and didn't like the ARVN."

Phu Cuong, April 2010

***

CHAPTER 14

A South Vietnamese–North Vietnamese War, 1973–74

The signing of the Paris Peace Accords on January 27, 1973 marked the beginning of a radically new type of Vietnam War—no more U.S. advisors, no more U.S. artillery, naval gunfire, or air support. Pacification, as the Americans and South Vietnamese had attempted to practice it, was virtually dead. CORDS ceased to exist on February 27, 1973 when a tiny fraction of its capabilities was transferred to an office under the U.S. ambassador. No such thing now as Vietnamization.

Old Training and The New Face of the War

After the war, North Vietnamese Colonel Bui Tin reflected on the American army and its Vietnamization attempt:

> In my opinion, the organization and equipment of the American forces were formalistic and cumbersome, and therefore totally unsuitable for contending with conditions on the ground in Vietnam, its climate and above all the nature of a struggle that was rooted in the people. The same was true of the Saigon army. Under American influence, its organization and weaponry lacked any flexibility. Even its uniforms were too heavy.[1]

There is more than a little truth in his statement, as borne out by photos of diminutive Vietnamese under American steel helmets which produced massive headaches and seemed to swallow the individual. We saw many Vietnamese units solve the problem by wearing only the light helmet liners, even during contact with the enemy—no protection at all. After all, was the reasoning, the enemy wore light pith helmets, jungle hats or caps, usually not steel helmets. Much more troublesome than their equipment, Bui Tin said, was that "the Saigon army only knew how to fight American-style. It had forgotten its basic roots and lost its self-confidence."[2]

Interestingly, our U.S. military schools and colleges not only short-changed American officers by not teaching to the war we were fighting and projecting ahead to those we might have to fight, but Vietnamese officers ironically felt that "[Vietnamese] commanders given U.S. schooling got very little benefit from it.... What little they did learn did not apply to the situation in Vietnam, where the enemy and the terrain required a different type of warfare than that taught at American defense colleges."[3]

The enemy—Viet Minh, Viet Cong, NVA—had learned from necessity how to fight a People's War. They had organized in different configurations to meet specific needs, from local fighters, recruiters, and administrators at the hamlet and village level up to division-size forces, and they had gained years of experience in doing so. Contrasting with the People's War strategy of the enemy in which the people supported them through compassion or compulsion or some combination of the two, the South Vietnamese never were able similarly to organize their people to fight a People's War. Nguyen Ba Can, Speaker of the House in Thieu's government and, near the end of the war, briefly Prime Minister, said,

> It is important to consider that there were two categories of people in [South] Vietnam. One category had to fight for the other category—I mean the armed forces. Only the armed forces had the responsibility to fight the war, in the opinion of the people. The people remained outside of this. They were not involved in the fight. It was the opposite of a "people's war." The way we conducted war, we should have realized that in the long run we had to lose it.... To sum up, the war was lost from its inception.[4]

MACV was disestablished on March 29, 1973 and replaced by a Defense Attaché Office, Saigon. It had only a small contingent of military staff. Except initially for certain replacement supplies and equipment—and by congressional action that too would soon be severely curtailed—South Vietnam would be on its own.

Of course, neither the South nor the North respected the Accords. Both sides continued a land grab begun in late 1972. Armed clashes and political proselytizing by both sides among the South Vietnamese people continued.

The International Commission

The Accords provided for an International Commission of Control and Supervision (ICCS) which had many duties, among them to supervise the cease fire and compliance with other restrictions on actions. It was to report on how the Accords were being followed. Two Communist countries, Hungary and Poland, and two non-Communist nations, Canada and Indonesia, were its members. Canada resigned after five months, replaced by Iran, at that time, politically a U.S.-leaning, non-Communist country under the reign of Shah Pahlavi.

The ICCS consisted of various field teams from all sides of the war, each of which comprised representatives of all four ICCS nations. These teams had diplomatic status and were to have freedom of movement in order to carry out their tasks.

The establishment of ICCS headquarters at Tan Son Nhut airbase on the northwestern edge of Saigon created an interesting coincidence. South Vietnam's enemies from Hanoi and from the PRG of South Vietnam now set up offices in the capital which to date they had tried and failed to take by revolutionary violence.

Since the U.S. was the only signatory more or less trusted by the North, and since it had a multitude of aircraft ready at hand in South Vietnam, initially it was American aircraft and their crews which flew team members into Saigon and to various places in Vietnam where they needed to travel to execute their duties. Ironically in ICCS there was a strange mingling of former enemies within South Vietnam, basically no longer shooting at one another. Except verbally, and there was a lot of that.

General Tran Van Tra had been Deputy COSVN Military Commander in 1969 when my task force had fought against his units. Then he was commander of the 1972 Easter Offensive attack on Loc Ninh/An Loc, the crucial northern gateway to Saigon. He was appointed head of the military delegation of the PRG.

A pickup of the general and his small staff was arranged for the air strip at Loc Ninh. Tra wrote,

> On 1 February 1973, a flight of U.S. helicopters landed, commanded by an American lieutenant colonel who was accompanied by a puppet officer. The U.S. major commanding my helicopter was very polite, carefully inspecting my seat, then stepped down, stood at attention and saluted, invited me to board the helicopter, fastened my safety belt, then sat down in his seat. The helicopters took off and headed straight for Saigon along Route 13.

Tra flew over An Loc which in 1972 he had tried so desperately to take, and which I remember so well from my convoy duties and two postwar visits. He said, "The flock of helicopters followed Route 13 past villages along the route. All of those places had been the location of many fierce battles between us and the American and puppet troops over the course of many years."[5] The general flew over what had been my Thunder III, II, and I fire support bases. He and I had both lost men in battles on and along that road, he many more than I.

Tra continued,

> The helicopters landed in the military part of the airfield [Tan Son Nhut]. Our delegation thanked the crew members and shook their hands. Looking neat in the tidy insignia-less liberation army uniforms, we formed into an orderly line on the runway. The officers carried briefcases and wore revolvers. The enlisted men wore floppy jungle hats and carried backpacks and AK rifles. Everyone wore the famous rubber sandals. I [didn't] know whether the Americans and their puppets understood the significance of that or not. Vietnamese and foreign reporters wrote, "They entered Saigon, capital of the Republic of Vietnam, in the same rubber sandals they wore during Tet of 1968."

Tra said, accurately,

> The most important aspect of the agreement, and the first matter that had to be implemented, was the ceasefire.... But after 28 January 1973, the day on which the ceasefire took effect (and until 30 April 1975) [when Saigon was overrun], it was ironic that there was not a day on which the guns fell silent on any of the battlefields in South Vietnam.[6]

The pending departure of almost all Americans from Vietnam came to a head in March. Tra reported,

> In the morning of 15 March 1973 USARV, the U.S. Army Command in Vietnam, conducted a flag-folding ceremony and [hurried] out. In the afternoon, MACV, the U.S. Military Assistance Command in Vietnam ... also pulled down and folded its flag. Whether by accident or by clever design, the next day the military delegations of the DRV and the PRG of the RSVN drove into the courtyard of that "Pentagon of the East." The two delegations got out of their cars and advanced directly into the reception room, past two rows of American MP's who stood at attention and saluted, in order to attend a party organized by the major general who headed the U.S. delegation. We laughed, drank American whiskey, and talked about the weather and peace in Vietnam.... Thus the U.S. troops also got out. But ... they left behind all kinds of weapons, military bases, and even officers in civilian clothing, to prop up the Thieu regime.[7]

Saigon's Decisions and Actions

To many observers in late 1972 and early 1973, it seemed that GVN had emerged from the Easter Offensive in better shape than their enemies. In fact, South Vietnamese General Tran Van Don (who in the last weeks of the war rose to become Deputy Premier and Minister of Defense) said of the period right after the Paris Accords were signed, "Strangely enough ... our military situation at that time was probably the best it had ever been, including the time of maximum buildup of U.S. forces in our country.... In fact, at that time, we had the best control over our highways, roads, and other lines of communication that I can remember since the relatively safe days right after the 1954 Geneva Accords."[8]

General Don was correct in that the enemy was sorely stressed. At the time, the effective combat strength of South Vietnam's main forces was much greater than that of the PAVN and Viet Cong. In addition they still had many of their RFs, PFs, and PSDFs whereas their enemy's regional and local forces had suffered much more. General Tra confirmed, "In 1973 our cadre and men were fatigued, we had not had time to make up for all our losses, all units were in disarray, there was a lack of manpower, and there were shortages of food and ammunition."[9] Contrary to that situation, in late 1972 just before the Peace Accords came into effect, the Americans had kicked into high gear their programs called Enhance, and Enhance Plus, which loaded GVN with replacement equipment—in fact, as became evident, more than it could train soldiers to maintain and operate.

RVNAF had been helped for years by the U.S. Vietnamization program. No good deed goes unpunished? Vietnamization had done virtually everything to help the Vietnamese military except to remove U.S. advisors from Vietnamese high-level staffs and combat units. Had this been done, the Vietnamese would have been forced to use their own artillery, airlift, logistical and tactical air support for troops in contact. They would have had to exercise fully their own planning, command and control. Unfortunately, there never had seemed to be a right time to do that. ARVN performance had always been so demonstrably questionable that no one in sufficient authority, South Vietnamese or American, was willing to risk the losses that might have resulted from battles without the support U.S. advisors brought. But in early 1973, with U.S. advisors no longer on the scene, there is scant evidence that Thieu prepared his forces to solve that critical problem of self-reliance.

What he did do was to institute "the Four No's": No territory or outpost would be given up to the enemy; there would be no coalition government; no further negotiation with the enemy; and no tolerance for Communist or neutralist political activity. This strategy, if it can be called such, was meant to stiffen the resolve of the South Vietnamese to build a secure nation which would resist and repel their enemy.

Hanoi's Decisions and Actions

On Hanoi's side, the most encouraging aspect of the situation for them in the early months of 1973 was that whereas General Don could report accurately that travel along the coastline was quite safe for ARVN, the situation inland was different. PAVN units could move relatively securely from Hanoi south through a corridor along the Annamite Chain all the way down to positions near Loc Ninh. All headquarters of the DRV "conducted a general review of the situation and goals of the first six months of 1973." The result, taking only one instance of actions around Quang Tri, is representative of many that occurred throughout South Vietnam. In the region around the nearly defunct Demilitarized Zone,

> The Military Region Command used provincial and district local force troops, supported by guerrilla forces, to hold our front lines directly in contact with enemy forces. This enabled the Military Region's main force units to be gradually withdrawn from the defense lines in northern Quang Tri and pulled back to base areas for reorganization and consolidation.... They strengthened their combat posture and stayed ready to advance into the lowlands when an opportunity presented itself.[10]

Creation of Four Corps Headquarters, and Improvements to Roads and Pipelines

Two major events revealed the North's determination to finish the war. They created four corps headquarters, and they made vast improvements to their roads and fuel pipelines to the South.

Lack of NVA corps commands had greatly decreased the effectiveness of combat actions. Trying to coordinate so many individual infantry divisions and separate regiments, plus regiments and brigades of air defense, armor, artillery, engineer and many smaller technical and support units across such widely dispersed areas had led to confusion on the battlefields. The solution was to create, successively, four corps headquarters, 1st, 2nd, 3rd, 4th, similar to what the South Vietnamese had long possessed. By doing so, the North came into line with other modern armies. The official history stated, "Our army was now able to launch large-scale offensive campaigns using combined-arms forces in several different strategic theaters in order to bring the war to an end."[11]

Although General Giap had long been out of the business of being a battlefield commander, from his position as Defense Minister and Chairman, Central Military Party Committee, no doubt he felt great satisfaction in bringing PAVN to this point—formation of four modern army corps from its meager beginning: his command as "general" of that little band of 34 comrades at Pac Bo in 1944.

The second major event which revealed the North's intentions was the improvement and expansion of its logistics and communications networks within the South. Unfettered now by American air attacks, not only did the army greatly improve the Ho Chi Minh Trail on the western (Laotian-Cambodian) side of the Annamite Mountains range, but it also began construction of a new parallel, wide road on the eastern side, inside Vietnam itself, all the way down into Cochinchina. Dubbed "Ho Chi Minh East," this road enabled delivery of equipment and supplies directly to fighting units. Additionally, paralleling the strategic transportation and troop movement corridor was a petroleum pipeline network.

During 1973 Saigon was well protected by heavy ARVN concentrations and the strategic reserve of airborne and Marine units positioned around and within the city. Having interior lines, building logistical and combat unit strength was easier for the South than the North. Ominously, Thieu's forces were following his orders to dig in and defend its terrain—a Maginot Line syndrome?—while his enemy was building for highly mobile offensive action.

In North Vietnam the numbers of youths entering military service was up, and after they were trained they were sent south in large convoys. PAVN forces in both North and South Vietnam instituted training sessions of three to six months for political cadre and military units.[12]

Le Duan was overcoming problems that could inhibit his push to end the war. In mid-1973, Premier Zhou Enlai was encouraging Le Duan to "'relax' and stop fighting in the south for five or ten years."[13] As usual, the North Vietnamese cordially listened and then proceeded to do what they wanted—make plans to end the war as quickly as they could.

Contrasting Sides in the Story

Whereas earlier in this book the story played itself out largely at the levels of the people and the fighters themselves, now it necessarily focuses on what happened at the very top within Vietnam: on the one hand Nguyen Van Thieu alone; and on the other, Le Duan among a bevy of high-ranking officials who planned carefully, consulted often, and arrived at conclusions based on long experience.

The South Vietnamese side of the story is virtually that of Nguyen Van Thieu. Whereas Chairman of the Joint General Staff, Cao Van Vien, and his office provided necessary staff work, it was Thieu himself who set their agenda and shaped the process toward the final decisions which he made. One can be certain that every major decision on the South Vietnamese side that affected the outcome of the war was now entirely his, from conception to proclamation. Crucially, the commands which went out to his four corps and his strategic reserve during the vicious fighting which was to come were not shaped in any meaningful way by his highest-level staff. They were his, and his alone.

The situation on the North Vietnamese side was very different. Whereas no one doubted that Le Duan would have the final say, the careful, progressive work of the Politburo, the Central Party Military Committee, and its two senior generals, Vo Nguyen Giap and Van Tien Dung, were very much integral to the decision process.

On May 24 the Politburo met, and in speaking to the membership Giap used information obtained from spies in both General Cao Van Vien's office and Thieu's office, including the South's "urgent pacification plan from March to August 1973, the three-year pacification plan (1975–77), the five-year plan for the building of the puppet army (1974–79), the eight-year economic plan (1973–80)."[14] There was not much the North didn't know about what to expect.

Rehabilitation Operations by the North, 1973–74

Greatly concerned over not just personnel losses during the 1972 offensive, but also of equipment during this period in which China's patronage was reduced, Giap spurred prodigious efforts internally to rebuild. "During 1973–74 all units of the armed forces conducted a general inventory of property and finances and organized the retrieval, collection, and repair of equipment, thereby partially resolving some of our logistics and technical support problems."[15]

Units were told to reduce their expenditure especially of large-caliber ammunition, and to repair and use captured equipment. At upper echelons, great efforts were made to produce needed equipment, to move damaged equipment to the North for repair, to substitute low-caliber ammunition which was in good supply for larger caliber, to send repair teams with specialty tools to the battlefields to make on-site repairs, and to train many more technicians. At the same time, combat units on the battlefields were ordered to assist engineers in improving the road and pipeline networks needed for large-scale movement of equipment and supplies to the South. As a result, the North was able greatly to increase the flow of materiel to their units.[16]

The result of these rebuilding efforts was that in early 1974 PAVN units began increasing the number and strength of attacks on ARVN forces, and this continued throughout South Vietnam during the year. Even more ominously for the survival of South Vietnam's government, as it would turn out, some of its generals and civilians in high positions were beginning surreptitiously to contact the PRG about whether some kind of coalition government might be possible.[17]

The Thieu Government and Corruption

In June 1973, the North's Military Committee reported that "Quantities of weapons recently poured in by the United States fell into the hands of the Liberation Army." Quite certainly most of this was not the result of capturing weapons during battle, but dealings with corrupt South Vietnamese officials.

In my research I had found no evidence of this kind of corruption for personal gain on any significant scale in North Vietnam, so I asked Merle Pribbenow, the CIA expert on Vietnam, to comment. He agreed, saying in an email to me: "There were reported problems of pilfering of supplies at Haiphong harbor during the war, but I do not recall anything indicating that there was high-level corruption or that the problem was as serious and widespread as it was in South Vietnam."

Many South Vietnamese high-ranking officials commented on how damaging corruption was to their efforts during the last years of the war. General Cao Van Vien, South Vietnam's ranking soldier, was respected by all MACV commanders. Post-war he wrote that several high-ranking military officers to include province chiefs and two corps commanders—plus Thieu's assistant for security!—were publicly charged with corruption. The two corps commanders were temporarily removed from command, but Thieu took no action against his security assistant. By 1971, Vien said, corruption had become widespread in RVNAF.[18]

General Vien reflected on the period 1973–75:

> Finally, after many years of continuous war, South Vietnam was approaching political and economic bankruptcy. National unity no longer existed; no one was able to rally the people behind the national cause. Riddled by corruption and sometimes ineptitude and dereliction, the government hardly responded to the needs of a public which had gradually lost confidence in it.[19]

The United States was still providing some military aid to South Vietnam. General Tran Van Don, Thieu's Minister of Defense, said,

> With a team of young, but dedicated, technicians I determined that the greatest problem with the administration of the aid we did get from the United States … was with the organized

system of corruption at all levels of our administration. Of sixty generals and two hundred full colonels, fewer than one-third were "clean." A two-star general in the First Corps, Vietnam's most exposed area … illegally sold rice to the Communists … in the Highlands military region … all positions of command from district to provincial levels—even that of regimental commanders— were "purchasable." …. until 1973 President Thieu was relatively honest, but he changed after the signing of the Paris Peace Agreements…. he shut his eyes to what his family was doing.[20]

Giap said, accurately, of the 1973 U.S. withdrawal,

The U.S. troops had completely pulled out…. Business circles regretted the "fortune-making" time when U.S. troops were present. The wives of puppet soldiers no longer worked for Americans, polishing shoes or selling cigarettes around U.S. garrisons. Rice in the six western provinces no longer flowed to Sai Gon in the same high volume as in the past. Imports were reduced. Unemployment was rampant. Money was devalued very quickly. Prices increased by leaps and bounds. Corruption prevailed at all levels without exception. The army abounded with "ghost soldiers."[21]

Such soldiers did not exist. Names were included in army lists for wages that were supposed to be paid automatically to their families but were instead raked off by scheming military and civilian officials.

***

President Nixon in late 1972 had secretly promised President Thieu that the U.S. "would take swift and severe retaliatory action" against North Vietnam if it violated the Peace Accords. Again in a meeting with Thieu at San Clemente in April 1973 he emphasized that if South Vietnam needed assistance, "we would act as the situation required." Nixon did not doubt he could do as he promised. He was Nixon! But in May, the House cut off funds for financing directly or indirectly U.S. combat activities in, over or off the shores of North Vietnam, South Vietnam, Laos or Cambodia. Also, by June, Watergate revelations were cutting closer to Nixon himself and he was far more concerned with Nixon than with South Vietnam. Then too, Congress proved to be more resistant than Nixon believed and on November 7, 1973 overrode the president's veto and passed the War Powers Resolution (Act). This put further restrictions on the president's ability to conduct war without Congressional action.

Thieu and others of his administration had taken Nixon at his word. They were bitter and later denounced America for betrayal. How could a country not do as its leader had promised? They could not fathom, given their type of government, and indeed that of many countries in the world, that a U.S. president had no right to make such promises without the backing of Congress.

PAVN's Creation of a New Offensive Posture, 1974

By May 1974 PAVN had regained its strength throughout most of Vietnam. Whereas the United States had earlier supplied more equipment and other war materiel than the South could use, the Soviet Union and China, apparently with the exception of artillery and artillery rounds, had adequately supplied the North.

***

An ominous development for South Vietnam was that there would be no repeat of Enhance and Enhance Plus type aid of late 1972. For FY 1973 Congress had appropriated $2.27 billion in military aid; In FY 1974 it decreased to $1.1 billion, cut to $700 million in September 1974.

***

During late spring and continuing through the summer and fall of 1974, PAVN units struck at many spots near the coastal cities of Da Nang, Chu Lai, and Quang Nai in II Corps zone. Farther north, in I Corps, they attacked just south of Hue. ARVN was able to hold them out of Hue, but the ring around the city was closing.

As it turned out, the attacks in III Corps zone north of Saigon were the critical successes for PAVN, although Giap and the Military Committee did not at first recognize this. Early in April, General Tran Van Tra's 7th Division overran the fire support base at Chi Linh on the Song Be River. This opened up an avenue for attack on Chon Thanh on Route 13, the critical post south of the An Loc outpost. The loss of this post and of others at Tay Ninh opened up the routes to Dau Tieng and the Michelin plantation. Critical positions along Route 13 which led into Saigon were now threatened all the way from An Loc south to Ben Cat. Then an NVA attack swept south along the Saigon River through Ben Chua, which had given us so much grief, and down into the Iron Triangle. Another arm of the attack went west to An Dien where I had had troops defending the bridge into Ben Cat. If these attacks had succeeded, ARVN to the north on Route 13 would have been cut off, and the road south would have been open to Phu Cuong, the last major ARVN position north of Tan Son Nhut on the northwestern edge of Saigon. But they did not succeed. ARVN counterattacks had given Thieu's forces breathing time.

Political Generals, and the Nature of GVN Military Forces

President Thieu, a general who had come to power in one of the coups after Diem's assassination, like Diem carefully crafted both civilian and military promotions, often down to district and battalion levels. Politics trumped merit. It was more important for a president to remain in power, even to the point of stationing his trusted elite reserve units close by as "palace guard" than to chance a strictly merit promotion. Earlier, in a few extreme cases, he had had to remove political favorites and replace them with more competent men. In October 1974, though, considerably upset that his top commanders had lost terrain to the enemy's strategic raids—the cardinal point in his four no's was not to give up positions—he relieved three of his four corps commanders, retaining only Ngo Quang Truong of I Corps. Gone was General Thuan, commander of III Corps, who, as a Thieu favorite and former 5th Division commander, had been most unimpressive when he worked with our 11th Armored Cavalry and 1st Infantry Division, and who had sold munitions and equipment to the enemy.

Thieu was soon to need all the competence and courage he could get from his commanders. Whereas ARVN had regained many of the positions it had lost, with the winter dry season already started, the enemy was in a greatly advantageous position. In an arc centered on Route 13 only 60 miles north of Saigon, General Tran Van Tra was building his combat capability by training his units and receiving considerable amounts of fuel, weapons, ammunition, and other war materiel from the nearby terminus of a main branch of the Ho Chi Minh Trail and pipeline.

After the war, General Don proposed reasons for the defeat of GVN. For one thing,

> We did not adopt correct military strategy to deal with the inexorable Communist steamroller. We spread our forces too thin, trying to maintain a presence in and defend each province town, an ambition clearly beyond our capability. Although by this time we had an armed force of over one million men, such a method of defense did not have a chance for success.[22]

Don also said that the nature of GVN's military forces was that families often lived in or near the defensive positions, thus virtually precluding mobility in response to an enemy attack. A soldier's natural inclination was to protect his family, and this interfered with his unit's ability to withdraw so they could fight another day.

The North Plans for the Dry Season, 1974–75

Giap and his Central Military Committee had worked during the summer of 1974 on a plan for the coming dry season when good trafficability would favor mobility in the attack. The plan contained guidelines for continuing operations in 1975–76 and was approved by the Politburo in October. Giap commented on the need for conserving resources in certain areas: "Heavy guns and tanks must be used thriftily; since the signing of the Paris Agreement, both the Soviet Union and China had stopped dispatching artillery to us."[23] Many meetings had preceded the Politburo's conference, and all high-level cadre had had a chance to contribute to the plan through its many revisions before Le Duan and the Politburo approved it—and the plan would continue to be tweaked as events developed.

Giap reported that on December 13, 1974 the Phuoc Long Province campaign began. Dong Xoia, a village we had secured in 1969, was "liberated," resulting in capture of a large store of artillery, shells, and rifles. A relieved Giap said, "The concern over a shortage of shells, which had been weighing heavily on my mind for some time, was now alleviated!" The province headquarters town of Phuoc Binh (Song Be) fell on 31 December. "For the first time in the South, a province—one near Sai Gon—had been entirely liberated."[24]

Phuoc Long Province was the ultimate test of Vietnamization. Giap noted that the South had fought back entirely using its own resources—and lost. He could not know it at the time, but the victory was to have far greater significance. Almost five months earlier, President Nixon had resigned in order to avoid impeachment for Watergate crimes, and now, President Gerald Ford did not counter with an American attack, as Nixon had promised to Thieu if such a thing were to happen. This signaled that the South indeed would be on its own for the rest of the war.

**

A patter of criticism of President Ford for not supporting South Vietnam failed to consider both the War Powers Act and the realities of any American military response. Congress would not have sanctioned such a move, and even if it had, the Phuoc Long situation did not lend itself to the quickest form of American reintervention, B-52 bombing. The North Vietnamese units around Phuoc Long were not massed and therefore not susceptible to the kind of bombing that had saved An Loc in 1972, and a timely insertion of sufficient U.S. ground forces would have been logistically and tactically an impossibility. Above all, the American people, profoundly thankful to be out of Vietnam, would not have supported such an attempt. Three weeks later, at a press conference [January 21, 1975], a reporter asked, "Mr. President, are there circumstances in which the U.S. might actively reenter the Vietnam war?" The president replied, "I cannot foresee any at the moment."

How much did U.S. withdrawal from the war and subsequent cuts in aid to the South Vietnamese determine the outcome to a decades-long war? Not much. On December 31, 1974 when Phuoc Long fell, the hour was late. Ho Chi Minh long ago had tapped into the two thousand years of resentment against foreign domination. Not his Communism, but his nationalism, his beliefs and conduct as a revolutionary, allowed him first to inspire, then shape and ultimately control a Vietnam-wide movement that would never give up on its idea of independence and union.

**

Success in Phuoc Long kicked Giap's Military Committee and the Politburo into high gear. The official Communist history *Victory in Vietnam* states,

> During the final days of 1974, after hearing reports from our battlefield commanders … the Politburo foresaw that a strategic opportunity might appear earlier than anticipated. For this

reason, in addition to the basic two-year plan for 1975–1976, the Politburo ordered that another plan be drafted so we would be ready to seize any opportunity to liberate the South during 1975.[25]

Historically, Ho and Giap had fought their war by taking time—lots of it—to prepare carefully and ensure that to the best of their abilities whatever they undertook would be successful. This was the Confucian way, the Viet Minh way. When Le Duan became powerful in the late 1950s, he was of a different mentality. He wanted to finish off the war in the South right away. Now, at the end of 1974, having met with a huge, relatively unexpected success quite quickly and easily in "liberating" Phuoc Long Province, not only Le Duan but Giap and others of the Politburo and Military Committee smelled blood in the water and were circling for the kill.

CHAPTER 15

Revolutionary Violence, the Final Act, 1975

Giap said, "The core belief of the current Central Committee Plenum was that the revolution in the South must continue its march along the path of revolutionary violence."[1] That term, "revolutionary violence," had been central to the ideology of Communist parties ever since Lenin.

Marx and Engels, in *The Communist Manifesto*, never used the term, but stated, "The Communists openly declare that their ends can only be attained by the forcible overthrow of all existing social conditions." Lenin, embroiled in an actual uprising of the proletariat, took this belief to its logical conclusion, asserting in "The State and Revolution" that revolutionary violence was the sole means of achieving overthrow of the bourgeois state since its leaders would not give up power in any other way. From early in his rise in the Party, Le Duan had enthusiastically advocated that concept. In his 1956 treatise, "Tenets of the Revolution in South Vietnam," he had proclaimed that the road to victory was that of revolutionary violence. And here, in early January 1975, with the Phuoc Long Province victory, the end was in sight.

Crucial Ban Me Thuot

For some months before that victory, the Military Committee and Politburo had made many revisions to their overall plan for 1975–77, and always they came back to the Central Highlands as the critical area to strike in their march on Saigon, in particular the large village of Ban Me Thuot, 100 miles north of Phuoc Long on Route 14. General Leclerc had recognized its importance in controlling access to points east and south, and had it seized in his northward sweep in Cochinchina in late 1945. Because of its advantageous position as the crossroad of trade routes, by 1975 Ban Me Thuot in the western Central Highlands had grown larger into what might be called a small city, and a strong South Vietnamese garrison had long been stationed there. NVA units were already relatively close to the city. Capture of it could lead to control of Route 14 to the south to Phuoc Long Province, and Route 21 east which intersected with strategic Route 1 on the coast. Route 1 ran all the way south along the coast from Hanoi to Nha Trang, Cam Ranh, Phan Rang, and Phan Thiet, all large cities heavily defended by Thieu's forces. Thus it was possible that capture of Ban Me Thuot would result in cutting South Vietnam in half, trapping all forces north of Nha Trang, and opening up Route 14 all the way south to Chon Thanh on Route 13 below An Loc. If Ban Me Thuot were to fall, Saigon would be in great danger.

The official history stated,

> Throughout the years of the resistance war against the French and on through the resistance war against the United States, the Central Highlands had always been a strategically important battlefield for both ourselves and the enemy. It was an area suitable for mobile operations and could support combat operations by main force units in Vietnam and throughout the Indochinese Peninsula.... On orders from the General Staff, between late December 1974 and February 1975 reinforcement units for the campaign began arriving at their designated assembly positions.[2]

Senior General Van Tien Dung was sent down from Hanoi by the Politburo to take charge of the campaign. Dung said, "This time we must effect a change quite different from those of any previous campaign."[3]

Dung said that their enemy at the beginning of 1975 had 1.3 million troops, including 495,000 main force men, 375,000 regional force (RF) troops, and 381,000 civil guards (PF and PSDF troops). That information as well as the positioning of those troops was based on reports from spies in Thieu's office, his general staff, and the offices of other high-ranking officials. The numbers generally accorded with what South Vietnamese officials later acknowledged. In addition, Thieu had a significant air force whereas the North had relatively few planes and they did not factor into the battle. Thieu had a significant advantage in numbers but had caused a terrible handicap when he insisted that his commanders must not yield ground. Dung had many fewer fighters in all categories, but he would fight using highly mobile forces. He had the initiative—attack—whereas Thieu, by fixing his units rigidly in place, would defend. It would be an uneven fight from the beginning.

Dung set up his headquarters west of Ban Me Thuot in forest that was tinder dry. He had problems with forest fires burning communication lines, and with elephants pulling down branches on which the lines were strung. Because he concentrated his forces in that area he had an advantage over Thieu's men five to one in infantry; in tanks and armored cars he was slightly superior, and he had twice as many artillery pieces. Dung told his staff what they already no doubt knew: "In the final phase of revolutionary war, in conditions where we are stronger than the enemy, we definitely must carry out annihilation attacks and liberate the towns and cities.... For the attack on Ban Me Thuot we are in a stronger position than the enemy." He pointed out that he had three divisions whereas the enemy had only one main-force regiment and some RF/PF security forces in position. "The battle for Ban Me Thuot is the key opening battle of the campaign," he exhorted them.[4] Early in March he was ready, and he issued orders.

The Battle for Ban Me Thuot

Dung wrote, "On the night of March 9 at 2:00 a.m. artillery and rockets poured down, and small arms and RPG fire added to the din. Tanks, armored cars and troop transports roared in toward town from all directions." Soldiers of Thieu's 23rd Division fought back fiercely as fighter bombers supported them in counterattacks, but by mid-morning on March 11 the division headquarters and all major defensive positions had been overrun. The next day the South Vietnamese strongly counterattacked, and at the height of it, communications failed at Dung's headquarters. He wrote, "Disturbed by the bombs and shells of the battlefield, a herd of elephants started 'evacuating' past our headquarters, headed for the Vietnam-Cambodian border. The rush threatened to flatten the headquarters, but the elephants just missed it and the only casualties were broken telephone lines."[5]

By March 12, most of the fighting around Ban Me Thuot was over, the city had fallen, and NVA formations were thrusting eastward toward the sea. Le Duan commented in a Politburo meeting, March 24, 1975, "Our victory is bigger than we expected. Ban Me Thuot marks a turning point and the beginning of a great general offensive to liberate South Vietnam.... The general offensive has begun; the Central Highlands opened the door. We will follow up by attacking Danang. Finally, we will liberate Saigon."[6]

As General Dung was attacking Ban Me Thuot, PAVN forces throughout South Vietnam were attacking almost everywhere. For example, the Dau Tieng–Michelin plantation area had been assaulted by the 9th Division beginning March 4, and they now occupied the base camp area in the rubber which we had battled through six years earlier. North of Ban Me Thuot, all was in chaos. PAVN was attacking hard-pressed ARVN units, and the ARVN counterattacks were not succeeding.

Thieu Abandons His "Hold at All Costs" Strategy

Shortly after Ban Me Thuot fell, President Thieu was forced to confront the failure of his absolute "no"—no giving up terrain. He quickly formed a new plan of defense which, according to some of his top generals, was the fateful decision which caused the ultimate collapse. He ordered that Ban Me Thuot be retaken and a final defensive line established in an arc roughly from the sea just north of Nha Trang to just north of Ban Me Thuot, then southwest the entire length of the border with Cambodia.

General Vien wrote,

> President Thieu's decision to switch strategy from "hold at all costs" to "hold as you can" was inevitable; he had no other alternative. The unfortunate thing was that this alternative was implemented too late and without appropriate planning and preparations. Therefore this sudden decision came as a hard psychological blow, with all the undertones of defeat.[7]

No other instance shows more clearly the disastrous effect of Thieu running a one-man show all those years. He would not trust his General Staff and corps commanders with studying options and devising contingency plans a year or so earlier because he knew everything better than anyone else. There must be no yielding of positions or even contingency plans drawn. In contrast were General Dung, Giap, the Military Committee, and Politburo who had planned together for years, sharing the single-minded goal of unifying the country under socialism and working as a team toward that end.

General Dung Orders Go, Go, Go

General Dung ordered attack—attack without delay. His troops had to forget the traditional manner of using time to carefully prepare their moves. He told his commanders, "The old ways of thinking, organizing, and acting ran counter to the demands of the newly developing situation.... It was not as if the enemy were organized, waiting for us with defenses prepared; they were disorganized, falling apart."[8]

South Vietnamese General Lam Quang Thi said rumors of Thieu ordering that all of I Corps and part of II Corps be abandoned, and that a new line be established intersecting the sea at Nha Trang to the south led to panic in I and II Corps. "These rumors were in part responsible for mass desertions in certain units as officers and soldiers asked themselves: 'Why do we have to fight to defend Danang and Hue while it has been agreed that the new line would lie somewhere [south] ... between Ban Me Thuot–Nha Trang'"?[9]

General Dung bemoaned the loss of even one day when they waited until dark to move on the roads to avoid the South's air attacks. These strikes were at high altitude, no doubt because of the antiaircraft fire, and he said, "when they dropped their bombs their aim was not precise, yet we did not send our troops into battle during the day—waiting, late, wasting time."[10] No more Confucian patience here. The general had to tell his commanders to go, go, go. They responded and they went, during daylight and darkness, slowing only sometimes to scarf up enormous quantities of abandoned equipment, munitions, fuel, vehicles, even aircraft. Before the battles, Giap had worried about having enough artillery and shells since the Chinese had stopped supplying them. No worry once battle was joined. They had more of everything than they could use, captured from their enemy or, in the case of food, mostly given to them by the people.

Disastrous Withdrawal

Thieu's withdrawal orders caused disaster. The forced withdrawal is the most difficult military maneuver to conduct effectively. Unless withdrawals are anticipated and planned carefully, they usually start from a crisis situation, an inability to hold a position which negatively affects the mind and performance of units. Maintaining contact among units is difficult, and an unexpected enemy thrust can cause a rupture that can lead to chaos.

Even before orders went out to South Vietnamese units to withdraw, soldiers' families and civilians were fleeing the oncoming destruction, clogging roads and impeding the withdrawal. Hue fell, and Route 1 south was a tangled mess of vehicles, soldiers, and civilians fleeing. Da Nang was next, and so on down the coast as columns of PAVN troops made their way through throngs of desperate people, past bodies, pushing aside destroyed vehicles to open the road ahead.

General Lam Quang Thi had been commander of I Corps Forward and at times acting commander of the corps. He said,

> By March 25, the situation was rapidly approaching chaos. Soldiers deserted to take care of their families. Police desertions mounted, and bands of armed stragglers roamed the streets. Shooting incidents between soldiers and police were reported. Food and water were running short and people panicked when they saw the evacuation of U.S. personnel and Vietnamese employees of the U.S. consulate. Civilians and soldiers fought to board commercial and American ships to flee the city. The airport was invaded and military aircraft seized by panicking soldiers. Bands of hungry, thirsty children wandered aimlessly in the streets, demolishing everything that happened to fall into their hands.
>
> I flew my wife to the airport. She and the family of Brigadier General Khanh … boarded one of the last military flights out of Danang [headed for Saigon] under heavy MP escort.[11]

As the enemy entered the city, Thi and other generals fled by whatever means, air and sea. Thi's helicopter made it to an LST offshore at night. I Corps commander General Truong and another general separately swam out to sea and were picked up by a U.S. Navy ship. Thi and his aide later flew in their damaged helicopter to Saigon where he picked up his family.

***

As Da Nang was falling, a White House memo on March 25 shows that President Ford was meeting with top officials. The president said, "I regret I don't have authority to do some of the things President Nixon could do."

***

By April 2, the coastal cities of Qui Nhon, Tuy Hoa, Nha Trang and Cam Rahn were taken, with only some isolated spots of defenders still holding out. All of I Corps and II Corps essentially had collapsed. By mid-April, Cambodia and Laos were on the verge of falling to the Communist forces of their countries. Worse for the South Vietnamese, Phan Rang, the last major defensive position on the coast, had fallen. Thi said,

> The fall of Phan Rang was a fatal blow to President Thieu's concept of [establishing] a new South Vietnam [behind the defensive arc that Thieu had ordered held]. It was also a fatal blow to his morale as ARVN units, before leaving the town, bulldozed and leveled the graves of his ancestors as the ultimate expression of hatred and anger.[12]

General Dung, commanding the massive PAVN movement southward, told of his logistics chief coming upon a broken-down truck and finding two sloppily dressed drivers repairing it. This officer asked,

> "Say, what unit are you from? Don't you think that's a ridiculous, inappropriate way for victorious troops to dress?" The drivers answered, "Sir, we're POWs." At this time over the whole battlefield, and in all units, our soldiers were using people who had previously been in Saigon's armed forces to drive and repair all kinds of vehicles.... In our advancing columns American M113 [armored personnel carriers], M-48 and M-41 tanks, 105mm and 155mm artillery pieces, and PRC-25 radios began gradually to make their appearance.[13]

I Corps and II Corps had been lost, and to the south in III Corps, the situation was critical for the South Vietnamese forces. Tran Van Tra's 9th Division, having taken Dau Tieng, cut Route 22 south of Tay Ninh and fought off ARVN counterattacks. Tay Ninh Province was now isolated from Saigon. An Loc and Chon Thanh on Route 13 were evacuated as the NVA moved in and now owned the terrain on which our Thunders III, II, and I FSBs had stood. The northern gateway to Saigon that we had kept closed was being burst open.

On April 3, General Dung was driven to Loc Ninh where cheering throngs received him. He was a short distance to the west at COSVN headquarters on April 8 when a motorcycle approached and Kissinger's nemesis at the Paris Accords, Le Duc Tho, got off. He brought the invigorating news that the Politburo had approved a plan for the liberation of Saigon. Dung was to command the campaign to be named in honor of Ho Chi Minh, and Tran Van Tra was to be one of his two deputy commanders. Le Duc Tho told the assembled commanders and staff that the Politburo said everyone must be focused on victory: "They have five divisions. We have fifteen divisions, not to mention our other strategic reserve forces."[14]

The Beginning of the End

On April 9 the final thrust began principally with a massive attack on Xuan Loc near what had been Blackhorse base camp where, seven years earlier, I had joined

11th Cav. The official Communist history, *Victory in Vietnam*, reported, "Xuan Loc was an important gateway to Saigon.... The 7th Division made the main assault."[15] In 1969 we had fought battalions of this division's 165th and 209th Regiments in the Michelin and along Route 13.

***

While the desperate battle at Xuan Loc was taking place, on April 10 America watched on TV as President Ford addressed Congress: "I have received a full report from General Weyand. He advises that the current military situation is very critical, but that South Vietnam is continuing to defend itself with the resources available. However, he feels that if there is to be any chance of success for their defense plan, South Vietnam needs urgently an additional $722 million in very specific military supplies from the United States. In my judgment, a stabilization of the military situation offers the best opportunity for a political solution."

But at this very late date, with the enemy in Xuan Loc ready to move on Saigon, the U.S. could do little except plan for evacuation of remaining U.S. and selected South Vietnamese personnel, which it did. Congress would provide funds only for evacuation efforts.

***

On April 21 President Thieu resigned, transferring power to Vice President Tran Van Huong. During a TV address to the South Vietnamese people he bitterly, tearfully read from Nixon's 1972 letter pledging "severe retaliatory action" if North Vietnam threatened the South. Thieu said, "The United States has not respected its promises. It is inhumane. It is untrustworthy. It is irresponsible."

A few days later Thieu and his family flew out to Taiwan.

On April 23 President Ford addressed the convocation audience at Tulane University. He said, "We, of course, are saddened indeed by the events in Indochina. But these events, tragic as they are, portend neither the end of the world nor of America's leadership in the world.... Today, America can regain the sense of pride that existed before Vietnam. But it cannot be achieved by refighting a war that is finished as far as America is concerned."

This, a week before Saigon fell.

***

On April 23, the U.S. evacuation of Saigon began. South Vietnamese General Don said that by the 26th, "Sixteen enemy divisions equipped with armor and heavy artillery were tightening their ring around Saigon."[16] General Dung had moved his advance headquarters down from Loc Ninh to the Long Nguyen Secret Zone just west of Chon Thanh near the spot where my task force had turned west to attack toward the Michelin plantation six years earlier.

On the 27th, President Huong stepped down in favor of General Duong Van Minh ("Big Minh") who appealed for a cease fire and was ignored. On the 28th and 29th, PAVN forces were shelling Saigon and Tan Son Nhut. On April 29, Merle Pribbenow, the CIA officer who helped me so much by translating enemy histories and providing invaluable insights, caught one of the last helicopters out. Ky and General Ngo Quang Trung took off by helicopter and landed on an American aircraft carrier. Generals Vien, Thi, and families were evacuated by the Americans. Big Minh and his wife bravely stayed behind, Minh futilely believing that he could negotiate an acceptable government with the conquerors.

The ARVN IV Corps commander and his deputy committed suicide, as did the ARVN 7th Division commander. The 5th Division commander shot himself in his headquarters at Lai Khe, which had been our 1st Infantry Division headquarters and one of QuarterCav's logistics and maintenance locations after we moved north out of Di An.

The official Communist history *Victory in Vietnam* states: "The Campaign Headquarters decided to attack Saigon from five directions: northwest, north-north-east, east-southeast, west, and southwest." Of the five, my men and I had fought in the first three. In the northwest, the NVA 3rd Corps was to strike from the Tay Ninh-Dau Tieng area to seize Tan Son Nhut and the South Vietnamese General Staff Headquarters. From the north-northeast, 1st Corps was to target Phu Loi and destroy the 5th Division at Lai Khe and Thu Duc. The thrusts from the east and southeast would employ two corps, the targets of which were Binh Hoa and Independence Palace in Saigon.

The End for Di An District

On April 29, the Lai Khe base was heavily shelled during the night, Ben Cat District Town was under attack, and National Route 13 was interdicted between Phu Cuong, the province capital, and Lai Khe. Phu Cuong was penetrated by NVA sappers. The fighting had reached Di An District. Nguyen Minh Chau, my friend, the incredibly brave, capable Marine who had been promoted to lieutenant colonel, described his last days:

> The situation at that time was extremely tense. The district government and the district military headquarters were hurriedly working on a defense plan against enemy tanks.
>   I had to stay with my soldiers and the people until the end.... My in-laws were worried about their grandchildren, so they took all my children down to Saigon to stay with them, leaving me free to carry out my duties. My wife, however, refused to leave and stayed at the

base to give me moral support. Seeing this, the soldiers and the local civilians felt more at ease and less worried....

All my RF soldiers, PF soldiers, and all the district, village, and hamlet officials obeyed their orders and were determined to remain at their posts to fight to the end. However, on the night of 29–30 April, we were abandoned and left helpless because we lost all contact with the Bien Hoa Province Military Headquarters.... A North Vietnamese regiment accompanied by T-54 tanks had moved down from the direction of Tan Uyen to the [northern part of] Di An district and was sitting there, waiting.

I discovered many years later that my Binh Co family was directly in the path of NVA forces rushing on Saigon and could have been in great danger during fighting. General Giap said, "Division 312 (Army Corps 1) made preparations to attack Binh Co and Binh My." The battlefield commander of NVA forces, General Dung, said, "It was the first time in the decades of resistance [in this part of South Vietnam] that trucks of the regional logistics section and the logistics departments of all the zones could come down from the east ... all the way to Binh Co and Binh My north of Tan Uyen."[17]

But as NVA units bore down on the two hamlets, great good fortune seems to have intervened. The ARVN units evacuated. During my 2010 visit there, my girls from Binh Co, now grown women with families, told me that the night after ARVN left, they had been on their sleeping mats, eyes wide open, holding one another close as they heard the NVA tanks clanking and grinding and trucks passing harmlessly by during the night.

Chau continued,

Our only choice was to fight as long as we could. We did not know whom we could rely on for help, so all we could do was entrust our fates to God. It was a night filled with terror and anxiety. Everyone, from officers and officials down to privates, had an anti-tank rocket, a machinegun, or a rifle in his hand and waited up the entire night for the enemy to approach our perimeter.... When we looked toward Saigon we could see the lights of helicopters landing and taking off. We guessed it was the Americans evacuating their people. We were all very shaken. We had no idea what would be the final fate of Di An district and of all of South Vietnam.

The next morning at 10:00 we heard the voice of General Duong Van Minh over Saigon Radio ordering all units to lay down their weapons and surrender. This news hit everyone, from officer to private, like a bolt of lightning, and the entire compound where the soldiers' families lived and the local population all burst into tears. I immediately used my radio to order all soldiers and district, village, and hamlet officials to destroy all documents and leave their units, wishing them and their families well and saying a few words of farewell, with my heart full of such sadness and bitterness that I could not stop my tears. 30 April 1975 ended my military career, a career that had lasted exactly 21 years, because I had joined the army in April 1954.[18]

The End for South Vietnam

Finally, with PAVN forces closing in on Saigon from multiple directions, as the official history relates,

A North Vietnamese tank entering the smashed-down gate of Independence Palace, April 30, 1975. This tank and all tanks in the column are fl ying the fl ag of the Provisional Revolutionary Government (PRG) of South Vietnam, an act of comeraderie which soon faded as the North clamped down and established totalitarian control. (Roger-Viollet/TopFoto)

> At 10:45 A.M., the lead tank … crashed through the palace gates and roared into the grounds of Independence Palace. A number of cadre and soldiers … marched into the Palace conference room and took puppet President Duong Van Minh and his entire cabinet prisoner. At 11:30 A.M. on April 30, 1975, the flag of the Revolution was raised in front of the main building of the Independence Palace complex.[19]

***

Addendum

After the Fall of Saigon

When General Tran Van Tra's International Control Commission duties were finished in 1973 he had gone back from Saigon to Hanoi and then down south again as COSVN commander. As a deputy to General Dung during the final campaign, on April 30, 1975, the day Saigon fell, he was at the command headquarters in the Long Nguyen Secret Zone just west of Chon Thanh, very near where we had turned west off Route 13 for our attack toward the Michelin. Tra said,

> Suddenly a cadre gleefully brought in a tape recorder and placed it on the table: it was the voice of Duong Van Minh announcing his unconditional surrender over the radio and ordering the

puppet troops to throw down their weapons and surrender. Everyone gathered around, listening silently. Everyone jumped with joy. Le Duc Tho, Pham Hung, and Van Tien Dung, who were very moved, hugged and kissed one another and firmly shook hands.[20]

General Dung also described what it was like at the command headquarters when they got the news of surrender.

> We wept. Yes, those tears were reserved for this day of total victory which so many generations had fought for with all their devotion and with all their passion, committing their lives to it.... Our thought, our first thought in that first moment of victory was of our beloved Uncle Ho.... Uncle's arm was still beckoning affectionately, calling us to his embrace ... beating time for us as we sang. The song was one which Ho was especially fond of leading groups in singing—Ket Doan—"Unity."[21]

The next day, Tra received word that the Politburo had appointed him chairman of the Military Management Committee of Saigon-Gia Dinh, and he quickly departed for Saigon. He said, "Our convoy left the command headquarters [and] passed through the Dau Tieng rubber plantation [the Michelin]."[22] In doing so, he drove through what had been our Fire Support Base Doc six years earlier where we had lost men and had killed and wounded many more of his in a fierce night battle. Then he crossed the ford we had bridged for our attack into the Michelin to strike into units of his 7th Division, resulting in the largest battle ever fought in the historically bloody plantation. A few days later General Giap flew down, and he and General Dung hugged in shared jubilation.

***

General Creighton Abrams, MACV commander, had said at his WEIU briefing on August 29, 1969, a few weeks after I returned home: "In the whole picture of the war, the battles don't mean much."[23] He was in charge. He was right. But during my command of Task Force 1–4 Cav, we lost 43 men either directly under my command, or in fights over which I had command authority. Twenty-one of them were killed in "battles," the big ones to which Abrams was referring. It is hard, very hard, to acknowledge that Abrams was right. I had long known I would have an agonizing tough time answering parents, wives, or children on what their loved one died for if they asked me. I do know they were courageous, fine young men who died while doing what their country asked of them as they were looking out for one another, and that is the best answer I could give. I believe that many combatants in that very long, heart-rending war—French, French Union, American, Free World Forces, South Vietnamese, North Vietnamese—might say the same.

CHAPTER 16

Conclusion: "You Cannot Kill an Idea With Bullets"

***

"You know, you never beat us on the battlefield."

Colonel Harry G. Summers, Chief, Negotiations Division,
Four Party Joint Military Team
Hanoi, a week before the fall of Saigon

———

"That may be so, but it is also irrelevant."

Colonel Nguyen Don Tu, Summers' North Vietnamese counterpart

***

The Vietnamese were conditioned by two thousand years of revolt against foreign occupiers. When they lost, as most often they did, they prepared for another try, time after time. The leaders of the few times they won were legends, revered down through the centuries.

Our story has been one of events *within Vietnam* and the people in that country who in large measure caused the events or took part in them. The high-level politics of Washington, Paris, Beijing, and Moscow—well revealed in many histories of the Vietnam War—provided a framework within which our autopsy progressed. There was no monolithic Communism, controlled by Moscow. Vietnamese Communism was uniquely Vietnamese. The leaders of both North and South Vietnam, contrary to frequent accusations, were not mere puppets of the foreign powers which supported them. They sought and accepted outside help and advice but ultimately danced to their own tune, often to the frustration of their supposed masters.

Independence. Unity. Two words, a single concept. How to convey it to the masses in order to create an independent, unified nation?

Much of it did not have to be conveyed. A deep yearning was already there.

This narrative has been an exploration from the point of view of a combatant, a soldier-scholar who needed to know what the war in which he fought and lost soldiers killed and wounded was about—really about. He was assisted by another combatant with keen insights to the war and its participants.

Post World War II, the Western World came to believe that containment was a strategy that could prevent the spread of Communism which was threatening to engulf countries of Southeast Asia, and perhaps beyond.

The French had ruled Indochina for a hundred years, and now, after World War II they sent an expeditionary force to re-establish control. If they could defeat Ho Chi Minh, his government, his army, they would in fact be contributing to stopping the spread of Communism. At least that is how the American government saw it, and sent massive aid. But France's nine years of war succeeded only in strengthening the resolve of Vietnamese seeking independence.

Enter the Americans. Why couldn't the Americans contain Communism just by assisting the South Vietnamese with the world's best military? Others had posed that question, but early in the American intervention, Kennedy had concluded, "It is their war. They are the ones who have to win it or lose it. We can help them, we can give them equipment, we can send our men out there as advisors, but they have to win it, the people of Vietnam."

The Americans were superbly proficient in fighting a different kind of war, a war of massive firepower applied at the right time and place. But the Americans were not trained to fight the kind of unconventional war that Vietnam presented. Americans set about fashioning the South Vietnamese armed forces along the same lines as their own. Big mistake. The American military was not organized, equipped, or trained to fight a war against men and women who had learned how to conduct People's War across two decades. And now the South Vietnamese military was similarly handicapped. North Vietnamese Colonel Bui Tin reflected on the American army and its influence on ARVN: "The organization and equipment of the American forces were formalistic and cumbersome, and therefore totally unsuitable for contending with conditions on the ground in Vietnam, its climate and above all the nature of a struggle that was rooted in the people. The same was true of the Saigon army. Under American influence, its organization and weaponry lacked any flexibility."

Clearly, the South Vietnamese government needed to work among the people and win their support. Pacification programs were necessary. But America took charge. Pacification should have been a Vietnamese endeavor, and it was not. After the Tet '68 offensive, Robert "Blowtorch Bob" wanted pacification expanded. He had designed a program and wanted it implemented—now!

Vietnamization went hand in hand with pacification. The South Vietnamese needed to learn how to plan, launch, and support combat operations all by themselves. But their dependence on U.S. advisers who provided crucial air and other support sapped their self-reliance. The enemy's Easter Offensive in early 1972 was a profound test of Vietnamization. It showed that the South Vietnamese desperately needed American help. An Loc and Quang Tri were two critical points which had to hold against vicious assault. Lieutenant General Ngo Quang Truong, the South's best field commander, commented on An Loc and Quang Tri, praising U.S. support obtained through the advisers. He wrote, "An Loc [was] saved only because of timely B-52 strikes." He continued, "Quang Tri city certainly could not have been retaken, nor could ARVN forces have held at Kontum and An Loc had it not been for the support provided by the U.S. Air Force."

At the top levels, enemy civilian and military leaders were dedicated Vietnamese Communists. Lower down, the motivation was mostly patriotism—compulsion to do their part in creating an independent, unified country. Our enemy generally were tough fighters, used to hardship and danger. I marveled at the little men we pulled from holes and tunnels in the jungle. Some of them had been existing there for years. They smelled terrible, like the jungle rot that was their life. Some had had terrifying B-52 strikes hit among them. Some of them changed sides, but the bulk of them fought until captured, often wounded. I was astonished at the bravery of individuals and units. It took guts to attack armored cavalry in a fire support base, but they came at us; and it took guts to stand up in lanes of rubber trees to fire RPGs and AKs at our attacking armored vehicles, but that is what they did. As we were killing and wounding them, they killed and wounded us. When their unit was badly hurt they would retire to a base camp and fill the vacant ranks with recruits, some of whom had just arrived from North Vietnam. They would regroup, retrain, and come back at us on another day.

Ho Chi Minh told his early fighters that the loyalty of the people was much more important than guns. If they had the people, they had everything. His people fought for a cause they believed in.

In my 2005 visit back to Binh Co, seeking to find my "family," I discovered that the only thing remaining from our rebuilding of the two houses and the school in 1968 was the metal roof of the family's house. It now was on the new, concrete house of Luong, the youngest of the three girls. The termites had loved our American-supplied lumber and had eaten the two houses and school down to the ground. Perhaps that could be taken as a metaphor for the whole American effort were it not for the several cattle I saw behind Luong's house. They turned out to be the offspring a few generations later of the young bull and heifer I had Tom Witter deliver to them in 1969. These livestock and a treadle sewing machine had given the family a decent chance of surviving the hardships of the war.

The French could never have won. It was too late, the world had shifted too much against colonialism, and the enemy was too much strengthened by an inbred idea of independence and unity. General Leclerc fought the enemy and came to conclude, "You cannot kill an idea with bullets." He urged his government to "Make a deal, at all costs."

We Americans could never have won. Our character, world opinion, and the likelihood of China coming into the war—perhaps resulting in a nuclear World War III—would never have allowed what would have been required: a brutal crushing of North Vietnam by invasion supported by massive area bombing as in World War II, followed by occupation of long duration. America's forces were trained and equipped to fight wars using massive firepower. The war in Vietnam needed a different approach. General Abrams concluded, "In the whole picture of the war, the battles don't mean much." He was right. Colonel Summers said to his North Vietnamese counterpart, "You know, you never beat us on the battlefield." Colonel Tu replied, "That may be so, but it is also irrelevant." Colonel Tu was right.

The South Vietnamese could never have won. As circumstances developed, they needed foreign troops in massive numbers to ensure their survival; they were plagued by corruption and favoritism in political and military appointments; they failed to offer their people a cause around which they could rally; and their forces too often victimized the people they were charged with protecting. When I returned to Vietnam in 2010 and found the four women from Binh Co who had been children in 1968–69, one of my questions was whether they had been afraid of the VC? Of the Americans? Their answer was, "We were not afraid of them. But we were afraid of and didn't like the ARVN." Their response speaks volumes about the South Vietnamese failure to win.

***

Some have said the war was lost because America left the war and Congress cut appropriations for the South Vietnamese. The causes went far deeper—into the character of the people, into the determination of one side to persevere no matter how long or what the sacrifice. How much longer should the U.S. have stayed; what number of names on the Vietnam Wall beyond the 58,318 should we have accepted; how much more than three-quarter trillion dollars should we have spent; how much longer should we have supported a government that could not gain the support of its people; how much longer should we have supported a military which had superior numbers of personnel and equipment but could not defeat its enemy? How long? Years? Decades? How long?

According to authoritative U.S., French, and Free World sources, in addition to America's casualties, other losses for the Indochina and Vietnam wars were: French Union forces 89,797 dead and missing; RVNAF 220,000; Free World 35,282; Viet

Minh, Viet Cong, and PAVN 1.1 million. How many civilians in North and South Vietnam, and in Cambodia and Laos were killed, wounded, disabled? No reliable figure can be given, but probably more than two million.

Vietnamese had fought foreigners for two thousand years, and our enemy was determined to fight for as long as it took. The lengthy mural that Hal Moore had seen in Hanoi showed only a couple inches as America's portion in the history of the Vietnamese struggle for independence. Had America not pulled out, would another inch or two, or even a foot or more have brought victory in Vietnam?

Ho Chi Minh had indeed tapped into the two thousand years of resentment against foreign domination. Not his Communism, but his nationalism, his beliefs and conduct as a revolutionary, allowed him first to inspire, then shape and ultimately control a Vietnam-wide movement that would never give up on its idea of independence and union.

To me, and to many Americans, Vietnam was a tragedy beyond comprehension. We had lost many fine young Americans, and the war had torn our country apart. We wanted the South Vietnamese to survive and prosper. Many South Vietnamese were courageous, giving, loving, industrious people. We had made friends, and we and they had suffered. Bonds are deep, and wounds are painful.

No general—French, American, South Vietnamese—could ever have brought victory. The war in Vietnam was unwinnable—lost before the French Expeditionary Force fired its first shot, before the South fielded its first soldier in the National Army of Vietnam, before the first U.S. advisor set foot in country.

An idea—*independence and unity*—would triumph over bullets.

***

The "Idea" is Not Forgotten

On April 30, 2015, at the 40-years celebration of the end of the war, marked by parades and speeches, "Prime Minister Nguyen Tan Dung praised 'the great victory in 1975' for ushering in 'an era of independence and reunification … '"
(*USA Today*, 8A, May 1, 2015)

Endnotes

Vietnam and other Indochina holdings in French, English, and Vietnamese are available at Texas Tech University, Vietnam Archives. Finding Aid for the William Haponski Collection of over 500 books plus extensive unit journals and other original source material: Texas Tech Item Number 25620000000.

Preface

1   U.S.G. Sharp, *Strategy for Defeat: Vietnam in Retrospect* (Novato, CA: Presidio, 1978), 271.
2   Adolphe Vézinet, *Le général Leclerc* (Paris: J'ai Lu, 1982), 239. All translations from French by author unless otherwise specified.
3   Harold G. Moore and Joseph L. Galloway, *We Are Soldiers Still: A Journey Back to the Battlefields of Vietnam* (New York: HarperCollins, 2008), 20.
4   Ibid., 25.

Chapter 1

1   Lloyd C. Gardner, *Approaching Vietnam: From World War II through Dienbienphu* (New York: W. W. Norton, 1988), 11.
2   William Colby, *Lost Victory: A Firsthand Account of America's Sixteen-Year Involvement in Vietnam* (Chicago: Contemporary, 1989), 16.
3   George W. Ball, *The Past Has Another Pattern, Memoirs* (New York: Norton, 1982), 364–67.
4   Bruce C. Palmer, Jr., *The 25-Year War: America's Military Role in Vietnam* (Lexington, KY: University of Kentucky Press, 1984), 24.

Chapter 2

1   Chester A. Bain, *Vietnam: The Roots of Chaos* (Englewood Cliffs, NJ: Prentice-Hall, 1967), 88–89.
2   William Duiker, *The Communist Road to Power in Vietnam* (Boulder, CO: Westview, 1996), 14.
3   Bui Tin, *Following Ho Chi Minh: The Memoirs of a North Vietnamese Colonel* (Honolulu: University of Hawaii Press, 1995), xi.
4   Dong Van Khuyen, in Lewis Sorley, ed., *The Vietnam War: An Assessment by South Vietnam's Generals* (Lubbock, TX: Texas Tech U Press, 2010), 67.

5   Bernard Fall, *Ho Chi Minh on Revolution: Selected Writings, 1920–66* (New York: Signet, 1967), vii.

6   Bernard Fall, *The Two Viet-Nams: A Political and Military Analysis* (New York: Praeger, 1965), 91

7   Douglas Pike, *History of Vietnamese Communism* (Stanford, CA: Hoover Institution Press, 1978), 1.

8   Fall, *The Two Viet-Nams*, 92–94.

9   Merle Pribbenow, trans. *History of the Dau Tieng Rubber Workers Movement (1917–1997) [Lich su' Phong Trao Nhan Cao su Dau Tieng]* (Ho Chi Minh City: Workers Publishing House, 2000), 31. Selectively translated for author by Merle Pribbenow. Vietnamese-language book available in Vietnam Archives, Haponski Special Collection.

10   Ibid., 38.

11   Fall, *Ho Chi Minh on Revolution*, 131.

12   Pribbenow, trans., *History,* 48.

13   Claude Hesse D'Alzon, et al., *La Presence Militaire Française en Indochine 1940–1945* (Vincennes: Publications du service historique de l'Armée de Terre, 1985), 25 Annexe 6.

14   David G. Marr, *Vietnam 1945: The Quest for Power* (Berkeley, CA: U California Press, 1995), 91.

15   Ibid., 174.

16   Pribbenow, trans., *History,* 49.

17   Cecil B. Currey, *Victory at Any Cost* (Washington, DC: Potomac, 1997), 60.

18   Duiker, *Communist Road to Power*, 71.

19   Pierre Brocheux, *Ho Chi Minh, A Biography* (Cambridge: Cambridge U Press, 2007) 79–80.

20   William Duiker, *Ho Chi Minh* (New York: Theia, 2000), 268.

21   Martin Shipway, *The Road to War: France and Vietnam, 1944–1947* (New York: Berghahn, 2003), 39.

22   Vo Nguyen Giap, *The Military Art of People's War*, Stetler, Russell, ed. (New York: Monthly Review Press, 1970), 67–68.

23   Duiker, *Ho Chi Minh*, 283.

24   Ibid., 287.

25   Fall, *Ho Chi Minh on Revolution*, 138–39.

26   Currey, *Victory at Any Cost*, 80.

27   Giap and Van Tien Dung, *How We Won the War* (Philadelphia: RECON Publications, 1976), 7.

28   Currey, *Victory at Any Cost*, 80.

29   *The 30-Year War, 1945–1975*, Vol. 1 (Hanoi: Gioi, 2002), 9.

30   Tran Van Don, *Our Endless War: Inside Vietnam* (Novato, CA: Presidio, 1978), 1–2.

31   Bui Diem, *In the Jaws of History* (Bloomington, IN: Indiana U Press, 1987), 20–24.

32   Archimedes L. A. Patti, *Why Viet Nam?* (Berkeley, CA: U California Press, 1980), 58.

33   Ibid., 83–84.

34   Currey, *Victory at Any Cost*, 88.

35   Patti, *Why Viet Nam?*, 129.

36   Vézinet, *Le général Leclerc*, 233.

37   Patti, *Why Viet Nam?*, 250.

38   Marr, *Vietnam 1945: The Quest for Power*, 463–64.

39   Peter M. Dunn, *The First Vietnam War* (London: C. Hurst, 1985), 134.

40   Ibid., 22.

41   Ibid., 202–203 (emphasis by author).

42   Christophe Dutrone, *Le Viet-Minh: de l'Indochine au Vietnam* (Paris: Éditions Les Indes Savantes, 2009), 52.

43   *The 30-Year War*, Vol. 1, 33.

Chapter 3

1 Vézinet, *Le général Leclerc*, 288.
2 Ibid., 238–39.
3 Ibid., 239.
4 Jean-Pierre Bernier, *Le Commando des Tigres: Les Paras du Commando Ponchardier, Indochine 1945–1946* (Paris: Jacques Grancher Éditeur,1995), 7.
5 Ibid., 40.
6 Historia, Hors Serie 24, *Notre Guerre d'Indochine* (Paris: Librarie Jules Tallandier, 1972), 164.
7 Jacques Massu, *Sept ans avec Leclerc* (Paris: Plon, 1974), 238.
8 *Coups de Massu,* December 1945, 14. A series of booklets available only at Texas Tech University, Vietnam Archives, Haponski Special Collection.
9 Massu, *Sept ans,* 244–45.
10 Yannick Guiberteau, *La Dévastation: Cuirrasse de Riviére* (Paris: Albin Michel, 1984), 43–44.
11 Bernier, *Le Commando des Tigres*, 66–68, 70.
12 Jean Leroy, *Fils de la Rizière* (Paris: Éditions Robert Laffont, 1977), 89.
13 Guiberteau, *La Dévastation*, 58.
14 Massu, *Sept ans*, 248–49.
15 Fall, *Two Viet-Nams*, 107.
16 Giap, *Banner of People's War, the Party's Military Line* (New York: Praeger, 1970), 12.

Chapter 4

1 *The 30-Year War,* Vol. 1, 42–43.
2 Journal Officiel le 22 août 1945.
3 Stein Tonnesson, *Vietnam 1946: How the War Began* (Berkeley, CA: U California Press, 2010), 36.
4 Vézinet, *Le général Leclerc*, 247.
5 Ibid., 252.
6 Tonnesson, *Vietnam 1946*, 39–40.
7 Vézinet, *Le général Leclerc*, 265.
8 Jean Lacouture, *Ho Chi Minh: A Political Biography* (New York: Vintage, 1968), 119.
9 Currey, *Victory at Any Cost*, 25.
10 Raoul Salan, *Mémoires: Fin d'un Empire, le sens d'un engagement, Juin 1899-Septembre 1946*. Vol. 1 (Paris: Presses de la Cité, 1970), 367.
11 Ibid., 380.
12 *The 30-Year War*, Vol.1, 380.
13 Vézinet, *Le général Leclerc*, 272.
14 Tonnesson, *Vietnam 1946*, 74.
15 Qiang Zhai, *China & the Vietnam Wars, 1950–1975* (Chapel Hill: U North Carolina Press, 2000), 11–12.

Chapter 5

1 Currey, *Victory at Any Cost*, 125–27.
2 Bui Diem, *In the Jaws of History*, 46.
3 Currey, *Victory at Any Cost*, 129.

4   Shipway, *The Road to War*, 235.
5   David Schoenbrun, *As France Goes* (New York: Harper & Brothers, 1957), 232–35.
6   Fall, *Ho Chi Minh on Revolution*, 196.
7   *The 30-Year War*, Vol.1, 82.
8   Truong Nhu Tang, *A Viet Cong Memoir* (San Diego, CA: Harcourt Brace Jovanovich, 1985), 11–16.
9   Leroy, *Fils de la Rizière*, 106, 115.
10 Shipway, *The Road to War*, 235.
11 Ibid., 251–52.
12 *The 30-Year War*, Vol.1, 91.
13 Giap, *Fighting Under Siege* (Hanoi: Gioi, 2004), 14.
14 Jean-Julien Fonde, *Traitez a Tout Prix …* (Paris: Édition Robert Laffont, 1971), 311–12.
15 *The 30-Year War*, Vol.1, 100.
16 Giap, *Fighting Under Siege*, 12.
17 Vézinet, *Le général Leclerc*, 278.
18 Ibid., 277–83.
19 Ibid., 285–86.
20 The Pentagon Papers, Gravel Edition. The Defense Department History of United States Decisionmaking on Vietnam. Vol. 1 (Boston: Beacon, 1971), 24.
21 Lacoutre, *Ho Chi Minh: A Political Biography* (New York: Vintage, 1968), 179.
22 Vézinet, *Le général Leclerc*, 286–90.
23 Or, "Negotiate, negotiate, negotiate, at any price." Fonde, *Traitez a Tout Prix …*, 344.
24 20ᵉ Siecle. *Guerre d'Indochine*. Vol. 1. *De la conquête de l'Indochine à de Lattre* (Paris: Trésor du Patrimonie. no date), 41.
25 Marvin Kalb and Elie Abel, *Roots of Involvement: The U.S. in Asia 1784–1971* (New York: W. W. Norton, 1971), 56.
26 *Unités Combattantes Indochine*—Official Publication of Ministry of War available only at Texas Tech U Vietnam Archives, Haponski Special Collection.
27 Giap, *Fighting Under Siege*, 62–63.
28 Ibid., 82.
29 *The 30-Year War*, Vol.1, 117.
30 Leroy, *Fils de la Rizière*, 126.
31 Guy de Chaumont-Guitry, *Lettres d'Indochine* (Paris: Alsatia, 1951), 32–36.
32 Ibid., 154.
33 Giap, *Fighting Under Siege*, 62–63.
34 *Historia* Vol. 1, 77.
35 *The 30-Year War* Vol. 1, 134.
36 Bui Tin, *Following Ho Chi Minh*, 10–11.
37 Giap, *Fighting Under Siege*, 143.
38 Leroy, *Fils de la Rizière*, 141.
39 Bui Diem, *In the Jaws of History*, 60–68.
40 Giap, *Military Art of People's War*, 88.

Chapter 6

1   Kalb and Abel, *Roots of Involvement*, 62.
2   Fall, *Ho Chi Minh on Revolution*, 183.
3   Zhai, *China & the Vietnam Wars*, 24.

4   *The 30-Year War*, Vol. I, 195.
5   *Historia* Vol. 1, 167.
6   Bui Tin, *Following Ho Chi Minh*, 14–15.
7   20ᵉ Siecle, *Guerre d'Indochine*, 81.
8   Fall, *Two Viet-Nams*, 115.
9   Yves Gras, *Histoire de la guerre d'Indochine* (Paris: Plon, 1971), 368.
10 Ibid.
11 *Historia* Vol. I, 168–173.
12 Giap, *The Road to Dien Bien Phu* (Hanoi: Gioi, 2004), 167.
13 Erwin Bergot, *Indochine 1951: Une Année de victoires* (Paris: Presses de la Cité, 1987), 141.
14 Gras, *Histoire de la guerre d'Indochine*, 367.
15 Pike, *History of Vietnamese Communism*, 83–85.
16 Bergot, *Indochine 1951*, 23.
17 Fall, *Two Viet-Nams*, 117.
18 Bergot, *Indochine 1951*, 178
19 Ibid., 141.
20 Henry Ainley, *In Order to Die* (London: Burke, 1955), 211.
21 Ibid., 29–30.
22 Ibid., 42–43.
23 Ibid., 46.
24 Ibid., 146.
25 Ibid., 221–22.
26 Valérie André, *Ici, Ventilateur!* (Paris: Calmann-Levy, 1954), 48.
27 United States Department of State "Foreign Relations of the United States, 1952–1954. Indochina" 1952–1954, Part 1, 6.
28 Bergot, *Indochine 1951*, 189.
29 Tran Van Don, *Our Endless War*, 6.
30 Bui Tin, *Following Ho Chi Minh*, 15.
31 Ibid., 40.
32 Currey, *Victory at Any Cost*, 81.
33 Michael Lee Lanning and Dan Cragg, *Inside the VC and the NVA: The Real Story of North Vietnam's Armed Forces* (New York: Faucett Columbine, 1991), 88–89.
34 Fall, *Ho Chi Minh on Revolution*, 228.
35 Giap, *Road to Dien Bien Phu*, 356.
36 Ibid., 385.
37 William C. Haponski, "Toward Dien Bien Phu: The Historical Context," in Geneviève de Galard, *The Angel of Dien Bien Phu* (Annapolis, MD: Naval Institute Press, 2010), 9.
38 Salan, *Mémoires* Vol. 1, 31–34.

Chapter 7

1   Geneviève de Galard, *The Angel of Dien Bien Phu*. Introduction, sketch maps, appendices by William C. Haponski (Annapolis, MD: Naval Institute Press, 2010), 17.
2   Ibid., 30.
3   Ibid.
4   Haponski, "Introduction," *Angel of Dien Bien Phu*, 10.
5   Martin Windrow, *The Last Valley: Dien Bien Phu and the French Defeat in Vietnam* (Cambridge, MA: Da Capo, 2004), 205–206.

6   Haponski, "Introduction," *Angel of Dien Bien Phu*, 10.
7   Windrow, *Last Valley*, 217.
8   Haponski, "Introduction," *Angel of Dien Bien Phu*, 11.
9   Ibid.
10 Windrow, *Last Valley*, 46.
11 Mark Atwood Lawrence and Fredrik Logevall, eds., *The First Vietnam War: Colonial Conflict and Cold War Crisis* (Cambridge, MA: Harvard U Press, 2007), 218.
12 Marcel Bigeard, *Pour une parcelle de Gloire* (Paris: Plon, 1975), 134.
13 Ibid., 135.
14 Windrow, *Last Valley*, 206.
15 Ibid., 242.
16 Ibid., 281.
17 Haponski, *The Angel of Dien Bien Phu*, "Appendices … D," 149–52, 155–56.
18 De Galard, *The Angel of Dien Bien Phu*, 50.
19 Giap, *Dien Bien Phu* (Hanoi: Foreign Languages 1984), 128–130.
20 Bernard Fall, *Hell in a Very Small Place: The Siege of Dien Bien Phu* (Philadelphia: J. B. Lippincott, 1967), 366.
21 Windrow, *Last Valley*, 497.
22 Fall, *Hell*, 373.
23 De Galard, *The Angel of Dien Bien Phu*, 83.
24 Ibid., 84.
25 Bigeard, *Pour une parcelle de Gloire*, 188.
26 De Galard, *The Angel of Dien Bien Phu*, 93.
27 Giap, *Dien Bien Phu*, 134.
28 Windrow, *Last Valley*, 624.

Chapter 8

1   Lam Quang Thi, *The Twenty-five Year Century: A South Vietnamese General Remembers the Indochina War to the Fall of Saigon* (Denton, TX: U North Texas Press, 2001), 72.
2   Fall, Ho Chi Minh on Revolution, 245.
3   Duiker, *Ho Chi Minh*, 456–57.
4   Ibid, 459.
5   Geneva Accords. For Unilateral U.S. Declaration, see Sagar, *Major Political Events in Indo-China 1945–1990*, p. 190.
6   Pike, *History of Communism*, 115.
7   Bui Tin, *Following Ho Chi Minh*, 66.
8   U.S. Department of State Bulletin, November 15, 1954, 736–37.
9   CD, BACM Research, Pentagon Papers: The Complete Report, Unredacted, IV.A.3.ix (16 Dec 54).
10 Ibid., IV. A. 3.ix (19 Dec 54).
11 Seth Jacobs, *Cold War Mandarin: Ngo Dinh Diem and the Origins of America's War in Vietnam, 1950–1963* (Lanham, MD: Rowman & Littlefield, 2006), 22–23.
12 Ibid., 32.
13 Lam Quang Thi, *The Twenty-five Year Century*, 88.
14 Ibid., 86–89.
15 Bui Tin, *Following Ho Chi Minh*, 54–55.
16 Tran Dinh Tho in Sorley, *Vietnam War*, 222.

17   Bui Tin, 60-61.
18   Theodore C. Sorensen, *Kennedy* (New York: Konecky & Konecky, 1965), 658–59.
19   Lawrence and Logevall, eds., *The First Vietnam War*, 77.
20   Cao Van Vien in Sorley, *Vietnam War*, 275.
21   Sorensen, 657.
22   Lawrence, 76.
23   William C. Westmoreland, *A Soldier Reports* (Garden City, NY: Doubleday, 1976), 63.
24   Ibid., 63.
25   Phillip B. Davidson, *Vietnam at War, The History: 1946–1975* (Novato, CA: Presidio, 1988), 314.
26   Maxwell Taylor, *Swords and Plowshares* (New York: Norton, 1972), 330–31.
27   Bui Tin, 41–42.
28   Merle Pribbenow, trans., *Victory in Vietnam: The Official History of the People's Army of Vietnam, 1954–1975.* The Military History Institute of Vietnam (Lawrence, KS: U Press of Kansas, 2002), 124–26.
29   Lien-Hang T. Nguyen, *Hanoi's War: An International History of the War for Peace in Vietnam.* (Chapel Hill, NC: U North Carolina Press, 2012), 28.
30   PAVN official histories make no distinction of "VC" divisions. All are listed as PAVN. The original "VC" divisions became more and more "PAVN" as NVA individual soldiers and units took positions within them.

Chapter 9

1   Samuel Zaffiri, *Westmoreland: A Biography of General William C. Westmoreland* (New York: Morrow, 1994), 106.
2   Westmoreland, *A Soldier Reports*, 38.
3   Ibid., 68.
4   Ibid., 75.
5   Ibid., 82.
6   CD, BACM Research, Pentagon Papers: The Complete Report, Unredacted, IV C. 8. iii.
7   Jay Taylor, *China and Southeast Asia: Peking's Relations with Revolutionary Movements* (New York: Praeger, 1974), 31.
8   http://www.archives.gov/research/military/vietnam-war/casualty-statistics.html.
9   Subsequently, this report was called into question and later deemed false.
10   Robert S. McNamara, *In Retrospect: The Tragedy and Lessons of Vietnam* (New York: Times Books, 1995), 181.
11   Bui Diem, *In the Jaws of History*, 338.
12   Zhai, *China & the Vietnam Wars*, 169–70.
13   Lien-Hang T. Nguyen, *Hanoi's War*, 76.
14   Pribbenow, trans., *Victory in Vietnam*, 182.
15   Westmoreland, *A Soldier Reports*, 83.
16   Bruce Palmer, *The 25-Year War*, 45–46.
17   McNamara, *In Retrospect*, 237, 239.
18   Dave Richard Palmer, *Summons of the Trumpet: U.S.–Vietnam in Perspective* (San Rafael, CA: Presidio, 1978), 117.
19   Harold G. Moore and Joseph L. Galloway, *We Were Soldiers Once ... and Young: Ia Drang, The Battle that Changed the War in Vietnam* (New York: Random House, 1992), 10.
20   Ibid., 26–27.
21   Ibid., 33, 36–37.

22 Ibid., 49–51.

23 Ibid., 55.

24 Ibid., 57, 60.

25 Ibid., 51.

26 Ibid., 62.

27 Ibid., 84.

28 Ibid., 192–93, 199, 200.

29 Larry Gwin, *Baptism: A Vietnam Memoir* (New York: Ivy Books, 1999), 155.

30 Ibid., 165.

31 Moore and Galloway, *We Were Soldiers,* 339.

32 Lewis Sorley, *Westmoreland: The General Who Lost Vietnam* (New York: Houghton Mifflin Harcourt, 2011), 95.

33 Palmer, *The 25-Year War*, 43.

34 Palmer, *Summons of the Trumpet*, 64.

35 Westmoreland, *A Soldier Reports*, 145–46.

36 Edward F. Murphy, *Semper Fi, Vietnam: From Da Nang to the DMZ Marine Corps Campaigns, 1965–1975* (New York: Ballantine, 1997), 7.

37 Victor H. Krulak, *First to Fight: An Inside View of the U.S. Marine Corps* (Annapolis, MD: Naval Institute Press, 1984) *180, 186.*

38 Ibid., 194.

39 Jack Shulimson, *U.S. Marines in Vietnam: An Expanding War 1966* (Washington, DC: U.S. Marine Corps, 1982), 13.

40 Philip Caputo, *A Rumor of War* (New York: Holt, 1977), *xix, xviii-xix, xix-xx.*

41 Ibid., 229.

42 Lewis W. Walt, *Strange War, Strange Strategy: A General's Report on Vietnam* (New York: Funk and Wagnalls, 1970), 112–114.

43 Caputo, *A Rumor of War*, 333.

44 Ibid., 334.

45 Tran Dinh Tho, in Sorley, *Vietnam War*, 262.

Chapter 10

1 William B. Rogers, *Cedar Falls–Junction City: A Turning Point* (Washington, DC: Department of the Army, 1974), 15.

2 Ibid., *v.*

3 Ibid., 58–59.

4 Ibid., 74–78, 158.

5 Palmer, *The 25-Year War*, 56.

6 Dinh Thi Van, *I Engaged in Intelligence Work* (Hanoi: Gioi, 2006), 153–54.

7 Ibid., 207, 211.

8 Ibid., 224.

9 Ibid., 227–36.

10 Merle Pribbenow, trans., *The Ten Thousand Day Journey: A Memoir [Chặng Đường Mười Nghìn Ngày]* Hoang Cam, Colonel General, as told to Nhat Tien (Hanoi: People's Army Publishing House, 2001), 200.

11 Ibid, 202–44.

12 Rogers, *Cedar Falls–Junction City*, 121.

13 Ibid., 127.

14 U. S. G. Sharp and W. C. Westmoreland. *Report on the War in Vietnam (As of 30 June 1968)* (Washington, DC: U.S. Government Printing Office), 137.

15 Rogers, *Cedar Falls–Junction City*, 155–159.

16 Richard H. Shultz, Jr., *The Secret War Against Hanoi: Kennedy's and Johnson's Use of Spies, Saboteurs, and Covert Warriors in North Vietnam* (New York: HarperCollins, 1999), 49.

17 Ibid., 8.

18 Lien-Hang T. Nguyen, *Hanoi's War*, 90–91.

19 Ibid., 102.

20 Giap, *Banner of People's War*, 77.

21 Palmer, *The 25-Year War*, 58.

22 Westmoreland, *A Soldier Reports*, 315.

23 Pribbenow, *Victory in Vietnam*, 224.

24 Sorley, ed., *Vietnam Chronicles: The Abrams Tapes 1968–1972* (Lubbock, TX: Texas Tech U Press, 2004), 66.

25 Westmoreland, *A Soldier Reports*, 335.

Chapter 11

1 Lewis Sorley, *A Better War: The Unexamined Victories and Final Tragedy of America's Last Years in Vietnam* (New York: Harvest, 1999), 18.

2 Ibid., 17.

3 Ibid., 18.

4 John C. ("Doc") Bahnsen, *American Warrior: A Combat Memoir of Vietnam* (New York: Citadel Press, 2007), 177–80, 185–92.

5 Richard A. Hunt, *Pacification: The American Struggle for Vietnam's Hearts and Minds* (Boulder, CO: Westview, 1995), 150.

6 Davidson, *Vietnam at War*, 614.

7 Ibid., 571–72.

8 Hunt, *Pacification*, 87.

9 11 ACR Quarterly Pacification Report, available NARA.

Chapter 12

1 Name disguised to protect him.

2 Tran Van Tra, *Vietnam: History of the Bulwark B2 Theatre*. Vol 5. *Concluding the Vietnam War* (Ho Chi Minh City: Van Nghe Publishing House, 1982), (on Internet), 76.

3 Pribbenow, trans., *7th Division: A Record [Su Doan 7: Ky Su]* Editorial Supervision: 7th Division Party Committee and Headquarters, Lt. Gen. Nguyen The Bon et al. (Hanoi: People's Army Publishing House, 1986), 90.

4 Ibid, 89.

Chapter 13

1 Pribbenow, trans., *Victory in Vietnam*, 246.

2 Ibid., 243.

3 Ibid., 246–50.

4   Westmoreland, *A Soldier Reports*, 388.
5   Tran Dinh Tho, in Sorley, *Vietnam War*, 545.
6   Richard M. Nixon, *No More Vietnams* (New York: Arbor House, 1985), 149.
7   Bruce Palmer, *The 25-Year War*, 102–103.
8   Truong Nhu Tang, *A Viet Cong Memoir*, 147.
9   Ibid., 164–166.
10 Ibid., 172.
11 Ibid., 160.
12 Colby, *Lost Victory*, 277–78.
13 Ibid., 288.
14 Bruce Palmer, *The 25-Year War*, 112–13.
15 Nguyen Duy Hinh, in Sorley, *Vietnam War*, 592, 595.
16 Pribbenow, trans., *Victory in Vietnam*, 283.
17 James H. Willbanks, *The Battle of An Loc* (Bloomington, IN: Indiana U Press 2005), 65–66.
18 Ngo Quang Truong, in Sorley, *Vietnam War*, 660.
19 Truong Nhu Tang, *A Viet Cong Memoir*, 207.
20 Sorley, *Vietnam Chronicles*, 872.
21 Ngo Quang Truong, in Sorley, *Vietnam War*, 663–64.
22 Nixon, *Memoirs* (New York: Grosset and Dunlap, 1978), 113.
23 Tran Dinh Tho, in Sorley, *Vietnam War*, 246.
24 Nixon, *Memoirs*, 734.
25 Nixon, *No More Vietnams,* 120, 124.

Chapter 14

1   Bui Tin, *Following Ho Chi Minh*, 57.
2   Ibid., 61.
3   Stephen T. Hosmer et al, *The Fall of South Vietnam: Statements by Vietnamese Military and Civilian Leaders* (New York: Crane Russak, 1980), 89.
4   Ibid., 56–57.
5   Tran Van Tra, *Vietnam*, 9, 12–14.
6   Ibid., 11.
7   Ibid., 25.
8   Tran Van Don, *Our Endless War*, 229.
9   Tran Van Tra, *Vietnam*, 33.
10 Pribbenow, trans., *Victory in Vietnam*, 336.
11 Ibid., 342–44.
12 Ibid., 350–53.
13 Zhai, *China & the Vietnam Wars*, 207.
14 Giap, *General Headquarters in the Spring of Brilliant Victory* (Memoirs) (Hanoi: Gioi, 2013), 44n1.
15 Pribbenow, trans., *Victory in Vietnam*, 347.
16 Ibid., 347–50.
17 Truong Nhu Tang, *A Viet Cong Memoir*, 232.
18 Cao Van Vien, in Sorley, *Vietnam War*, 298–99.
19 Ibid., 826.
20 Tran Van Don, *Our Endless War*, 235–37.
21 Giap, *General Headquarters*, 50.
22 Tran Van Don, *Our Endless War*, 230.

23   Giap, *General Headquarters*, 106–07.
24   Ibid., 117–118.
25   Pribbenow, trans., *Victory in Vietnam*, 359.

Chapter 15

1   Giap, *General Headquarters*, 56.
2   Pribbenow, trans., *Victory in Vietnam*, 362–63.
3   Van Tien Dung, *Our Great Spring Victory: An Account of the Liberation of South Vietnam* (New York: Monthly Review, 1977), 34.
4   Ibid., 44, 48–49.
5   Ibid., 62–63, 83.
6   Pribbenow, trans., (email to author): Comrade Le Duan's Comments in a Politburo Meeting Held 24 March 1975, After our Victory at Ban Me Thuot, 213.
7   Cao Van Vien and Dong Van Khuyen, in Sorley, *Vietnam War*, 873.
8   Van Tien Dung, *Our Great Spring Victory*, 87.
9   Lam Quang Thi, *The Twenty-five Year Century*, 357.
10   Van Tien Dung, *Our Great Spring Victory*, 87.
11   Lam Quang Thi, *The Twenty-five Year Century*, 360–361.
12   Ibid., 377.
13   Van Tien Dung, *Our Great Spring Victory*, 142.
14   Ibid., 158.
15   Pribbenow, trans., *Victory in Vietnam*, 406.
16   Tran Van Don, *Our Endless War*, 249–50.
17   Van Tien Dung, *Our Great Spring Victory*, 174.
18   Nguyen Minh Chau, "Happy and Sad Memories of a Time of War" [Ky Niem Vui Buon Trong Thoi Chinh Chien], *KBC Hai Ngoai*, Issue 18, June 2003, pp. 59–66, translated by Merle L. Pribbenow, Jr.
19   Pribbenow, trans., *Victory in Vietnam*, 420–421.
20   Tran Van Tra, *Vietnam*, 199–200.
21   Van Tien Dung, *Our Great Spring Victory*, 247.
22   Tran Van Tra, *Vietnam*, 200.
23   Sorley, ed., *Vietnam Chronicles*, 59.

Selective Further Reading

The French War

Ainley, Henry. *In Order to Die* (London: Burke, 1955). *Foreign Legion memoir, author's name is a pseudonym.*

Bergot, Erwin. *Indochine 1951: Une Année de victoires* (Paris: Presses de la Cité, 1987*). Focusing on De Lattre.*

Bernier, *Le Commando des Tigres: Les Paras du Commando Ponchardier, Indochine 1945–1946* (Paris: Jacques Grancher Éditeur,1995).

Galard, Geneviève de. *The Angel of Dien Bien Phu* (Annapolis, MD: Naval Institute Press, 2010).

Fall, Bernard. *Hell in a Very Small Place: The Siege of Dien Bien Phu* (Philadelphia: J. B. Lippincott, 1967). *Dien Bien Phu.*

Massu, Jacques. *Sept ans avec Leclerc* (Paris: Plon, 1974).

Vézinet, Adolphe. *Le général Leclerc* (Paris: J'ai Lu, 1982) *Account of Leclerc by his chief of staff.*

South Vietnamese Authors

Bui Diem. *In the Jaws of History* (Bloomington, IN: Indiana U Press, 1987).

Lam Quang Thi, *The Twenty-five Year Century: A South Vietnamese General Remembers the Indochina War to the Fall of Saigon* (Denton, TX: U North Texas Press, 2001).

Tran Van Don. *Our Endless War: Inside Vietnam* (Novato, CA: Presidio, 1978).

North Vietnamese/VC Authors

Bui Tin. *Following Ho Chi Minh: The Memoirs of a North Vietnamese Colonel* (Honolulu: University of Hawaii Press, 1995).

Dinh Thi Van. *I Engaged in Intelligence Work* (Hanoi: Gioi, 2006).

Fall, Bernard. *Ho Chi Minh on Revolution: Selected Writings, 1920–66* (New York: Signet, 1967*) Translated writings.*

Giap, *The Military Art of People's War*, Stetler, Russell, ed. (New York: Monthly Review Press, 1970).

Giap. *Dien Bien Phu* (Hanoi: Foreign Languages 1984).

Giap and Van Tien Dung, *How We Won the War* (Philadelphia: RECON Publications, 1976).

Truong Nhu Tang. *A Viet Cong Memoir* (San Diego, CA: Harcourt Brace Jovanovich, 1985).

American Authors

Duiker, William. *Ho Chi Minh* (New York: Theia, 2000).

Haponski, William C. *One Hell of a Ride: Inside an Armored Cavalry Task Force in Vietnam* (Createspace, 2009).

Hunt, Richard A. *Pacification: The American Struggle for Vietnam's Hearts and Minds* (Boulder, CO: Westview, 1995).

Jacobs, Seth. *Cold War Mandarin: Ngo Dinh Diem and the Origins of America's War in Vietnam, 1950–1963* (Lanham, MD: Rowman & Littlefield, 2006).

Moore, Harold G. and Galloway, Joseph L. *We Were Soldiers Once … and Young: Ia Drang, The Battle that Changed the War in Vietnam* (New York: Random House, 1992).

Moore, Harold G. and Galloway, Joseph L. *We Are Soldiers Still: A Journey Back to the Battlefields of Vietnam* (New York: HarperCollins, 2008).

Palmer Jr., Bruce C. *The 25-Year War: America's Military Role in Vietnam* (Lexington, KY: University of Kentucky Press, 1984).

Palmer, Dave R. *Summons of the Trumpet: U.S.–Vietnam in Perspective* (San Rafael, CA: Presidio, 1978).

Shultz, Richard H., Jr. *The Secret War Against Hanoi: Kennedy's and Johnson's Use of Spies, Saboteurs, and Covert Warriors in North Vietnam* (New York: HarperCollins, 1999).

Sorley, Lewis S. *Westmoreland: The General Who Lost Vietnam* (New York: Houghton Mifflin Harcourt, 2011).

Walt, Lewis W. *Strange War, Strange Strategy: A General's Report on Vietnam* (New York: Funk and Wagnalls, 1970).

Index